Reading and Writing
AMERICAN HISTORY
An Introduction to the Historian's Craft

VOLUME 1
THIRD EDITION

PETER CHARLES HOFFER
University of Georgia

WILLIAM W. STUECK
University of Georgia

PEARSON
Custom Publishing

Cover art: *The Hunter's Return*, by Thomas Cole, 1845, courtesy of Amon Carter Museum, Forth Worth, Texas.

Printed in the United States of America
10 9 8 7 6 5 4

Please visit our web site at www.pearsoncustom.com

ISBN 0–536–72820–8

BA 996802

JC

PEARSON CUSTOM PUBLISHING
75 Arlington Street, Boston, MA 02116
A Pearson Education Company

Contents

11 BIG QUESTIONS: INEVITABILITY, MORALITY, AND THE LESSONS OF HISTORY

Civil War and Reconstruction   207

To the Teacher

If your institution has a history requirement, as ours does, most students in your survey course will be conscripts. The course is part of their core curriculum. The reason they *should* take history—the reason that it is required for a liberal arts education—is obvious to us, but students may find that reason distant and abstract. At the outset, we face the obstacle of persuading students of the relevance of the past.

Today's students are very present minded. This perspective may result from the general widening of opportunities for undergradute education, or from the increasing pressure on young people to find a niche in the business or professional world before they leave college. Some universities have catered to those demands, allowing their professional schools to infiltrate undergraduate education and impose a dizzying load of preprofessional courses on students in the second and third years of undergraduate study. The ideal of a liberal-arts education, like the ideal of college as a sanctuary from the blooming, buzzing confusion of the workplace, has receded in the face of anxious careerism. Even if history courses offer a humanistic perspective on modern values, we cannot blind ourselves to the realities of college life. Students will leave our classrooms and step into a world whose distractions are so numerous and enticing that the past may not seem relevant.

History courses compete for students' time and attention not only with extracurricular demands often hostile to scholarly inquiry but with many other courses in the undergraduate curriculum. In a sense, we sell history in a buyer's market. Our effectiveness as teachers can be measured by the extent to which we can persuade our students to give their history course at least the same time and effort they devote to other courses. One way to do this is to load the class with extra reading and outside assignments. If every instructor in every other course—all sellers in this market—adopted this stratagem, our increased demands would be effectively neutralized by the across-the-board escalation of the workload, in the manner of the "prisoner's dilemma."

There is another, better way to convince students that history is relevant: offer them the chance to become an apprentice historian—a *doer* rather than a consumer. If history is the vital connection between past and present, then training in the skills and methods of thinking about history is more than a legitimate way to attract students' attention; it is an integral part of the introductory course. Students who begin to *do* history will appreciate the study of history as no passive reader of textbooks can, no matter how hard he or she studies.

We know from experience that, because there is so much to cover in American history surveys, little time remains to deal with basic questions of historical methods and skills.

Mindful of this fact, in *Reading and Writing American History*, Third Edition, we combine a manual on historical methods, a set of exercises that help students to hone their skill in using those methods, and a reader in primary and secondary sources that runs parallel to the chronological progression of topics in the survey course. *Reading and Writing American History*, Third Edition, is also suitable for methods courses for the history major.

A Manual

The old proverb "The teacher opens the door, the student must walk through it" has guided our plan for the book. We bring students face to face with the basic questions that every history teacher and scholar confronts. We begin by explaining why history is such a vital field of study and how every culture's conception of history gives its members a sense of identity. We treat basic problems in the philosophy of history, including the difference between fact and opinion and the ways in which historians use historical evidence. We introduce primary and secondary sources, source criticism and classification, and explain how to find historical sources and specific facts.

Subsequent chapters cover a wide range of reading and writing skills, from how to use the library to how to construct an essay. We introduce varieties of historical analysis, including causation, change and continuity, reasoning by analogy, the role of the individual in history, and the use of numbers.

A Workbook

Every point we make is reinforced by exercises. Some can be performed on the spot. Others require a trip to the library. Some exercises are textual, and we provide the text. Others require students to *find* the text. We have included nontextual materials—maps, pictures, and graphs—so that students can *see* the past as well as read about it. The materials cover a wide range of subfields in American history.

The methods treated in each chapter build on lessons in previous chapters. Within chapters, each exercise rests on those that come before it. The first exercise is often a "think piece," requiring students to ponder a historical question; subsequent exercises entail more writing. Because we understand that grading so many written exercises would be no mean task, many exercises are designed for "self-grading" or for class discussion. Space is provided for out-of-class assignments. The pages are perforated so that you can require students to turn in their work, and they are three-hole-punched so that students can retain their work in one place. We encourage you to pick and choose among the exercises and assignments, personalizing the course.

A Reader

Most exercises include readings, which allow you to link training in methods and skills to the substance of your course. These selections include primary and secondary sources and mix traditional and current historical concerns. Students are thus exposed to both the classics of historical writing and the most recent contributions. Many selections serve as springboards for discussion as well as skills practice.

The reading selections in each chapter are keyed to the chronological progression of events in American history. This chronological progression not only allows you to couple instruction in skills and methods to your lectures and discussions but also make this book a supplement to your textbook or to other required readings. We have found in our own teaching that the best way to ensure learning is through repetition. The selections in *Reading and Writing American History*, Third Edition, afford you the opportunity to repeat lessons using a variety of relevant materials.

New to This Edition

When the first edition of *Reading and Writing American History* was published in 1994, we were confident that college and university administrators and teachers regarded American history as the centerpiece of a college education. In the years since then, the college survey course in American history has faced two stiff intellectual tests. The present edition of *Reading and Writing American History* is designed to respond to these challenges.

The first challenge grows out of an invitation college and university instructors have issued to themselves to incorporate the many different voices of Americans in the basic undergraduate curriculum. Most independent colleges and state university systems still require the study of history as part of the liberal arts core, but the survey course in American history is no longer an automatic choice for students or their teachers to fulfill this obligation. Multicultural programs and diversity requirements have created special courses that provide other options to students.

The authors of *Reading and Writing American History*, Third Edition, are committed to the idea that the survey in American history is *the* multicultural course, for there is no nation that compares with ours in its ethnic diversity. We are truly one people made up of many peoples. This edition attempts to capture and explore fully that diversity by adding additional readings, exercises, and discussion materials on Native Americans, African Americans, and women. We have broadened the geographical scope of the volumes to include the peoples of the Southwest and the Caribbean.

The second trial that the American history survey course faces arises from the technology and information revolutions of our time. Many schools have introduced a computer literacy component to their basic undergraduate requirements. History may seem incompatible with such futuristic courses, but the fact is that historians have long used and valued the computer. Quantitative historians have relied on computer-driven software to calculate statistical associations and researchers have built computer databases from historical sources to study elections, population, and economic changes over time. More recently, many historical collections, archives, and libraries have gone online to make information available to users of the Internet and the World Wide Web. A number of history courses are now either entirely "online" (for example in "distance education") or rely on Web-based sets of documents. To meet the challenge of computer-aided instruction, we have added to this edition up-to-date facts on word processing software and Web sites for historians, along with rigorous exercises on computer-assisted library searches and Internet research in historical sources. The result, we hope, is a work-text that combines the training in skills and ways of thinking that have long made history the "mother of all intellectual disciplines," with the most modern techniques and information sources for students of history.

Acknowledgments

The final version of *Reading and Writing American History*, Third Edition, was a collaborative endeavor. The authors have worked together at every stage of the project; Volume 1 is the work of Peter Hoffer, and Volume 2 is the work of William Stueck. Our colleagues provided incisive and helpful comments. For this edition, we are grateful to Edward Larson, Peter Moore, Nan McMurry, Diane Trap, and Michael Winship at the University of Georgia, William James Hoffer at Seton Hall, N.E.H. Hull at Rutgers, Camden, and Daniel Mandell, at Truman State University, and Jennifer Carlson and Sharon Stevens, at Pearson Custom Publishing.

P.C.H.
W.W.S.

To the Student

We live in what the old Chinese proverb called "interesting times." Opportunities for personal achievement and community growth abound, but the dangers of modern life are just as close at hand as the prospects for progress. After the terrorist attack on the World Trade Center in New York City on September 11, 2001, every American has become aware of how history touches our lives. Not only do the motivations of the terrorists echo age-old animosities, history shows us parallel after parallel of such conduct and its causes. Those who do not learn these lessons, as the philosopher George Santayana wrote nearly a century ago, are fated to repeat them.

History is all around us; history shapes our lives; history can teach us who were are and how we gained our hopes and fears. But that is not all the study of history can offer us. The study of our early history teaches us to understand and value differences in points of view from our own, to see a world from the standpoint of people who had none of our modern conveniences and whose ordinary lives were filled with far more danger and sadness than our own. In these days of uncertainty about terrorism, the dwindling supply of natural resources, and the abuse of technology, these lessons about the past are vital reminders that we must learn to respect one another and the planet on which we live together.

There is a special reason for studying early American history: it is one of the most dramatic and sweeping stories that anyone could retell. It begins with the greatest migration in all history, peoples from Europe and Africa journeying across a vast sea to new homes. Here they encountered other peoples, Native Americans, themselves recently arrived on the east coast of North America. The stories of how these people interacted, of imperial war and tangled wilderness giving way to new communities, of broken hearts and trails of tears, of ideals of rights and liberties, of famous leaders that Americans still lionize and everyday heroes who raised families and worked the land, of slaves who toiled for others' profits and dreamed of freedom, of the tragedy of Indian removal and the triumph of capitalism, of the emergence of a great nation and the travails of a civil war—nothing can match this story.

1: *What Is History, and Why Should We Study It?*

Native Americans and Old World Peoples

In a classic oldie video, the singer Madonna prides herself on being a material girl in a material world. There is much truth in what she sings, for everywhere today we are surrounded by evidence of the triumph of technology. "Material Girl" can be seen on videos that we download from the Web, a technology that did not exist a generation ago. The pace of change in our world is so rapid that images and words collapse into "white noise," a discord of sights and sounds that blurs past, present, and future.

The study of history can rescue you from this buzzing confusion, giving you a sense of your place in time. History enables you to recognize the powerful forces that shaped your world and links you to the men and women who made those forces. History teaches you that your lives and aspirations are the culmination of the hopes and fears, the labors and loves, of people in the past.

Exercise 1: History in Your Pocket

As concerned as you are with the present and the future, you are a historian. Take a moment to look through your pockets, wallets, and bags. There you will find evidence that ties you to the past. A sales receipt, a snapshot of your family, a driver's license, your college ID card—all place you in the stream of history. You carry history in your head as well as in your pockets. Memories of old acquaintances, places you have seen, and homes in which you have lived are history you can call forth with a blink of the eye.

Scrutinize the evidence you have found in your pockets and bags. If you were a historian in the future, and you came upon this collection of evidence, what might it tell you about the people who lived during this period? What ideas were important to them? What material things and personal relationships did they value? Pick three pieces of evidence from your pocket, wallet, or bag and in the spaces below, briefly indicate how they might serve as historical evidence.

1. _____

_____

_____

2. _____
   _____
   _____
   _____
3. _____
   _____
   _____
   _____

The Meanings of the Word *History*

The word *history* has three meanings. First, history is a necessary part of human culture. Every cultural group formulates and expresses in words and images a conception of the origin of the group. Such collective, deeply embedded ideas of the past give the group a sense of identity and coherence. Without history, the group would lose its grasp on reality, just as an individual who forgot his or her past would have amnesia. A people's history also tells individuals what is good and bad, what they must do to survive and prosper, and how to pass their values on to new generations.

Second, history is a substantive body of information that scholars assemble about what people did, thought, felt, and perceived in the past. This collection of facts is sometimes overly compressed in the classroom into mind-numbing lists of names, dates, and places. Such lists are incomplete and misleading because they do not convey the richness, drama, and irony of human endeavor.

Third, history is a way of studying past events, a mental "discipline" in which you sift evidence from surviving sources, fashion facts from evidence, and weave them together into a coherent story. The three main sections of this chapter consider the three domains of history in detail.

History and Identity

It will be easier to grasp the basic truth that history gives you your identity and values if you mentally transport yourself to a less cluttered and crowded time. Imagine that you are a Pilgrim on the deck of the *Mayflower* in the middle of the Atlantic Ocean in the fall of 1620. It is cold and damp in the hold of the ship, frigid and wet on deck. You can hear the creak of the rigging and the thump of the waves on the hull, the cursing of the sailors, and the cries of the other Pilgrims' children.

In that perilous time and place, you have no trouble understanding your place in history. You are going to the New World to escape religious persecution in Europe. If there had been no wars of religion raging across the face of Europe, there would have been little reason for you to flee. If you survive the voyage, you will find a haven on the far shore because companies of merchants seeking rare minerals and furs have already built trading posts there. Without the rise of commerce and the age of discovery, there would be no companies sending their agents in search of gold and beaver pelts. You will find that shore because navigators developed compasses and because shipbuilders learned how to rig their boats for ocean travel. Standing on the deck of the *Mayflower*, you know how and why you are part of history.

Today, the Pilgrims' survival in the New World is celebrated with the holiday of Thanksgiving, but students of American history should learn another, more important lesson from this handful of determined immigrants. They believed with unshakable faith that a knowledge of history was a vital part of their lives. For them, history was filled with lessons and directions for conduct and belief; it told them what they must do to carry out their mission in the New World.

The Pilgrims were a small group of men and women in the great stream of English-speaking immigrants to the Atlantic shore. In that migration they joined Africans from many nations and several other European peoples, including Dutch, French, German, Irish, Portuguese, Spanish, and Welsh. Some came willingly; others wore chains on their ankles and wrists. Some longed for ease and luxury; others expected hardship. Waiting on the shore were Native Americans who spoke many dialects and practiced customs as varied as those of the Europeans. All of these peoples relied on written accounts or orally transmitted stories about their past to remind them of who they were and what made them distinct.

The peoples who met on the Atlantic coast of North America in the sixteenth and seventeenth centuries had well-developed views of their origins and a strong sense of their identities. The Native Americans of the pre-contact period used songs, stories, and speeches to link the past and the present. These accounts moved back and forth through time, uniting the history of their people with natural events and supernatural forces.

The English-speaking explorers and settlers had a more linear, or straightforward, idea of time that fit their sense of self. English adventurers like John Smith, founder of the Virginia colony, sought personal glory and regarded history as a story of conflicts among great men, clashes that featured the rise of England's power and the submission of its enemies. English Protestant reformers, including the Pilgrims, had a different personal mission—to free the church from corruption—and saw history as a series of divine verdicts upon human weakness. The Pilgrims' idea of time began with creation and ended with redemption of the saved.

Exercise 2: What Our Histories Reveal About Us

Following are an excerpt from an Iroquois folktale, a reproduction of an Iroquois religious mask, a Hopi legend, a selection from William Bradford, a leading Pilgrim, and from John Smith. Each relates to a historical event in the life of its creator's people. At the same time, each reveals the way in which its creator conceptualizes his people's values and place in history. The introductions to each piece provide information to help you understand what you are reading. After each are questions for you to answer.

Note that all of these selections record or recall the voice of the original historical figures. The language will thus seem unfamiliar to you. These are called *primary sources*, and we will discuss them in detail in Chapter 3.

A The Iroquois Indians in what is now New York State were surrounded by enemies and constantly fought to protect themselves, extend their territory, obtain captives, and maintain their honor. Their longhouses were surrounded by wooden walls, and bands of warriors periodically marched off to raid the villages of their neighbors and rivals, the Algonquin-speaking peoples of New England and Canada.

Raiding was an extension of the hunt for game. Like all hunter-gatherers, the Iroquois believed that they and the animals they hunted shared the world, and that only by hunting in certain set ways could that sharing benefit both the Iroquois and the animals. Hunters not only learned how the animals lived but taught themselves to think like the animals. The animals themselves told the Indians when the seasons of the hunt should begin—frogs along the streams signaled the beginning of the fall hunt, for example—and the Iroquois called to the animals of the hunt with song. Woodland lore and Indian custom merged in Native American rituals. After the hunt was over, the Iroquois lovingly returned the animal remains to the forest to ensure that the supply of animals would never diminish.

The warrior-hunter is a predator, and the Iroquois had to learn to control the aggressiveness that raiding and hunting bred. The following Iroquois folktale explains how the first Indians learned to master their own aggression.

This is a saga concerning the first people—the ancient people—the people of the beginnings—who live now and who lived also when the earth was new, and, therefore, was young. . . .

In the land of the sunrise . . . there was situated a village of these first people. . . . There came a day when one of the young men, "He-Who-Cleaves-the-Sky-in-Twain," resolved to form an expedition to make a raid westward into the distant regions through which pass the daily path of the sun.

So to promote his design [he] induced his friends to prepare a great war feast . . . he announced to the public assembled there his purpose of leading a troop of warriors far into the west . . . to slaughter unknown men and to obtain the scalps of alien peoples as tokens of their prowess and their courage in warfare. In response to this appeal twenty-eight young virile men volunteered to be members of the war party.

As these warriors traveled on they finally reached a place in which they found the habitations of a people whom they did not know, but these unoffending persons they ruthlessly killed and scalped. After this bloody exploit they journeyed westward. . . . These bloody exploits were repeated wherever they found a village of people dwelling on the line of their march. This bloody work continued for many moons.

About this time they fell in with a person, a male man being, whose towering stature reached one-half the height of the tallest trees. [One of the warriors said] "I think that the next move to be made is to decide to kill this man being whom we have met in this place . . . so let us attack him at once."

So deploying they at once began to assault him by shooting their arrows at him, and by striking him with their war clubs and with their stone hatchets; but they could not make any impression on him; they failed to harm him in the least.

At last the strange man being said to them, kindly, "What is that you desire to do? Do you imagine that you can kill me?" Then they answered, "That is, indeed, our purpose, as it has been our design in making our journey hither to kill all persons who might fall in our way, no matter who they might be."

To this frank admission of their purpose to kill him, this strange man being replied, "The purpose for which you are banded together is not good. And from this time forward you must utterly renounce it and strictly desist from carrying it out. It is quite impossible for you to kill me. And I came to meet you here for the purpose of giving you this counsel. I watched you on your way to this place, and I saw with grief that you killed many people. I want you to know that the reason why I came to meet you is that you have now committed wrongs enough on innocent people. And I want you to know that if you will not cease from committing these wrongs you yourselves also shall perish."

Then He-Who-Cleaves-the-Sky-in-Twain replied, saying, "We are very thankful to you for this good counsel, and we will try to abide by it." . . . Then the strange man being merely replied, "Do you then start on your journey." And while they listened to him with bowed heads he vanished from them; they did not know or see whither he went.[1]

1. What motivated He-Who-Cleaves-the-Sky-in-Twain when he set out on his journey?

2. What did his warriors regard as proper conduct then? _____

_____

_____

3. To what physical object does the teller of the folktale compare the mysterious "man being"?

_____

_____

4. What does this comparison suggest about the relationship between nature and moral goodness in Iroquois thinking? _____

_____

_____

5. What did the warriors learn from the man being, and how did the lesson change their concept of themselves? _____

_____

_____

6. What lessons did the folktale teach the Iroquois who heard it? _____

_____

_____

B Like their neighbors and rivals among the Native American peoples, the Iroquois believed that the world was filled with spirits. Some of these, like the man being, were benevolent and taught the Native Americans how to live and prosper. Other spirits were dangerous and malevolent; they had to be placated or fooled, or they would bring death and destruction. Some spirits were animals and lived in the forests and fields with the Indians. Others were manifestations of the earth, sky, rain, and sun. Sometimes a shaman or medicine man supervised this folk worship, but more often than not a group of men were charged with keeping harmony between the Indians and the spirit world.

During important Indian religious ceremonies, dancers and singers wore masks. For example, the False Face Society of the Iroquois were healers, and their songs and dances had the power to cure the sick. Each of the false faces they wore had its origin and place in Indian folk stories. The face in Figure 1.1 is "Crooked Mouth," who dared to challenge the earth and was bent by an onrushing mountain. The face was carved from a living tree by members of the Onondaga tribe of the Iroquois nation. The eyes are copperplate. The hair is from a horse's tail. Such faces, like the folktales of the Iroquois, did not capture a particular moment in time but tied past to present, and present to future.

FIGURE 1.1 *"Crooked Mouth"—Iroquois Medicine Mask*
Courtesy of the Cranbrook Institute of Science

1. How might such a mask play a role in curing a sick person—assuming that the sick were afflicted with evil spirits? _____

_____

_____

2. The carving, care, and use of the mask were restricted by custom to only those individuals who had been initiated into the secrets of the society. How might such men gain power and status from their participation in the healing rites? _____

_____

_____

3. How did the mask remind the Onondaga of who they were and how they were expected to behave? _____

_____

_____

   C The Hopi of what is today New Mexico spoke a different language from the Iroquois and lived in different surroundings. To the Hopi, home was a stone and mortar dwelling on a plateau or against a cliffside in a region of mountain, desert, and gorge, often next to forty or fifty other family dwellings. For this reason, the Spanish called the Hopi a "pueblo" (town) people. Hopi today believe they are the descendants of older Native American settlers, called "Anasazi" (ancient ones), who lived to the north and were driven from their homes by drought, war, and their own disobedience to their gods. For all southwestern pueblo Indians, water was not merely a necessity of life, it was a source of spiritual power. Water management was vital if large numbers of people were to dwell together in peace; thus water gods had to be treated with dignity and politeness.

The legends of the Hopi are filled with lessons, like the Iroquois' folktales. The storytellers of the Hopi weave together the memory of historical events, passed down by word of mouth, with Hopi religious beliefs. In these legends gods, heroes, spirits, and animals mingle as equals. The legends "reinforce the bonds of ethnic and cultural identity and create a sense of continuity" between past and present.[2] With the invasion of the Spanish, much changed for the Hopi. Driven from their homes, forced to adopt at least outward trappings of a foreign religion, the Hopi coped by mixing the new Christian beliefs with older Hopi rituals and stories, and thereby regained, after two centuries of strife, a measure of local autonomy. The legends, from which we have taken the following selection, link the preinvasion world with the present generation's concern for harmony and respect for nature.

The elders of the village of Soongoopavi (sometimes pronounced "Shungopavi") wanted to change the course of a nearby spring so that they could bring additional lands under cultivation. They chose volunteers to bring offerings to the powerful water spirits of the spring, but they got more than they bargained for. Faced with the ruin of their village, they turned to a neighboring village's shaman. Please read the selection and answer the questions that follow.

At the spring itself there was life, too. Apparently, some very powerful beings had made their home there. These beings were Water Serpents that had their own way of life. Wherever a spring exists, these creatures can be found. It is due to the Serpents disgorging water that a well springs up from the ground. In this way they supply water for all other living things. They possess the knowledge of providing moisture at any location. And because they were responsible for the flow of the spring there, the leaders of Shungopavi tried to persuade the Serpents to do something for them. They were hoping that the Serpents would enlarge the spring to the point where large masses of water would spill down the slopes in that area.

At first not all of the leaders were in favor of this request. But some of the more obstinate ones persisted and changed the minds of the others. When at long last the Shungopavis all agreed, the village chief and the heads of the different ceremonial societies met at the home of the village chief. With all of them now sharing the same intentions, they were determined to carry out their goal. "Let us begin at once so it won't be too long before the Serpents make the fields for us on which we can plant." The leaders were unanimous in this decision. . . .

By now, the head of the Serpents had decked the altar with the prayer items he had received. Then all those of high rank who had a place at the altar stepped up to it and sat down next to it. Since they had given their word to help the villagers, they now began to pray for this undertaking. While the priests were performing the ritual, the other Serpents began writhing. As a result, the water in the spring above them started to slosh about, and the ground began to shake. . . .

The cliff walls along the northeast side now really began cascading down. At the village of Shungopavi, too, the homes of the people started to shake and to collapse. . . .

Whenever a cliff came tumbling down, the entire mass would land in one huge piece at the bottom. . . . This had not been the intention of those in favor of this undertaking. The people of Shungopavi themselves could not stand the earth tremors anymore. They were so frightened by now that they began to abandon the village. Everything was chaos and pandemonium. . . .

All this time the catastrophe continued. The entire earth kept on trembling. Whenever a cliff cracked, it would crash down. Things could not go on in this manner. The people of Shungopavi were scared, so they sent a messenger to the village of Walpi. There he was to fetch a shaman who had distinguished himself at his trade. The messenger informed the medicine man that he was needed immediately, and brought him back to Shungopavi. He escorted him to the location where the Shungopavi leaders hatched all of their plans.

When the shaman arrived, he went in to the men and found them still huddled around their altar. Immediately he took out his crystal and peered through it at the chiefs. He saw that every one of them was evil. "What a wretched bunch you are!" he exclaimed. "You've committed a wrong against the people. You seem bent on destroying everyone. Why on earth did you plan such a thing? Every one of you is bad. You had no business doing this. You think you know it all. Really, you Shungopavis are full of vanity," he chastised them. "It was your desire to do a great feat and to experiment with something. You ought to know that you are not to do these things. This world is supposed to stay the way it was created. It does not behoove us to alter it in any way. Some of you must have known this. So why did you persuade the others to go along with you?" he scolded them. . . .

This chain of events accounts for the fault in the present community of Shungopavi. If ever these events should recur, this fault will split open and destroy the village. It is said that if the rituals are not being carried out properly, Shungopavi in its entirety will sink into the ground. The time for this prediction is now at hand.[3]

1. What actual event do you think the legend recalls? _____

_____

_____

2. How did the village leaders expect to change the lay of the land? _____

_____

_____

3. What happened as a result of their plan? _____

_____

_____

4. What was the fault of the village leaders, according to the shaman? _____

_____

_____

5. What is the moral of the legend? _____

_____

_____

D In the social life of all peoples there is a mixture of conservatism and custom, on the one hand, and the desire for improvement, on the other. The same combination of motives and necessities that led the leaders of Shungopavi and He-Who-Cleaves-the-Sky-in-Twain to act as they did drove early modern Europeans to examine their lives. Some of them resolved that change was necessary in order to preserve what was good and important in their way of life. For the Pilgrims, a small sect of English men and women who had fled their native land to preserve the purity of their faith, the prospect of still further change brought both fear and joy. As they pondered an opportunity to escape the corruptions of Europe and find a haven for themselves in the New World, one of their leaders, William Bradford, began a journal. Such journals were common among radical Protestant sectaries, for in the journal they could plot the course of their own spiritual pilgrimage and record evidence of salvation in the signs of God's favor. Please read the selection and answer the questions that follow.

It is well known unto the godly and judicious, how ever since the first breaking out of the light of the gospel in our honourable nation of England, (which was the first of nations whom the Lord adorned therewith after the gross darkness of popery [Roman Catholicism] which had covered and overspread the Christian world), what wars and oppositions ever since, Satan hath raised, maintained and continued against the Saints [pious ones] from time to time, in one sort or another. Sometimes by bloody death and cruel torments; other whiles imprisonments, banishments and other hard usages; as being loathe his kingdom should go down, the truth prevail and the churches of God revert to their ancient purity and recover their primitive order, liberty, and beauty.

But when he could not prevail by these means against the main truths of the gospel, but that they began to take root in many places, being watered with the blood of the martyrs and blessed from heaven with a gracious increase; he then began to take him to his ancient stratagems, used of old against the first Christians. That when by the bloody and barbarous persecutions of the heathen emperors he could not stop and subvert the course of the gospel . . . he then began to sow errors, heresies and wonderful dissentions amongst the . . . professors [people] themselves, working upon their pride and ambition, with other corrupt passions incident to all mortal men . . .

When as by the travail and diligence of some godly and zealous preachers, and God's blessing on their labors, as in other places of the land, so in the North parts [of England], many became enlightened by the word of God and had their ignorance and sins discovered unto them, and began by His grace to reform their lives and make conscience of their way, the work of God was no sooner manifest in them but presently they were both scoffed and scorned by the profane multitude . . . Which, notwithstanding, they bore sundry years with much patience. . . .

Yet seeing themselves thus molested, and that there was no hope of their continuance there [in England] by a joint consent [the Pilgrims] resolved to go into the Low Countries [the Netherlands today], where they heard there was freedom of religion for all men.[4]

1. According to Bradford, what perils did the first English Protestants face? _____
_____
_____

2. Who (or what) was the root of the trouble—the "he" in the account?_____
_____
_____

3. How did the persecution transform the Pilgrims' view of themselves?_____
_____
_____

4. According to Bradford, what motivated the Pilgrims' actions throughout—that is, how did they identify themselves as a group? _____

E John Smith was a contemporary of William Bradford. In fact, Bradford and other Pilgrims were studious readers of Smith's *A Description of New England*, published in 1616. Known then and now for his participation in the establishment of the Jamestown colony in 1607, Smith was a mercenary soldier, explorer, writer, and business entrepreneur, a type of macho English go-getter in many ways the very opposite of the pious Pilgrims. Bradford had effaced himself—he was only God's instrument. Smith saw himself at the center of history. For him, the project of colonization was a personal as well as public goal. But like Bradford, he knew that history taught lessons to those willing to learn from it. In particular, he wanted the history of his voyage to New England to teach the English that they could and should compete with Spain and Portugal for control of the New World.

> It would be a historie of a larger volume, to recite the adventures of the Spaniards, and Portuguese, their affronts, and defeats, their dangers and miseries; which with such improbable honor and constant resolution, so far beyond belief, they have attempted and endured in their discoveries and plantations, as may well condemn us, of too much imbecility, sloth, and negligence.... And though we see daily their mountains of wealth (sprung from the plants of their generous endeavors) yet is our sensuality and untowardness [awkwardness] such, and so great ... that we either so neglect, or oppress and discourage the present ... [and] fear that which is not, and for fear ... force such against their wills to be idle or as ill [used].... Who is he [that] hath judgment, courage, and ... industry or quality with understanding, will leave his country, his hopes at home, his certain estate, his friends, pleasures, liberty and the preferment sweet England doth afford to all degrees, were it not to advance his fortunes by enjoying his desserts [labors]? ... [and] to make them more abound in honor, by heroic deeds of action, judgment, piety, and virtue.[5]

1. What virtues does Smith celebrate in this passage? In what ways are these masculine traits?
   _____
   _____

2. What lesson does he want his English readers to take from his short account of England's rivals? _____
   _____
   _____

3. What values or benefits does Smith see in colonization, and what obstacles does he warn of?
   _____
   _____

4. How does Smith show his resentment at being kept on the bench while others got to go abroad? _____
   _____

Differences and Similarities: Why History Is Two-Faced

As Exercise 2 demonstrates, the era of the founding of European colonies in North America differed markedly in many respects from our own. There appear to be similarities as well, but the differences are quite striking, and they lend our study of history much of its excitement. Without assuming some degree of similarity between the past and the present, however, you could never begin to guess the motives of men and women who lived before you. Thinking about the past is like taking a trip to a country whose customs are exotic and intriguing, but some of whose guides speak your language. You enjoy the differences but are reassured by the similarities.

History always faces in two directions. One face looks backward, seeing differences between past and present. History's other face looks directly at you and requires you to re-create the feelings and perceptions behind those very differences. You cannot perceive differences unless you make comparisons and connect the past and present.

Some of the differences between modern life and life in the seventeenth century are so overwhelming precisely because they touch every aspect of daily life. For example, most of us take for granted that we can control light and darkness, heat and cold, with the flick of a switch. In the seventeenth century, the distinction between day and night, warmth and chill, was sharp and beyond the control of many people. The French historian Lucien Febvre was struck by this difference between the modern world and its predecessor:

> What does the contrast between night and day mean to us . . . of the twentieth century? Practically nothing at all. A switch, a movement of the arm, and sunlight gives way to electric light. We are the masters of light and darkness. . . . [But people in the seventeenth century] were not masters of light, especially the poor who did not even have oil-lamps or candles to light when night came on. Their life was divided . . . into day and night, white and black, absolute silence and the noisy bustle of work. . . . Today, there is heating everywhere. . . . Anybody going into [a] house in the [seventeenth century] in January felt the cold . . . the silent dark cold of heatless dwellings. You shivered in anticipation, in the same way as you had been shivering all the time in church. Just as you shivered in the king's palace despite the big fireplace that devoured whole trees. . . . So can we really believe that a life of this sort fashioned in [people] the same mental habits and the same ways of thinking and feeling, the same desires, the same actions and reactions as our own life does in us?[6]

If Professor Febvre was right in claiming that the world of 1600 was so profoundly different from our own that we cannot assume that men and women then felt or did as we do, how could anyone begin to write a history of that time? Febvre was not arguing that it is impossible to know what people did and thought in the past but only that we must always take into account the differences between the modern world and the world 400 years ago—or 50 years ago, when he wrote.

Exercise 3: Discovering Differences

Following are three pieces of evidence about customs and thought in seventeenth-century Europe—ways of life that the European settlers brought with them to the New World. Examine the selections and illustration, and ask yourself in what ways people 300 years ago differed from people today. How were they similar? More specific study questions follow each of the passages.

A   Slavery was not offensive to most seventeenth-century Europeans. Though it did not flourish on the continent of Europe or in the British Isles, slavery was planted in Latin America by the Spanish and Portuguese. They bought men and women captured in war in West Africa and transported them to the Caribbean, Mexico, and Central and South America to work on plantations and in mines alongside the Indians that the Europeans enslaved. To facilitate the African slave trade, the Portuguese, followed by the Spanish, the French, the English, the Dutch, and finally the German and Swedish traders, built forts on the coast of West Africa. As slavery became a fixture of the labor system of the American colonies, the slave trade became more and more lucrative. The European nations that engaged in it fought wars to determine which country's traders would control which portions of the West African coast.

Some Christian leaders objected to slavery or sought to curb its worst abuses. Although the medieval theologian Thomas Aquinas believed that slavery was part of the natural order of the world, and later religious thinkers like Martin Luther and John Calvin did not see any contradiction between Christianity and human slavery, other Christians argued that slavery violated the basic precept of human equality that Christianity proclaimed. The following passage is a segment of the reply that a Jesuit teacher in Angola wrote to a Roman Catholic priest in Brazil. The priest, Father Sandoval, was worried that the Africans had been captured illegally. The teacher, Luis Brandaon, countered with legalistic reasons why the priest should not trouble himself with doubts about the slave trade.

> Your reverence writes me that you would like to know whether the negroes who are sent to your parts have been legally captured. To this I reply that I think your reverence should have no scruples on this point, because this is a matter which has been questioned by the Board of Conscience in Lisbon, and all its members are learned and conscientious men. . . . Since the traders who bring those negroes [to Brazil] bring them in good faith, those inhabitants [the Portuguese who had plantations in Brazil] can very well buy from such traders without any scruple, and the latter on their part can sell them, for it is a generally accepted opinion that the owner who owns anything in good faith can sell it and that it can be bought. . . . Besides, I found it true indeed, that no negro will ever say he has been captured legally. Therefore your reverence should not ask them whether they have been legally captured or not, because they will always say that they were stolen and captured illegally, in the hope that they will be given their liberty. . . . And to lose so many souls [that is, potential converts to Christianity] as sail from here [as slaves]—out of whom many are saved . . . does not seem to be doing much service to God.[7]

1. What three arguments does the teacher offer the priest to quiet the latter's doubts about the legality of slavery?

   a. _____

   b. _____

   c. _____

2. Does the teacher's letter hint at any underlying mercenary reason why the slave trade should continue uninterrupted? _____

   _____

   _____

3. How does the teacher's view of slavery differ from yours? _____

   _____

   _____

B In the first half of the seventeenth century, London was a study in motion and contrast: the homes of the wealthy stood next to the hovels of the poor; bustling businesses and shops abutted pestholes and "rookeries" of crime. Periodically, epidemics of smallpox, bubonic plague, and tuberculosis swept off whole neighborhoods of people, but fire was the worst danger. In 1666 much of the housing shown in Figure 1.2 was destroyed by a great fire. Such conditions prompted many young English men and women to leave London and emigrate to the colonies.

FIGURE 1.2 *The Cheapside-Cornhill District of London, 1658*

1. Look at the illustration. Why was fire such a great danger in mid-seventeenth-century London? _____

_____

_____

2. In what two ways was getting about in such a city different from travel in a major city today? _____

_____

_____

3. Think about hygiene and food. What smells would be different? How might eating habits have differed? Why? _____

_____

_____

4. Was pollution worse or better? (Hint: think about heating.) _____

_____

_____

5. Did the city sound different then? _____

_____

_____

C Seventeenth-century Europeans believed that the world was filled with spirits and demons. Many Christians, including educated officials and clergymen, feared that their neighbors consorted with the Devil and practiced witchcraft. Catholic and Protestant magistrates tortured and executed suspected witches (people who had made pacts with the Devil) throughout Europe. Europeans brought their fears of witches to the American colonies.

The vast majority of the victims of the great witch scare were women, most often poor and either very old or very young. In 1652 a French court tried Suzanne Gaudry for witchcraft. At first she confessed, convinced by other peasants that a confession would save her. Later, realizing that the court intended to execute her regardless of what she said, she recanted her confession. The judges then ordered her tortured to find out whether she had told them the truth.

> This prisoner, before being strapped down, was admonished to maintain herself in her first confessions [to witchcraft] and to renounce [the Devil]. She said she denies everything she has said [during her first forced confession] and that she has no lover [witches were assumed to have taken the Devil as a lover]. Feeling herself being strapped down, says that she is not a witch, while struggling to cry.
>
> Asked why she fled outside [her village when the prosecutors came after her] says that God [forbids her to say she is a witch]. And upon being asked why she confessed to being one, said that she was forced to say it.
>
> Being a little stretched on the rack [a torture] screams ceaselessly that she is not a witch, invoking [God's name and the Virgin Mary]. Being more tightly stretched upon the torture rack, [and] urged to maintain her confessions, [she] said that it was true that she is a witch and that she would maintain what she [now] had said.[8]

1. What was Gaudry's suspected offense? What had she supposedly done? _____

_____

_____

2. In what ways was her treatment different from the treatment accorded a defendant today?

_____

_____

3. What made Gaudry change her testimony? _____

_____

_____

4. Does the passage suggest to you any reason why women were prosecuted for witchcraft ten times as often as men? _____

_____

_____

Historical-Mindedness: The Discipline of History

As the study of history enables you to develop your sense of identity and recognize differences and similarities between the past and the present, you begin to confront some of your own prejudices about other peoples. Ironically, the more you study the past, the more prejudice and bias you encounter, for narrow-mindedness and hate were much in evidence in past times. You glimpsed this intolerance in the selections you read in Exercise 3. Properly taught, history can reverse prejudice and help you understand the experiences of others.

True, you have certain values, and these dictate to a large extent how you see the past. You have in your mind a mental map of the outside world with visual and verbal signposts that enable you to process new information. If the study of history is to be possible at all, you must assume that you share with people from the past some similar ideas, attitudes, and views of the world, at least enough to be able to understand something of their experience. At the same time, the study of history sharpens your awareness of the differences between your mental map and the mental maps of people who lived in the past.

Historians call this imaginative intellectual endeavor *historical-mindedness*, meaning that they try to see the past as those who lived in it saw it. Is this imaginative leap back in time really possible? We know that we can see the past only in our mind's eye. The "noble dream" of historical objectivity, to which past generations of "scientific historians" clung, held out the possibility of recapturing the past "as it actually was." Few historians still adhere to this position. However we may attempt to free ourselves of bias, however hard we may work to transcend the limitations of our mental map, we know we cannot reproduce the past in a test tube as a chemist in a laboratory can reproduce a chemical compound by following a formula. We can nevertheless strive to think critically and imaginatively about the past, and that enterprise is well worth the effort.

Your historical-mindedness will grow as you work through the exercises *in Reading and Writing American History*. At this stage of your study of historical methods, however, you are still dependent on what historians tell you. Your first step toward critical and imaginative thinking about the past requires you to begin to separate historical facts from historians' opinions. A historical fact is an *educated conclusion* about what happened in the past, reached through assembling pieces of evidence. "Facts" do not speak for themselves; they are statements historians make.

An opinion, by contrast, is a conviction, a persuasion, or a feeling that may or may not be based on fact but that rests on the writer's or speaker's own attitudes toward facts. It is a *judgment*. One historian's opinion about the past often differs from another historian's opinion precisely because opinion is an expression of the individual's state of mind. Historical-mindedness is an act of imaginative re-creation, and historical accounts will always feature both facts and opinions.

It is sometimes difficult to distinguish fact from opinion, but note the differences in the following examples. "It was raining yesterday" is a factual statement about the weather. "It was a rotten day yesterday" is an opinion about the weather. "The Puritans and the Indians mistrusted each other" is a historical fact. "The Indians should never have trusted the Puritans" is an opinion.

Exercise 4: Fact and Opinion

Try your skill at separating fact from opinion. Read each passage; then circle the facts and underline the opinions in each. We have circled one fact and underlined one opinion in the first passage to get you started. Be prepared to explain the reasons for your choices in class.

Note that the following selections are not original pieces of evidence (primary sources) but instead are taken from the work of historians (secondary sources, treated in detail in Chapter 4).

A Nineteenth-century historian Francis Parkman wrote a series of books on the conflict between Native Americans and European emigrants in seventeenth- and eighteenth-century North America. He traveled the paths of the Iroquois and the Algonquin and read the accounts of English and French settlers, but he was no lover of Native American ways. A descendant of the founders of New England, he believed strongly that God and nature had ordained a British victory in the struggle against the Native Americans. Note, for example, his use of words like *savages* and *civilization*.

> In Indian social organization, a problem at once suggests itself. In these communities, comparatively populous, how could spirits so fierce, and in many respects, so ungoverned, live together in peace, without law and without enforced authority? Yet there were towns where savages lived together in thousands, with a harmony which civilization might envy. This was in good measure due to peculiarities of the Indian character and habits. . . . That well-known self-control, which, originating in a form of pride, covered the savage nature of the man with a veil. . . . Though vain, arrogant, boastful, and vindictive, the Indian bore abuse and sarcasm with astonishing patience. Though greedy and grasping, he was lavish without stint, and would give away his all to . . . gain influence and applause, or ingratiate himself with his neighbors.[9]

B In the next selection, Professor Alden Vaughan of Columbia University, also a descendant of the founders of New England, comments on the same Native American peoples whom Parkman described. Vaughan focuses on the different ways in which Indians and Europeans wage war. The Native Americans fought small battles, little more than raids, for honor, to gain prisoners to replace lost population, or to persuade the vanquished to submit themselves to their victors. Europeans waged all-out war to control territory or scourge their religious enemies. The difference between Parkman's and Vaughan's mixture of facts and opinions reflects the century of growing sympathy for the Indians' rights and way of life separating the times in which Parkman and Vaughan wrote, but Vaughan is not an apologist for the Native Americans by any means. Circle the facts and underline the opinions.

> It may be that war among the New England tribes served more of a symbolic role than did European warfare [in Europe]. Various reasons for fighting [among the Indians]—petty grievances, revenge, defense of honor, and saving face—could perhaps be met by a show of courage without the wholesale slaughter that would only lead to prolonged and costly warfare. And since each tribe was small in membership, it had strategic as well as humanitarian reasons to avoid heavy casualties; this undoubtedly encouraged the Indians to wage the cautious kind of battle that the [English in New England] found so ludicrous. While it is not true that the white man introduced the Indians to the art of war, it may well be that he taught the red man how to practice it more energetically.
>
> In contrast to the mildness of Indian warfare was the fury with which the red man destroyed many of their [male adult] captives. . . . Male captives were often tortured to death in ways more fiendish than any inquisitor [like the torturers of suspected witches] ever devised.[10]

C In this selection, the late Francis Jennings, longtime director of the Native American Studies Program at the Newberry Library in Chicago, contributes his own general account of the relations between the English and the Native Americans. Jennings has little use for Vaughan's views and calls the confrontation between Native Americans and Europeans "the invasion of America." Does this phrase give a clue to his opinion about who was at fault for the destruction of Native American ways of life? Was the arrival of the Europeans in fact an "invasion"? Circle facts and underline opinions.

> A basic rule was that any given Englishman at any given time formed his views [of Native Americans] in accordance with his purposes. Those who came for quick plunder saw [Indian] plots and malignancy on every side; in a mirror image of their own intent, [these Englishmen's] savages were sinister and treacherous . . . much as the English saw Turks and Spaniards who were likewise fit objects of prey and likewise intransigent about accepting [the role the English assigned to them]. . . . When Indians were regarded as partners in a profitable trade, they appeared less threatening, and their vices were excused. When they resisted eviction from lands wanted by the colonizers, they acquired demonic dimensions. When they were wanted as soldiers for war against the French, the martial abilities of these [Indian] demons were appreciated rather than decried. In short, like the most modern of architects, the Englishman devised [an image of] the savage's form to fit [the Englishman's] function.[11]

D Colin Galloway is part of a new generation of Native American historians greatly influenced by anthropology. Indeed, the men and women in this group have been labeled *ethnohistorians* by some observers of their work. Ethnohistorians are Indian centered in their approach, trying to see the world of the natives through their own eyes. The accounts may or may not be supportive of native motives and actions but are always empathetic. In the following passage, Galloway describes the structures and rhythms of eastern woodland Native Americans' public speaking. Circle the facts and underline the opinions. As you read the selection, you will notice that the exercise of separating fact from opinion has become measurably harder. Why do you suppose that might be so?

> Even in translations that rob them of nuances and fluency, Indian speeches [from the seventeenth and eighteenth centuries] display oratorical power and testify to the richness and importance of the spoken word in native American cultures. Their metaphors and symbolism offer insights into how the speakers conceived of their universe and their place in it. . . . Until lately, Hollywood movies have created an impression that Indians spoke monosyllabic utterances, breaking away from "how" and "um" only to deliver stock phrases like "white man speak with forked tongue." In reality, Indian orators spoke well and at length. . . . Indian speakers employed rich images and powerful metaphors in their talks, but they also used humor, irony, sarcasm, anger, body language, and dramatic silences. Public speaking was an important part of Indian life, and oratorical prowess a common, respected, and often necessary skill. Indians did not give orders to their people—many North American Indian languages contain no imperative voice [command form of predicates]—they enlist their support through persuasion and influence.[12]

Relations between Native Americans and European-Americans are the subject of one of the saddest chapters in our history—sad because the encounter could have turned out much differently, because there were so many misconceptions on both sides, and because for so long historians failed to see through their own prejudices and their own need to give excuses for the many treacheries on both sides. Facing such gripping and argumentative points of view, how can you dissociate fact from opinion? Must you conclude that all historical arguments are just opinion, and therefore that one is just as true, or false, as another? What do you think?

_____

_____

_____

_____

_____

Historical-mindedness, the goal of all history students, cannot provide you with absolute truths, but it will change you. It will teach you to look for the difference between fact and opinion and help you to understand and appreciate the peoples of the past.

Notes

[1] Adapted from "He Whose Body Is Divided in Twain," an Iroquois folktale, reprinted in Frederick W. Turner III, ed., *The Portable North American Indian Reader* (New York: Viking Press, 1973), 50–54.

[2] From *Hopi Ruin Legends*, collected, translated, and edited by Ekkehart Malotki. (Lincoln: University of Nebraska Press, 1993). Reprinted by permission of Ekkehart Malotki.

[3] Ibid., 27, 33, 35, 45.

[4] William Bradford, *Of Plymouth Plantation, 1620–1647*, ed. Samuel Eliot Morison (New York: Modern Library, 1952), 3–4, 8, 10.

[5] John Smith, *A Description of New England* [1616] in Karen Ordahl Kupperman, ed., *Captain John Smith: A Select Edition of His Writings* (Chapel Hill: University of North Carolina Press, 1988), 247

[6] Lucien Febvre, "History and Psychology" in Febvre, *A New Kind of History and Other Essays*, ed. Peter Burke, trans. K. Folca (New York: Harper & Row, 1973), 7–8.

[7] Brother Luis Brandaon to Father Sandoval, March 12, 1610, in Elizabeth Donnan, ed., *Documents Illustrative of the History of the Slave Trade to America* (Washington D.C.: Carnegie Institute, 1930), 1:123–124.

[8] Alan C. Kors, and Edward Peters, eds., *Witchcraft in Europe, 1100–1700: A Documentary History* (Philadelphia: University of Pennsylvania Press, 1972), 274–275.

[9] Francis Parkman, *The Jesuits in North America* [1867], in Samuel Eliot Morison, ed., *The Parkman Reader* (Boston: Little, Brown, 1955), 41.

[10] Alden T. Vaughan, *New England Frontier, Puritans and Indians*, 1620–1675, rev. ed. (New York: Norton, 1979), 40.

[11] Francis Jennings, *The Invasion of America: Indians, Colonization, and the Cant of Conquest* (Chapel Hill: University of North Carolina Press, 1975), 59.

[12] Colin G. Galloway, *The World Turned Upside Down: Indian Voices from Early America* (Boston: Bedford Books, 1994), 11–12.

2: *The Elements of Style: Outlines, Paragraphs, and Papers*

Encounters in the Americas

At sea in the fall of 1492, Christopher Columbus kept a journal. He intended it as a present for the king and queen of Spain, and he planned to give it to them when he returned from "The Indies" with the riches of Asia in the holds of his three caravels. Even for the boldest of explorers—the "Admiral of the Ocean Sea," as Spanish royalty dubbed Columbus—writing was important. Without it, he could not recount the wonders he expected to find, the routes he would travel, and the character of the people who waited on the other shore. Columbus finished his journal, and it was truly filled with marvels—islands of sweet-smelling trees whose harbors, he judged, would safely welcome the entire fleet of Spain; fish and birds never seen by Europeans; and gentle natives who (he was certain) wanted to convert to Christianity and submit themselves to Spain's benevolent rule. Columbus expected that the journal would confirm for him his place in history, for it preserved the achievements of his voyage.

Ironically, the original journal was lost, but before that happened, Columbus's letters and reports were translated, and the message of riches spread among Europe's educated readers. Writing made Columbus famous. But writing for him was never easy, and it is not easy for most of us. The novelist Ernest Hemingway, who gave us *For Whom the Bell Tolls* and other superb novels, once admitted that he continuously feared that he would never be able to write another word. The winking cursor on the word processor screen holds a similar terror for many writers today. How can you avoid writer's block, the paralysis that sometimes visits when you must tackle an essay exam, complete a theme, write a book review, or prepare a term paper?

A good general rule came from the late historian Carl Becker, a wonderfully fluid and persuasive writer. His work on the Declaration of Independence remains deeply moving. In Richard Ford's recent Pulitzer Prize–winning novel, *Independence Day*, the narrator keeps a copy of Becker by his bed and plans to give it to his teenage son—a tribute to any writer. In 1942, Becker told a group of college students that the secret of his success as a writer was simple: he read and wrote constantly. Becker was right: the more you read, the better sense you have of good style; and the more you write, the easier writing becomes. In his youth, Benjamin Franklin wanted to write well and found models in English magazine essays. He copied these down word for word, waited a bit, then tried to rewrite them from memory. When Becker needed someone to quote to prove his point, he turned to Franklin. James Axtell, a leading Native American specialist, has summarized all of this advice: "What the historian should be preoccupied with are the qualities of good historical writing: accuracy, clarity, conciseness, disinterestedness, and vigor." The historian has to "love words."[1]

Is Writing History an Art or a Science?

Even the most famous historical writers in past centuries could never agree about whether they were literary figures or scientists. The controversy is still going strong. Should historical writing be modeled on the literary essay or the scientific report? Is written history a branch of literature or a type of science? Until the twentieth century, most historians regarded themselves as men and women of letters. At that time, a "man of letters" had considerable status in society. Thomas Babington Macaulay, perhaps the greatest stylist among nineteenth-century English historians, made a conscious decision to model his writing on the best examples of literature. His historical scholarship and his love of writing meshed perfectly and made his *History of England* one of the most admired works of literature as well as scholarship.[2]

Professor Jacques Barzun of Columbia University, a tireless modern advocate of Macaulay's position, has repeatedly warned against the dangers of regarding history as a science. He scorns "the 'theology of science' . . . [that] attracts impatient minds who fear that their free thoughts, however solidly based, will not command assent, whereas they know that the forms of science compel belief."[3] The magnetic attraction of "scientific history" worries Barzun because "The bloodless categories of classes and factors, forces and trends [characteristic of history-as-a-science writers] lack even the spare beauty of geometric figures. They are indistinct and unimaginable."[4]

Whether or not you agree with Barzun's opinions, he is quite correct that since the turn of the century the ideal of scientific precision has captivated many historians. In 1902, English historian J. B. Bury told an audience of future historical writers that "If, year by year, history is to become a more powerful force for stripping the bandages of error from the eyes of men . . . and advancing the cause of intellectual and political liberty, she will best prepare her disciples . . . by [reminding] them that . . . she is herself simply a science, no less and no more."[5]

Bury wrote before World War I, when European scholars truly believed that there would be universal peace because the science of history taught statesmen how to avoid war. The First World War shattered that faith, and World War II buried the broken pieces of it. Nevertheless, the dream of a scientific history still flourishes. As one modern historian recently reported, "The development of behavioral theory flowing from careful empirical studies and the refinement of statistical and mathematical models aided by modern computer technology have brought remarkable changes in the social sciences. These advances have convinced many historians that the marriage of science and history is now possible. At least, they argue, historical writing might become more scientific than it has been."[6] In the 1970s and 1980s, the proliferation of social histories and the rise of quantitative historical methods seemed to push history even further into the social science category. In recent years, the pendulum may be swinging the other way. Recently, historical scholars writing on such diverse topics as the Indian raids on colonial Deerfield, Massachusetts, the Lewis and Clark expedition, and the causes of the Civil War have invented dialogue, much as would authors of historical novels. History-as-art again flourishes.

Exercise 1: History—Story or Report?

Undoubtedly, writing history requires artfulness of two sorts: artifice and artistry. Your account is artificial because primary sources do not speak for themselves. You must arrange evidence into fact and fact into argument. What is more, your account must be artistic—adorned with compelling language—if it is to capture the assent of a reader. At the same time, writing history also demands the attentiveness of the scientist; you must prove or disprove hypotheses with thorough and thoughtful accuracy. Without taking sides in this debate, try this short exercise: lay any of your written history assignments alongside one of your laboratory reports and one of your English composition essays. Which of the last two pieces of writing does your history piece most closely resemble? Why?

_____

_____

_____

Analysis, Narration, and Depiction

Good historical writing may take many forms: sweeping syntheses and narrowly focused studies, textbooks and picture books, sprightly essays for general readers and densely argued articles for specialists. Historians even contribute op-ed pieces to newspapers. Prize-winning Civil War historian James McPherson recently reminded us that we must try harder to reach out to a wide audience if we wish history to regain its pride of place among the humanistic enterprises. To judge from the many bookcases devoted to historical subjects at giant bookstore chains like Barnes and Noble and Borders, historians have taken up this challenge. To appeal to broad readership as well as to communicate with colleagues in the profession, historians blend three types of writing.

The first type of writing is analytical. Analytical history is argumentative: it marshals evidence to persuade you that a particular thesis or theme is correct. Analytical history sometimes employs tables, graphs, and other quantitative materials, or borrows concepts and methods from anthropology, economics, psychology, and sociology. Today, much social and cultural history features analytical writing. The second genre of historical writing is narration. It traces an event or a group of people over the course of time. The story may be only a brief episode, or it may cover many years. Narration stresses chronological sequence. Military and political history often feature narratives. The third type of historical writing is depictive. Depiction re-creates a time and place in the past so that the reader can feel that he or she is actually there. It is lush with detail and may rely on literary devices as the author strives to excite the reader's imagination. Recent environmental and Native American histories offer superb depictions of lost worlds. No doubt you are thinking that the histories you have read frequently combine these forms, but you can build your skills as a writer, and your activity as a reader of history by learning the distinctions among these approaches to historical writing.

Exercise 2: Analysis, Narrative, and Depiction

A bird's-eye view of the Atlantic Ocean after 1500 would show a steadily increasing flow of people from east to west. Europeans and Africans were leaving their old homes and finding new ones in the Caribbean islands and coastal areas of the Western Hemisphere. At first, Native Americans were welcoming, but as the Europeans made themselves odious—capturing and carrying off natives or forcing them into slave labor, ignoring native hospitality customs, and revealing that they were not visitors but exploiters—some natives began to resist. European arms and European diseases to which natives had no natural immunity so weakened the Americans that they could not stop the European advance. As native populations plummeted, Europeans purchased or captured West Africans and brought them as slaves to plantations in the Americas.

Over the past few decades, American historians have begun to tell all these stories of the encounter between newcomers and natives, using analytical, narrative, and depictive forms of writing. For Exercise 2, we have excerpted six short passages from recent historical accounts of the first meeting of native and newcomer. Your job is to decide which of them are primarily analytical, which narrative, and which depictive, and then to explain your choice.

A After a month and a half of sailing west, Columbus's mariners were restive. False sightings of land had raised their hopes, which the empty expanse of sea at dawn dashed. The captains of the other ships in his small fleet thought about turning back. Rumors of mutiny spread from the sailors' bunks to Columbus's ears, and he had all he could handle in persuading officers and men to stay the course. Historian Samuel Eliot Morison tried to sort out the various accounts in his biography of Columbus. Is the selection primarily analysis, narration, or depiction?

> On October 9, when the course was altered to W by N by reason of a southerly shift in the wind, a wind so moderate that the average speed was only a trifle over 2 knots, Martin Alonso and Vicente Yáñez came aboard the flagship, held a more or less stormy conference with Columbus in his cabin, demanded that the search for land be abandoned, and that advantage be taken of the southerly breeze to start home. But Columbus (supported by the birds) succeeded in persuading the brothers to carry on three more days, and they returned to their respective vessels. Then, at sunrise October 10, the trade wind made up fresh, sending the fleet along at a speed of 7 knots, which reawakened the fears of *Santa Maria's* crew that they would never be able to return. Hence the flare-up of mutiny that day. Columbus made the same promise to his men that he had to the Pinzons, and by nightfall the last danger of abandoning the Great Enterprise on the brink of success, was over.[7]

What kind of writing? _____ Explain your choice. _____

B In *European Encounters with the New World* British historian Anthony Pagden pondered the adjustments in thinking that Europeans had to make when they found that there was a densely populated continent where none had been imagined. Is his account analysis, narration, or depiction?

> The traveller, the discoverer, the settler, the immigrant, the missionary and the colonist: all such people came to America with battered ambitions, different expectations and different objectives. But if they were at all sensitive, they all in time came to see that, culturally at least, incommensurability [of the Old World and the New] was inescapable. In the real world beyond the high wooden walls of [the European's ships], the stark differences between worlds could not be reconciled by the simple transportation of samples, the identification of geological forms, the naming of the unfamiliar for the familiar.[8]

What kind of writing? _____ Explain your choice. _____

C Ramón Gutiérrez's controversial and thought-provoking *When Jesus Came, the Corn Mothers Went Away: Marriage, Sexuality, and Power in New Mexico, 1500–1846* described the changes wrought in Pueblo Indian life by the arrival of the Spanish. The Franciscan Order played a dominant role in the colonization of the Southwest. Is the selection here analysis, narration, or depiction?

> From 1581 to 1680, Franciscans provided the impetus for colonization in New Mexico. For most of this period the friars were virtual lords of the land. They organized the Indians into a theocracy that lasted until the Pueblo Revolt in 1680. What also differentiated the "Franciscan century" from the period of territorial conquest that preceded it was the promulgation of the 1573 Ordinances of Discovery, in which the king outlawed grand military expeditions such as those of Cortés and Coronado. "Discoveries are not to be called conquests," the Ordinance stated. "Since we wish them to be carried out peacefully and charitably, we do not want the use of the term 'conquest' to offer any excuse for the employment of force or the causing of injury to the Indian." Henceforth, only peaceful settlement directed by missionaries would be allowed into remote, hitherto uncivilized areas.
>
> The Franciscans' desire to carry the Gospel to New Mexico in 1581 was the logical outgrowth of the missionary enterprise they had begun in the Valley of Mexico in 1524. As the Indian *doctrinas* (parishes) they established to convert the natives were increasingly secularized and placed under episcopal control after 1572, the Franciscans had two choices. They could terminate their active ministry and retreat to conventual life or push into new missionary fields. The friars who entered New Mexico in 1581 chose the latter option, inflamed by millennial dreams and aglow with the spirit of apostolic renewal.[9]

What kind of writing? _____ Explain your choice. _____

D James Axtell explored Native American responses to the arrival of newcomers in *Beyond 1492*. One of his essays followed the trail of the "Black Robes"—the Jesuits—in the Abnaki and Huron lands around the St. Lawrence River. Indian religious beliefs and Christianity met head-on in these encounters. What type of writing did Axtell use to describe the process?

> Another force for change was equally new and audacious, but it appeared less dangerous because it wore a human face, however disfigured by unsightly hair. If diseases were the shock troops of the invasion of America, Christian missionaries were its commandoes, disguised in feminine black robes as members of a Peace Corps. Although they came bearing a message from a "Prince of Peace," they unconsciously bore a whole civilization that would not tolerate the America they had found. In its claim to universality and adamantine truth, evangelical Christianity had no room for "false gods," strange rituals, and local beliefs. It sought to bend the "pagan" and "infidel" worlds to its own will and vision of the good, true, and beautiful. In America as in China, "Christianity was a religion that changed customs, called into question accepted ideas and, above all, threatened to undermine existing situations." In countless instances, it not only threatened, it did so. As agents of change, missionaries in post-Columbian America had no human equals and only one strain of superiors.

Perhaps the best agents of all were the Jesuits. By history and design, the Society of Jesus was destined to change the American world. It was a fraternity designed for war, the greatest human engine of social change.[10]

What kind of writing? _____ Explain your choice. _____

E Whether in the Caribbean, the Lawrentian Basin of Canada, or the Piedmont of the Carolinas, as James Merrell reminded us in his prize-winning *The Indians' New World,* the meeting of native and newcomer always brought an unwelcome visitor—European pathogens. Diseases like measles, chickenpox, and malaria came to the New World from the Old. The worst of the invaders was smallpox, which wiped out over 75 percent of some native populations. Merrell tracked the effect of these epidemics on the natives' everyday life. Is his account analysis, narration, or depiction?

At the most fundamental level, disease played havoc with the relations that defined a person's identity. Everyone born in a piedmont town had automatically become part of a network of real or fictive kin. Houses, fields, food storage and preparation—all were divided on this basis. Kin taught children the ways of the world, from the secrets of making pots or arrows to the enemies of their people, from proper behavior toward one's fellow villagers to the mysterious forces controlling the universe. Kin punished with teasing, shaming, and ostracism those who forgot these lessons. Kin met to celebrate a young hunter's first kill or decide on the propriety of a marriage offer. Kin avenged one when one was harmed, took care of one in sickness, and mourned one after death. Small wonder that the most enduring memory among Indians taken out of the Carolina interior by Pardo's men was of a life surrounded by "children, grandchildren, and great-grandchildren."[11]

What kind of writing? _____ Explain your choice. _____

F William Cronon's *Changes in the Land: Indians, Colonists, and the Ecology of New England* demonstrated that both native and newcomer changed the face of the land. In this selection, he compared the effects of northern New England and southern New England land practices. Is this passage analysis, narration, or depiction?

The effect of southern New England Indian villages on their environment was not limited to clearing fields or stripping forests for firewood. What most impressed English visitors was the Indians' burning of extensive sections of the surrounding forest once or twice a year. "The Savages," wrote Thomas Morton, "are accustomed to set fire of the Country in all places where they come, and to burne it twize a yeare, viz: at the Spring, and the fall of the leafe." Here was the reason that the southern forests were so open and parklike; not because the trees naturally grew thus, but because the Indians preferred them so. As William Wood observed, the fire "consumes all the underwood and rubbish which otherwise would overgrow the country, making it unpassable, and spoil their much affected hunting." The result was a forest of large, widely spaced trees, few shrubs, and much grass and herbage. "In those places where the Indians inhabit," said Wood, "there is scarce a bush or bramble or any cumbersome underwood to be seen in the more champion ground." By removing underwood and fallen trees, the Indians reduced the total accumulated fuel at ground level. With only small nonwoody plants to consume, the annual fires moved quickly, burned with relatively low temperatures, and soon extinguished themselves. They were more ground fires than forest fires, not usually involving larger trees, and so they rarely grew out of control. Fires of this kind could be used to drive game for hunting, to clear fields for planting, and, on at least one occasion, to fend off European invaders.

Northern Indians do not appear to have engaged in such burning. Because they did not practice agriculture and so were less tied to particular sites, they had less incentive to alter the environment of a given spot. Their chief mode of transportation was the canoe, so that they had less need of an open forest for traveling. Moreover, many of the northern tree species were not well adapted to repeated burning, and northern forests tended to accumulate enough fuel at ground level that, once a fire got started, it usually reached the canopy and burned out of control.[12]

What kind of writing? _____ Explain your choice. _____

Historical Prose Organization and Style

Historical writing is as varied as the skills and interests of its authors. There is no one correct way to write about a historical time or subject as there is a single correct answer to a simple algebraic problem. But there are some guidelines, standards, and rules that will help you make your arguments clear and improve your prose style. The following suggestions will work for any kind of historical writing, from an essay examination to a full-dress research paper.

Using an Outline

An outline can be likened to the frame of a house. There are great gaps between the studs and the crossbeams, but you can visualize what the house will look like from the framing. The typical outline format looks like this:

    I. (Roman numeral)
      A. (Capital letter)
        1. (Arabic numeral)
          a. (lowercase letter)

The Roman numerals (I, II, III, . . .) in an outline designate major sections of a paper. The remaining subdivisions of the outline represent paragraphs and sentences. The capital letters represent topic paragraphs; they are to the section what a topic sentence is to a paragraph. The Arabic numerals (1, 2, 3, . . .) represent paragraphs or sentences with supporting arguments. The lowercase letters represent individual sentences or parts of sentences containing supporting evidence, illustrative details, and examples. The first part of an outline of the topic "Why English People Came to New England and Virginia" might look like this:

Motives for Early English Migration to New England and Virginia

    I. Religious reasons
      A. Desire to be free of religious persecution
        1. Pilgrims looking for a safe haven
          a. Flight from England to Leyden, in the Netherlands
          b. Founding of the Plymouth Colony

  2. The migration of the Puritans
   a. Puritans set out to reform English Church practices
   b. Toleration of Puritan dissent ends
   c. Puritans begin to see New England as a place to establish their churches
 B. Desire to spread the Gospel among the Indians
  1. Competition with religious views of Spanish and French colonizers
   a. Religion as a method to gain labor of natives
   b. Religion and warfare in the colonies
  2. Missionary impulses
   a. Religion in the colonial charters
   b. The first English missionaries

II. Economic reasons . . .

There are four common ways to organize an outline. The first is chronological; the second is topical; the third is spatial; the fourth is biographical. In a chronological outline the argument follows the time sequence of events. Your account follows the actual occurrence of past events step by step. Chronological organization is not fancy, but it is almost always workable. Imagine that you have been assigned an essay or face an examination question on the subject "The Rise of the Spanish Empire in the Americas, 1492–1680." You decide that your main points should include Columbus's voyages; the conquest of the Caribbean; Cortés in Mexico; Panfiló de Naervez, Ponce de León, and Hernando de Soto in Florida and the Southeast; Coronado and the conquistadors of the Southwest; the colonization of New Mexico; and, finally, the Pueblo Indian uprising of 1680. Each of these events can be assigned a date or chronological period. By arranging your main points according to their temporal sequence, you have begun to assemble a chronological outline.

Topical outlines are best when you are writing about an idea rather than telling a story. For example, if you were asked to write an essay or an answer to an examination question on "The Contributions of the Native Americans to Colonial Life" you might decide to focus on four key ideas: (1) the European borrowing of Native American foods like corn, potatoes, and chocolate; (2) the labor that Native Americans contributed to European exploitation of rare minerals in the Americas; (3) the way in which Native American modes of land use (for example, extensive surface burning to give new life to old fields) enabled Europeans to bring land under cultivation; and (4) the effects of Indian models of social organization (for example, the relatively high degree of freedom and status of women among many Native American groups) on European communities. These economic and social ideas do not have exact dates, so you should arrange your main points topically. You decide which to explore first, which second, which third, and which fourth.

A spatial outline is best when you are describing a scene or an event that has a geographical dimension. An essay describing the Four Corners region of the Southwest or the northern New England coast on the eve of the arrival of the Europeans would be best served by a spatial outline. In a spatial outline you travel from one place to another in logical order. For example, in the first case, you might move from the Rio Grande Basin north to the Anasazi lands of northern New Mexico and southern Colorado. For the latter, you might begin with the Acadian coast and move south, past the estuaries of the Penobscot and Kennebec Rivers down to the mouth of the Merrimack.

The last common type of outline is biographical. In it, you focus on the life of one person and organize your essay or answer around the major events in that person's life. Do not give equal weight in your outline to major events and trivial occurrences in your subject's life. You have only so much time and space, so concentrate on what is important or dramatic. If you were to write about a major political figure from the era of the great migrations, you might choose Moctezuma, whose vacillation gave to the Spanish the great city of Tenoch-titlán and brought low the Aztec Empire. Or you might choose Hernan Cortés, the son of an obscure Hidalgo (Spanish country gentleman), whose political savvy and military skill enabled him to topple an empire and make himself governor of "New Spain." Perhaps your choice will be Opechancanough, a Pamunkey from the Chesapeake Bay region who lived for a hundred years and saw firsthand the contest among Europeans and the conflict between Europeans and Native Americans. Opechancanough was taken to Spain as a youth in 1561, baptized as Luis de Velasco, and returned home to America to convert his people to Catholicism, but instead he helped drive out the Spanish. In 1621, when his brother, Powhatan, died, Opechancanough became chief of the confederation his brother had forged and led another uprising, this time against the English settlers of Virginia. The "Massacre of 1622" nearly wiped out the English colony. Opechancanough survived English retaliation to lead a last attempt at liberation of his ancestral lands in 1644. Had he been successful, his story would have been told by the children of an Algonquin-speaking nation in what is now Virginia. Whomever you select, your outline would begin with that person's family and early career, use the next Roman numeral to cover the person's rise to power, then continue through his or her major achievements, and finish with a section on his or her lasting significance.

Exercise 3: Good Outlines Make Good Grades

The best essay examination answers follow outlines. The question itself dictates the outline, and the outline then shapes the essay. Let us assume that you are to write an essay on the following topic: "Trace the steps by which the English established settlements on the North American coast. What were the key events in this process?" First, read your textbook section on the English colonies. Next, organize your thoughts and your information. We have provided an outline with empty slots for you to fill with appropriate facts from your textbook. Note that the question is a chronological one and your outline is thus chronological.

    I. The first English colonies (major topic)
      A. The southern colonies (subtopic)
        1. _____ (piece of evidence)
          a. _____ (detail or example)
        2. _____ (second piece of evidence)
          a. _____ (detail or example)
      B. _____ (second subtopic)
        1. _____ (piece of evidence)
          a. _____ (detail or example)
          b. _____ (detail or example)
   II. The evolution of English imperial policy
      A. _____ (subtopic)
        1. _____ (piece of evidence)
          a. _____ (detail or example)
      B. _____ (second subtopic)
        1. _____ (piece of evidence)
          a. _____ (detail or example)
  III. _____ (third topic)
      A. _____ (subtopic)
        1. _____ (piece of evidence)
          a. _____ (detail or example)

   B. _____ (second subtopic)
   C. _____ (third subtopic)
      1. _____ (piece of evidence)
         a. _____ (detail or example)

Every essay question suggests a structure for an outline. After reading the appropriate section of your textbook, write a brief outline for one of the following questions in the space provided below.

1. What were the major differences between the Spanish and the English colonies in North America?

2. Trace the causes and the course of the wars among the English and French settlers of North America and their native allies from 1607 to 1713.

3. What did the Atlantic Rim trade routes look like in 1500? In 1600? In 1700? What were the most important products that were carried on these trade routes?

4. Sir Walter Raleigh, John Smith, and John Winthrop were all leading figures in the early English colonization of North America. How were their lives similar? How were their experiences different?

_____

_____

_____

_____

_____

_____

_____

_____

_____

_____

_____

_____

_____

_____

_____

_____

_____

_____

_____

The Workhorse of Historical Prose: The Paragraph

You are reading a paragraph at this moment. The paragraph is the true workhorse of expository writing, explaining and illustrating your arguments. Every good paragraph has a topic sentence, telling the reader what to expect. The topic sentence need not be the first sentence of the paragraph, although it often is. Can you spot the topic sentence in this paragraph? The topic sentence need not report everything to come, but a well-structured paragraph keeps the reader interested and informed of your intentions.

Each paragraph should contain no more than one main idea. The sentences in the paragraph deepen, broaden, and embellish that idea. You might think of them as a team whose goal is to persuade and charm the reader. Thus paragraphs ought not be one sentence long (the team would be playing without all its members), nor ought they be more than fifteen to twenty lines in length (no game could go on with the regulars and all the substitutes on the field at the same time). Of course, there are exceptions to this rule. If there is one absolute rule about writing, it is that there are no absolute rules about writing. Dialogue, ordinarily typeset in paragraph form, may be only one sentence long, and great writers like William Faulkner and Washington Irving wrote paragraphs that ran on for pages.

Linkages within and between paragraphs—transitions—enable your reader to follow your argument or understand your story. "By contrast," "on the other hand," "if . . . then . . . ," and "but for" are common signals that a transition is coming. Transitions at the ends of paragraphs are particularly important, for they maintain the flow of your essay from paragraph to paragraph. Such transitions should foreshadow what is to come. If each paragraph is wholly self-contained, your argument will seem disconnected and jumpy. It is the balance between new ideas, arguments, and evidence on the one hand, and linkages on the other, that keeps your prose moving smoothly.

Macaulay was a master of transitions. In one essay, he glided from a paragraph on travel in late-seventeenth-century England to one on the state of the roads, to the next on highwaymen, and so on to the dreadful state of inns in the English countryside. Every step of the way, the reader follows, never realizing the range and diversity of Macaulay's subjects, or the difficulties that Macaulay overcame in making so many complex topics so accessible. With "subtlety and care" Macaulay made each transition a simple, supple joy for his readers.[13]

Exercise 4: Choosing a Topic Sentence

The first sentence of a well-written paragraph ordinarily announces the topic of the paragraph and tells the reader what to expect. The remaining sentences make supporting arguments and give evidence. But not all authors make the first sentence of the paragraph into a topic sentence. In some of the writing samples below, taken from accounts of the European migration to the Americas in the seventeenth century, we have tampered with the author's own sentence order, moving the topic sentence from the beginning of the paragraph and inserting it elsewhere in the paragraph. In each paragraph identify the sentence that you think should be the topic sentence. Then justify your choice.

A David Cressy's narrative of the migration of English men and women to New England features this paragraph on the trans-Atlantic voyage. Underline the sentence you would choose as your topic sentence. In the space provided below, explain your choice.

The ship became a liminal space, floating free of conventional considerations. Even the tyranny of time was transformed, since the daily round at sea had nothing in common with the rhythms of a Suffolk village or a London street. Such conditions, involving fellowship

in adversity and the pursuit of common goals, are well known to intensify group cohe-
siveness and group commitment, so it is not far-fetched to imagine a bonding among
Atlantic travellers of the kind that is found among veterans of other intensive group experiences. Betwixt and between the Old World and the New, the passengers could be likened
to participants in a protracted *rite de passage*, enjoying an intensive form of *communitas*
while separated from their normal regime. Confined for eight to twelve weeks or more to
a tiny wooden world, the travellers were thrust into intimacies that might never have
developed on land.[14]

B Many slaves came to the Americas in a far different fashion than the English voy-
agers. These West Africans' "rite of passage" was to be chained in the hold of a slave ship.
This so-called middle passage was a cruel introduction to the fact that slavery in the
Caribbean and the mainland colonies would be far more onerous than slavery had been in
their homeland. Peter Kolchin's depiction is harrowing. Underline the sentence you believe
to be the best candidate for a topic sentence, and explain your choice in the space below.

> Men were usually kept in chains, in holds; women and children, fewer in number, were
> sometimes allowed greater freedom of movement. Next came the transatlantic voyage, or
> "Middle Passage." In ships run by "tight packers," who deplored the waste of space pro-
> vided by holds five feet high and who consequently installed middle shelves, creating two
> levels of two and a half feet, slaves were often crammed together so closely they could
> barely move. If the weather was good, slaves would be taken on deck daily and "danced,"
> a painful exercise for those in chains thought to combat scurvy (caused, unbeknownst to
> anyone at the time, by a deficiency of vitamin C).[15]

C Far more slaves were taken to the British sugar islands in the Caribbean than to the
mainland colonies. Slaves suffered terribly on plantations there, as did the English, as
Richard Dunn explains in his classic study, *Sugar and Slaves*. Once again, underline your
choice for a topic sentence, and explain your reasoning in the space provided.

> Had the English pioneers been trying to escape from their acquisitive European cul-
> ture, had they been craving for peace, simplicity, ease, and innocence, they might indeed
> have found paradise in the Indies. But the English were looking for El Dorado, not Eden.
> They had geared themselves for wealth, excitement, and violent combat, so they fought
> and played feverishly in the enervating heat, exploited the labor of white servants and
> black slaves, risked sudden death from mysterious diseases or the annihilation of their
> profits in smashing storms and buccaneering raids. The expectations the English brought
> with them and the physical conditions they encountered in the islands produced a hectic
> mode of life that had no counterpart at home or elsewhere in English experience. This is
> what it meant to live beyond the line. The physical environment of the Caribbean islands
> *was* distressing to the early planters, especially when considered in conjunction with the
> social habits that they brought with them.[16]

The Elements of Style: Outlines, Paragraphs, and Papers

D The planters of the West Indies created a "little England" on their islands, and many even returned to their homeland rather than stay in the tropics. The settlers of the Chesapeake, James Horn argues, were similarly determined to re-create in the New World what they had left behind in England. Once more, underline your pick, and explain your reasoning in the space below.

> The majority of men and women who lived in Maryland and Virginia during the seventeenth century were born and raised in England. Most spent their childhood and early teens in rural and urban communities of southern and central England, specifically London, the Home Counties, and the Bristol region. Participants in a rich and variegated culture at local and national levels, they brought to the Chesapeake attitudes acquired during a formative period in their lives in the native country. Chesapeake society was part of English society, an offshoot of the parent culture.[17]

The Good Sentence

Paragraphs are usually composed of at least two sentences. Sentences may vary in length. Washington Irving and William Faulkner wrote sentences that were pages long; Ernest Hemingway preferred very short sentences. The best sentences are clear and easy to understand; length is not important. Consider the following example of two sentences: "Then the creeping murderer, the octopus, steals out, slowly, softly, moving like a gray mist, pretending now to be a bit of weed, now a rock, now a lump of decaying meat while its evil goat eyes watch coldly. It oozes and flows toward a feeding crab, and as it comes close its yellow eyes burn and its body turns rosy with the pulsating color of anticipation and rage." (You can find out what happens to the crab in John Steinbeck's novel *Cannery Row*.)

The author gets away with an involuted sentence because you can almost see the octopus slither toward its prey. Your sentences can be simple or complex, with multiple parts. Try to vary your sentences to keep your reader's interest. Sometimes simple is best. Sometimes the complexity of your thought can be conveyed only through complex writing. As a rule, it is bad form to address the reader directly—unless you are writing a book like *Reading and Writing American History*.

Whenever possible, write in the active voice rather than the passive voice. For example, write "Roger Williams had a problem. The leaders of the Massachusetts Bay Colony would not listen to his ideas about religious toleration," instead of "The problem was experienced by Roger Williams. His ideas about toleration went unheard." Avoid "animistic language," wherein you attribute human powers to inanimate objects or ideas. It is tempting to make the "Constitution speak of rights" or have "religious doctrines cause controversy," but in actuality it was the drafters of the Constitution who spoke of rights and religious sectaries who spawned controversies.

The best expository writing features strong and descriptive verbs. Do not rely on the verb *to be*. Vary your verbs. Feel free to use dramatic verbs as well as descriptive ones. When Roger Williams offered, advanced, presented, proposed, submitted, or voiced his views, he pleaded, cajoled, begged, threatened, whined, and lectured, as well as spoke.

Sentences are strings of words. The English language has over 8 million words, many of them borrowed from other languages. You need not know them all to be an effective writer. William Shakespeare used only 50,000 different words to delight and entertain four centuries of English-speaking people. Although your dictionary probably includes jargon (technical terms or very specialized, generally unfamiliar words) and slang (colloquial or street language), we urge you to refrain from using jargon and slang. Steer clear also of clichés.

"Weasel words" are catchall words or terms that usurp the place of stronger, more precise language. The most common weasel words—*thing, field, sector, area, factor,* and *aspect*—have precise meanings of their own. A thing is an inanimate object; a field may be plowed; a sector is a part of a map or plan; an area is a measure of two-dimensional space; a factor is a commercial agent or a mathematical operator; and an aspect is the appearance or demeanor of an object or a person. These words should not replace more precise delineators or names.

Do not make up new words. Avoid words ending in *ize,* such as *finalize* and *initialize*; use *finish* and *begin* instead. Do not add *wise* to the ends of your nouns. Do not overuse weak connectors like *however* and *nevertheless.* And remember that *while* and *since* denote duration of time; use *because* when you want to explain causation. Finally, avoid contractions; do not use *don't* in formal writing.

Correct English usage is a joy to read but not much fun to master. Here are some common stumpers *adapted* (made to fit), not *adopted* (taken exactly as is), from Walter Sullivan and George Core's delightful *Writing from the Inside* (1983). An *allusion* is a reference to a fact or a person; an *illusion* is a false impression. An *alternate* is a substitute; an *alternative* is a choice. *Blatant* means loud and obvious; *flagrant* means rude and obnoxious. To *compose* is to create; to *comprise* is to include or contain. *Continual* means regularly, at set periods; *continuous* means incessantly, without respite. *Disinterested* means neutral; *uninterested* means not interested. *Eminent* suggests respectability and esteem; *imminent* suggests immediately forthcoming; *immanent* means inherent and often is used to describe a deity's presence. *Exceedingly* means extremely; *excessively* means beyond any acceptable limit. *Farther* is used with distances; *further* is used with degree of effort. A *feasible* project is one you can accomplish; a *possible* project is one you might accomplish. To *imply* means to suggest; to *infer* means to deduce. *Oral* means spoken; *verbal* means relating to words. To *precede* means to come before; to *proceed* means to go on or to advance. *Sensual* means lewd; *sensuous* means appealing to the senses.

In the end, your prose style will be unique because you are unique, but it will not convey your message if you slip into errors of usage, grammar, and tone. For more on prose style, consult the latest editions of E. B. White and William Strunk's *The Elements of Style* and H.W. Fowler's *Modern English Usage.*

Exercise 5: Pick a Sentence, Any Sentence . . .

The following short samples from two of the finest stylists among modern professional historians demonstrate the power of superb historical writing. You feel you are there. Read each passage, paying special attention to the structure of sentences and the choice of words. How does the arrangement of the sentences build your expectations? What emotions and ideas does the choice of words and phrases evoke? Return to the passages and find the places that touched your feelings. Underline three of these and in the space below each paragraph explain how the phrase or sentence worked for you.

A At the beginning of the eighteenth century, Deerfield, Massachusetts, was still a frontier town. It had been raided in earlier days, but the rich meadowlands on the south side of the Deerfield River, a tributary of the Connecticut River, were too good to abandon. By 1703, however, war was again sweeping down from the north upon the village. John Demos's Parkman Prize–winning account returns us to the eve of the tragedy of the "Deerfield Raid" of 1704.

> Deerfield, Massachusetts. October 1703. Harvest over. First frost. The valley ablaze with autumn color: reds and yellows at the sides (along the forested ridges of East Mountain and the lower hills to the west), green of the meadows in between. The river low and languorous, a glassy rope snaked through the center. The most beautiful month, sunset of the year.
>
> Do the townspeople notice? No, they are fixed on the night ahead. Danger grows in darkening corners. Night of winter, night of want, night of war.
>
> They have, already, shocking news "from the eastward": the "mischief" done by French and Indian enemies along the Maine frontier. Will it be their turn next? They make what preparations they can. For some years past, Deerfield, like other exposed villages, has maintained a protective "fort" (or "stockade"). Within this central area of roughly ten acres, enclosed by a tall picket fence, the entire populace can be gathered in case of attack. The fence, however, has rotted in some places. And the housing within the fort falls far short of current need: perhaps a dozen regular dwellings, plus a few "cellars" and "small houses." (This, for a community of roughly 300.) So, they must rebuild the fence and create additional shelter inside.[18]

1. _____
   _____

2. _____
   _____

3. _____
   _____

B Martha Ballard was a pioneer woman, but she never went west. She lived on the Kennebec River, in Maine, bore nine children and buried three of them, was a midwife and nurse, prepared and dispensed folk remedies, and in the dead of winter crossed the dangerous ice whenever a neighbor called for aid. Born in 1735, she began a remarkable diary in 1785 and kept at it until her death in 1812. The diary is the basis for Laurel Thatcher Ulrich's Pulitzer Prize–winning book, *A Midwife's Tale* (1990), from which this excerpt is taken. Ballard has crossed the icy river to deliver Mrs. Byrnes's twins.

> Characteristically, the one obstetrical comment in the [diary] entry ("There was but a short space between the Births") is embedded in seemingly extraneous references to the weather, her journey, the names of the men who assisted her across the river and of the women who sat up with her through the night. The biological event fades into the clutter of social detail. Where is the center of the picture? Is it Martha Ballard scrambling up the icy bank, Mr. Dingley grasping one arm, Mr. Graves reaching toward her from above, while [her husband] Ephraim slowly turns his boat in the ice-rimmed river below? Is it Mrs. Byrnes, exhausted from her eight-hour labor, bearing down for the second delivery? Is it Mrs. Conry easing two perfect babies into the cradle, or the three drowsy women leaning toward the kitchen fire, the midnight cold at their backs, small clouds of mist above their whispers? There is no center, only a kind of grid, faint trails of experience converging and deflecting across a single day.[19]

1. _____
   _____
2. _____
   _____
3. _____
   _____

Term Papers and Research Papers

History is taught in almost every conceivable classroom setting in modern colleges and universities, from the small pro-seminar to the giant lecture hall. The vast majority of students in introductory history courses do not have the opportunity to write term papers or research papers. However, students in upper-level courses and "methods" courses for history majors may be asked to prepare research papers. The concluding pages of this chapter are directed to those students who face the daunting but rewarding prospect of carrying out such an assignment.

To write well on any historical subject, whether you are writing an essay answer for an exam or a full-fledged term paper, you must first know your subject. Students who are having trouble starting to write will often discover that they are not yet masters of all their material. More study or outside reading on the topic will solve that problem.

Thinking and Doing Research and Writing

In the midst of writing his famous history of England, Macaulay reported that he was always busy "thinking" and "doing." Like Macaulay, you have to think about your paper as a whole. Ask yourself what you want readers to learn from it. A good method for focusing your thoughts is to try to write down your theme or argument in no more than four lines. You must think through your arguments and plan how to prove each of them.

When Macaulay said that he was busy "doing," he did not mean only writing. Instead, he was constantly arranging and rearranging his evidence. Once you have enough evidence from primary and secondary sources to begin to see the general outline of your arguments, you can design a master plan for your paper. As you frame your master plan, continue to ask yourself whether you have enough material from your sources to support your arguments. Remember, writing and reading should loop around each other. Writing guides and directs further research. Do not hesitate to go back to the library to fill in gaps in your research that your writing reveals; then fill in those gaps with additions to your master plan.

Research

Your research will take you to libraries and archives. You probably have familiarized yourself with your school's library. Archives are buildings or parts of buildings that house collections of primary sources; they come in all shapes and sizes. The archive that houses United States documents, including the Declaration of Independence and the Constitution, is the National Archives in Washington, D.C. This giant rectangular building on the mall has two entrances. Every day thousands of Americans and foreign guests walk through the display area in the front of the building to view our Declaration of Independence and our Constitution. Thousands of researchers use the rear doors to spend the day reading and taking notes on millions of documents relating to diplomacy, government, war, and politics. The Library of Congress complex is located behind the Capitol. The ornate Jefferson building, shown in Figure 2.1, is a beautiful library containing almost every book ever published. The more functional Madison building across the street houses the papers of many famous and not-so-famous Americans in its special collections. Both are open to the public.

Not every archive is as spacious or imposing as the National Archives or the Library of Congress. In every state and many cities in our country there are historical societies and libraries that house collections of historical documents. The *Library of Congress Guide to Manuscript Collections* lists these, as well as collections of papers and manuscripts left to archives.

Archives collect and preserve two kinds of materials—public documents and private papers. Government archives like the State Archives of North Carolina in Raleigh or the State Library in Trenton, New Jersey, are the repositories for official state court records, legislative papers, and government-agency minutes and orders. State archives may also house private papers—letters, account books, family records, and similar primary sources. State and local historical societies are repositories of correspondence, diaries, account books, and unpublished writings. Sometimes the sources are famous men and women, sometimes less well-known people whose papers were lovingly preserved by their descendants and given to the historical society. "Keep every scrap of paper," Abraham Lincoln's secretary John Nicolay wrote to Lincoln's only surviving child, Robert Lincoln, "Everything is priceless."

In addition, there are many web sites on the internet that are or have links to primary sources. Some of these are associated with course materials for your history course. Pearson

FIGURE 2.1 *Interior of the Jefferson Building of the Library of Congress*
Courtesy of Kelly-Mooney/Corbis Images

Higher Education for example, has a number of web sites of this type. Blackboard™ is one of these. When you download a primary source (a document, letter, or other item) from these on-line sites, you must fully document the source just as if you went to the library and copied it by hand or on a photocopier. You need to include the entire web citation as well as the full reference to the document. (We'll have more to say about internet sources and web searches in Chapter 5.) Note that the restrictions on copying and the warnings about plagiarism that appear later in this chapter apply as well to materials taken from the web. In particular, you may under no circumstances characterize materials created on the web by another author or web provider as your own.

Taking Notes from Your Sources

Whether you find your primary and secondary sources at the library, the archive, or on the web, you have to take notes. Traditionally, scholars copied original documents in longhand, word for word. Some, like biographer Barbara Tuchman, used 4-by-6-inch note cards; others, like Milton Lomask, used sheets of 8½-by-11-inch paper. With the advent of modern photocopying methods, many scholars now prefer to ask the library or archive staff to photocopy primary sources. Some primary sources cannot be photocopied (the light and heat of the machine will destroy the document), but some archives will photograph the document and sell the microfilm. Most secondary sources can be photocopied, but the cost can become prohibitive.

Today many historians and history graduate students have replaced note cards and pens (or pencils, if they are working in a manuscript room) with laptop computers and note-taking software. Among the latter commercial offerings, a recent survey that we conducted indicated that Nota Bene™ is the favorite, but any word-processing software can be employed in this manner. Most recent versions of word-processing software have the ability to perform keyword searches, and some can index entries in a file alphabetically. If you feel comfortable with a laptop and have the appropriate software, most archives and libraries will let you use them to take notes. As with handwritten notes, you must double-check everything to make sure it is absolutely accurate.

Let us assume you decide to copy your sources on note cards or into your laptop. For each source you use, prepare a source or bibliography card or laptop entry. On this card or entry, write the exact title of the course, including the name of the collection in which it appears and the archive or library where you found it. If the source is published, write a full bibliographical citation. Keep your bibliography cards together, and back up your hard disk files with floppies.

If you are writing note cards, each card you use for transcribing quotations should have its own heading giving an abbreviated description of the source's title or the name of the collection and the particular source you are quoting. Remember to include page numbers for your quotations from printed sources. *Use only one side of each note card.* If your document or quotation needs more space, use additional cards. Number the cards consecutively. After you have finished copying the source onto the card, check word for word to be sure there is no error.

If you are using a laptop or other computer, keep the quotations on the same file as the bibliographical entry. Label the files so that you can sort through them easily. Keep a separate file or a notebook that lists the file names and their contents. Remember to back up everything on a floppy. Keep your note cards and floppies in a small box or closed bag. When the number of your note cards begins to swell, sort them by topic, author, date, event, or by the place they will go in your paper. Put all cards in the same category in an envelope, file folder, note-card box, or bundle.

You may want to take notes from some sources without copying them word for word. Head the note card or the laptop entry just as you would if you were copying the entire document or letter, and then, in your own words, summarize the gist of the source. This method is useful when you want to retain the important parts of a long document or take notes from a book or article. On the note card or in the entry, quote only those passages that best represent the author's thoughts or present them in the most dramatic or colorful language. Always include the page numbers when you have quoted or paraphrased from a printed source. Recheck your quotations to make sure they are correct.

A word to the wise: the most exasperating experience for a reader or researcher is recalling something important in a primary source but forgetting where you saw it. There is no way to prevent this from happening occasionally. The best rule is, when in doubt, take a note. Even when you have your laptop with you, carry around a notebook or note cards. The corollary to this rule is equally important: when you take a note, take down a full citation. A citation is a record of the source of your note. You do not want to repeat an archival search to find the origin of a quotation you already have. Good examples and good advice for note takers abound in Neil R. Stout, *The History Student's Vade Mecum* (1990) and Donald J. D. Mulkerne and Donald J. D. Mulkerne, Jr., *The Perfect Term Paper: Step by Step* (1988).

You may also want to keep a research diary. The research diary not only helps preserve a record of everything you saw but is a good place to jot down ideas for future research or notes for writing your theme or paper. Buy a spiral binder, and each day you go to the library or the archives, start a new page in the diary. Label it with the date, the assignment, the library or archive you are visiting, and the collections you use. Every time you copy a document or ask the archivist to copy a document, make a brief descriptive note in your diary. Some historians not only keep their diary entries in the spiral notebook, they copy the primary sources into the notebook as well. Even if you are using a laptop, a research notebook is a good idea. Laptops have been known to crash.

Exercise 6: Taking Notes

This exercise will give you practice in transferring information from your sources to note cards or notebooks. (The same techniques are useful in preparing book reviews.) The two paragraphs describe the changing racial composition of early South Carolina. Read each passage and the instructions that follow to complete the exercise.

> Throughout the first twenty-five years the documentary evidence suggests that most Negroes arriving in Carolina were brought in small numbers, by specific owners, from points in the western hemisphere. For example, in 1683 the ship *Betty*, "rideing att Anchor in the Roade of Barbadoes & bound for Ashley River in Carolina," took aboard six Negroes, along with two half-barrels of flour and two barrels of rum, for delivery "unto Bernard Schenckingh or to his Assignes." Upon their arrival, Schenckingh was to pay what must have been the standard shipping charge of fifty shillings per head for the group of slaves, which included four men (June, Meningo, Walle, Bache), one young woman (Cumboe), and a boy (Popler). Because of the direction of Carolina's mercantile ties and the broader patterns of the English slave trade, Barbados served as the main source for this small-scale commerce in Negro labor.[20]

Underline the words and phrases in the passage that you think are most important for a paper on race and labor in the early southern colonies. Next, using your own words, write three complete, grammatically correct sentences summarizing the author's main point. Be brief; accustom yourself to recording a lot of information with few words. We have put a heading on the note card for you.

Peter H. Wood, *Black Majority: Negroes in Colonial South Carolina from 1670 Through the Stono Rebellion* (New York: Norton, 1975), 45–46.

_____

_____

_____

_____

_____

During the first twenty-five years after the founding of South Carolina, roughly one out of every four settlers was a Negro. These first black Carolinians, scarcely more than a thousand in number, came from the West Indies, and most were retained as slaves by a small number of aspiring white immigrants from Barbados. During the quarter century after 1695 this racial balance shifted markedly, so that by the time the colony's Proprietors gave way to a royal government in 1720, Africans had outnumbered Europeans for more than a decade. But South Carolina's population, when free Indians are excluded, still totaled fewer than nineteen thousand people.[21]

Again, underline the key words or phrases; then summarize the argument on the note card below. Notice that you can now use a "short title" version of the heading on the first note card.

Wood, *Black Majority,* 131.

_____

_____

_____

_____

_____

First, Second, and Final Drafts

Let us assume that you have done enough research to begin writing. Your tentative outline, your note cards or laptop and research files, and your bibliography cards are at hand. You have allowed yourself enough time and space to begin, and you have found a quiet place in which to work. It is time for a first draft.

Some researchers prefer to wait until they have finished all their reading before starting to write. Charles Tilly, one of the foremost historians of early modern history, reminds his students to be on the lookout for additional "links in the chain of evidence." Tilly wants his students to ask themselves whether they can improve their account by adding one more person, place, or thing. Tilly's advice is priceless. For example, if you are writing about warfare in the northeastern woodlands, you should ask yourself whether your account would be stronger if you also looked at similar events in the western Pennsylvania forests. If you find that the additional links would not help to explain the main topic, then the chain has extended far enough, and your research is complete.

A few historians took this rule to an extreme. For example, the late Frederick Jackson Turner, one of the most forceful thinkers among early-twentieth-century historians, could never bring himself to write his definitive book on the relationship between the different sections of the United States before the Civil War. He always had more evidence to collect and more maps to draw. His dedication to completeness consumed him (an example of the holistic fallacy you will encounter in Chapter 4) and cost his readers a very good, if not perfect, book.

Other researchers do not delay writing. As the late English historian Edward Hallett Carr admonished his readers:

> The commonest assumption appears to be that the historian divides [the] work into two sharply distinguishable phases or periods. First, [he or she] spends a long preliminary period reading . . . sources and filling . . . notebooks with fact: then, when this is over, [he or she] puts away [the] sources, takes out [the] notebooks, and writes . . . from beginning to end. This is to me an unconvincing and implausible picture. For myself, as soon as I have got going on a few of what I take to be the capital sources, the itch becomes too strong and I begin to write—not necessarily at the beginning, but somewhere, anywhere. Thereafter, reading and writing go on simultaneously. The writing is added to, subtracted from, re-shaped, cancelled, as I go on reading. The reading is guided and directed and made fruitful by the writing: the more I write, the more I know what I am looking for, the better I understand the significance and relevance of what I find.[22]

Whether you wait until all your research is done, or begin writing as soon as you have something to say, be mindful that everything you write is a reflection on you. Neatness counts. For your first draft, use standard size (8½-by-11-inch), ruled paper (if you are writing the draft by hand) or bond (if you are typing or using a word processor). Double-space to leave room for insertions or corrections. Keep a dictionary and thesaurus handy. Do not worry if your first draft is longer than the assignment. It is easier to cut than to add. Tell your story from beginning to end. If you are blocked at a particular point, simply go beyond it. You can always return to a difficult passage or idea later. Put in all the quotations you are going to use. Alongside the quotation, at the bottom of the page, or on a separate sheet of paper, write down the full citation for each quotation you use, for protection in the event that a note card is lost or mutilated. If you are using a computer, put the footnotes or endnotes in the first draft. (See the next section for the rules of quoting and citing quotations.) Make a copy of your finished draft, and lay it aside for a day or two.

When you come back to your first draft, you may be disappointed that your writing is not as crisp or as colorful as you thought it was—first drafts are always disappointing to authors. Reread your text with the following questions in mind:

1. Did I make my points clear? Can another reader fully and immediately understand what I meant?

2. Does my paper have a beginning, a middle, and an end? Do I need to reorganize my arguments so that they flow smoothly from one to another?

3. Do I have enough evidence to support my arguments or illustrate my points?

4. Is my style fluid and my grammar correct? Would another reader enjoy my paper?

5. Have I properly used formal scholarly apparatus, quoting and citing according to the rules?

6. Have I made a real contribution on my topic? Do I seem to know what I am doing? Am I proud of my work?

In your second draft, revise the paper to respond to the questions you asked yourself. Do not hesitate to return to the library or archive or to seek advice from your instructor on difficulties. The second draft is still a working copy, but it should resemble the finished product. Have someone whose judgment you trust read your second draft after you have finished it. If your instructor offers to read second drafts, take advantage of the offer. Listen to criticism and further revise the paper if necessary. Make copies of every draft you submit.

Your third or "clean" version is the paper on which you will be graded. It should be neat and presentable. Type or print out your final paper double-spaced. Use 1-inch margins at the top, bottom, and sides of the paper. Number every page except the title page. Recheck your paper for spelling or factual errors. Hand it in with pride.

Quoting and Citing the Words of Others

Whether you are writing a theme, a book review, or a longer research paper, some of the words you use will be taken from your sources. When you copy words or ideas from primary or secondary sources, you must give credit to your source; otherwise you are guilty of plagiarism. Plagiarism is both cheating and theft, and offenders will always be punished severely. Your student handbook describes your school's rules on this offense, but take our advice: *Never do it.*

When using others' words or ideas, you may quote or paraphrase. A quotation is word-for-word borrowing. When should you quote? You may quote in order to prove a point you are making. The best proof will often be the words used in the source. Although this kind of quotation may be quite long (a "block" quotation), you should not quote any more of your source than you have to in order to prove your point. Long quotations tend to weary the reader. You also quote when you cannot say it better in your own words. You may quote short passages to enhance your own account; quotations of this sort are best merged into your writing a few words or sentences at a time.

The best term papers are those that bear the stamp of your own thinking and style. When one of the authors of this book was in middle school, his brother, then a college junior, returned home for the Thanksgiving Day holiday and announced that he had to submit a fifty-page history paper the following Monday. He then smiled and continued, "Don't worry. I'll find three or four books on the subject and quote whole pages from them. That should take up half the assignment. The rest I can make up myself." Can you guess the grade he received when he turned in his work? Do not submit a paper that is little more than a string of quotations.

Enclose all direct quotations in quotation marks (" "). If there is a quotation within the quotation (quoting an author who is quoting someone else), use single quotation marks inside the double quotation marks (" ' ' "). If your quotation is longer than five lines, set it off as a separate block of text. Indent five spaces from both margins. Do not use quotation marks at the beginning or end of block quotations.

If you have left out a word, phrase, or any other material from a quotation, use three dots (. . .), an ellipsis, to show the omission. If the missing material includes a period, add that to the ellipsis (. . . .). Do not leave out material that would change the meaning of the quotation. This is often done in advertisements for movies and books. The reviewer may have said, "The *Purple People Eaters* is the most terrible movie I have ever seen," but the ad says, "The *Purple People Eaters* is the most." When you quote, be fair to the spirit as well as the words of the author. You may add material to a quotation to explain a term in it or correct the author's error if you put your comments in brackets ([ ]). If you want to alert the reader to an obvious error in the question, you can put "[sic]" right after the error.

You may decide not to use a direct quotation but to rephrase what the source says and report it in your own words. Paraphrasing is perfectly legitimate scholarship. You can reduce a long quotation to a short paraphrase or capture the essence of a description or a conversation in a paraphrase. As in direct quotation, be sure that your paraphrase reflects the spirit of your source, and always cite its source.

Reference Notes

Whether you quote or paraphrase, you must give credit to your source. In historical writing, you use a reference citation to give credit. The reference citation can be placed at the bottom of the page (a footnote) or at the end of the paper (an endnote). Reference notes or citations are signaled in the text of your paper by a raised number. Each citation should contain the name of the author or editor, the title of the work, the publisher and place of publication, the date, and the pages quoted or cited. It should look like this:

    1. Arthur M. Schlesinger, Jr., *The Age of Jackson* (Boston: Little, Brown, 1945) p. (or pp., if more than one page), followed by the page number(s).

If the work is an article, include the title of the article, the title of the journal or magazine in which it appeared, and the volume number and date of the journal or magazine. A note to an article in a journal would look like this:

    1. John Lauritz Larson, " 'Bind the Republic Together': The National Union and the Struggle for a System of Internal Improvements," *Journal of American History* 74 (September 1987), p. (or pp., if more than one page).

If the work is an unpublished manuscript, include the author's name, the name of the recipient (if a letter), the date of the writing, the name of the collection in which you found the manuscript, the name of the archive or library where it is kept, and the page number if it has one:

    1. Frederick Douglass to William Lloyd Garrison, February 26, 1846, Frederick Douglass Papers, Yale University Library, New Haven, Conn.

A citation to a primary source that is published combines the forms for manuscript and published works:

    1. Frederick Douglass, "The Southern Style of Preaching to Slaves, January 28, 1842," in John W. Blassingame et al., eds., *The Frederick Douglass Papers* (New Haven: Yale University Press, 1979–), 1:17.

Note that Douglass's talk is in Volume 1 of his published papers but that there are additional volumes. When using a primary source cited in a secondary source or published in a collection, always give the full citation of the secondary source.

Citation of materials from the web has to be complete. For example, Stephen Aron's review of Alan Taylor's *American Colonies* in the online journal *Common-Place* should have the following citation:

Steven Aron, "Continental Visions: Review of Alan Taylor, *American Colonies.* New York: Viking, 2001" in *Common-Place* 3 (October 2002) *www.common-place.org/vol-03/no-01/reviews/aron.shtuml*

This full citation enables your reader to find the article on the Web.

The ruling concept behind citations is to give anyone using just your reference note enough information to find the exact words you read and quoted. There have been cases in which fine historians were sloppy in their reference notes, and minor errors in the notes—errors that did not weaken the argument in the body of the work—called the entire book or article into question.

Explanatory Notes

You may want to include in a footnote or an endnote material that explains, amplifies, or examines additional evidence about a point you have made in the text of your paper. Use an explanatory note to do this. The explanatory note may include references to one or more primary or secondary sources. These are usually enclosed in parentheses. The end result can look like a mini-paper. At one time, authors gave separate numbers or symbols for these explanatory notes, but now it is the custom to mix them in with the reference notes.

How many notes do you need? There is no set rule. You must provide a citation for every direct quotation and paraphrase, but note numbers for these may appear throughout the text or merely at the end of each paragraph. The former method helps the reader to find every reference but clutters your paragraphs with numbers. The block-citation method, in which all references that appear in a paragraph are given in a single citation signaled by one note number at the end of the paragraph, is more common than the multiple-citation form. It is easier and less distracting to block-cite, but an author can hide holes in his or her evidence in block cites more easily than in individual references. If you are asked to write a research paper for your course, your instructor may indicate a preference for individual or block citations. Manuals that offer models for citation include Kate L. Turabian, *A Manual for Writers of Term Papers, Theses, and Dissertations* (6th ed., 1996), and James D. Lester, *Writing Research Papers: A Complete Guide* (6th ed., 1996).

If You Word Process Your Papers

We strongly recommend that you prepare your papers using word processing software on a computer. Modern computers use function keys, a mouse, or a touch pad to move you about the paper at the blink of an eye. Alterations, additions, and revision are much easier, and all modern software programs for word processing allow you to set margins, do foot or end notes, change the spacing and font (type face), and number pages with a few key strokes. Your software will enable you to find and replace words. Microsoft Word™ and Corel WordPerfect™ are the two most popular programs. Versions of both are available for DOS and Apple operating systems.

To write well, you must write often and be willing to edit your own work. Invariably the papers that get the lowest grades are the ones that have not been revised. There are no shortcuts to good writing, but practice still makes perfect.

Notes

[1] James Axtell, *Beyond 1492: Encounters in Colonial North America* (New York: Oxford University Press, 1992), 21.

[2] I have taken this account from John Clive, *Macaulay: The Shaping of the Historian* (New York: Random House, 1973), 476.

[3] Jacques Barzun, *Clio and the Doctors* (Chicago: University of Chicago Press, 1974), 155.

[4] Ibid., 157.

[5] J. B. Bury, "The Science of History" (inaugural lecture as Regius Professor of Modern History, Cambridge University, 1902), reprinted in Fritz Stern, ed., *The Varieties of History* (New York: Meridian Books, 1956), 223.

[6] Harold D. Woodman, "Economics and Scientific History," *Journal of Interdisciplinary History* 5 (1974), 295.

[7] Samuel Eliot Morison, *Admiral of the Ocean Sea: A Life of Christopher Columbus* (Boston: Little, Brown, 1942), 290–291.

[8] Anthony Pagden, *European Encounters with the New World* (New Haven: Yale University Press, 1993), 41.

[9] Ramón Gutiérrez, *When Jesus Came, the Corn Mothers Went Away: Marriage, Sexuality, and Power in New Mexico, 1500–1846* (Stanford, Calif.: Stanford University Press, 1991), 46.

[10] James Axtell, *Beyond 1492: Encounters in Colonial North America* (New York: Oxford University Press, 1992), 155.

[11] James Merrell, *The Indians' New World: Catawbas and Their Neighbors from European Contact Through the Era of Removal* (Chapel Hill: University of North Carolina Press, 1989), 20.

[12] William Cronon, *Changes in the Land: Indians, Colonists, and the Ecology of New England* (New York: Hill and Wang, 1983), 49–50.

[13] John Clive, *Not by Fact Alone: Essays on the Writing and Reading of History* (Boston: Houghton Mifflin, 1989), 20.

[14] David Cressy, *Coming Over: Migration and Communication Between England and New England in the Seventeenth Century* (Cambridge: Cambridge University Press, 1987), 151.

[15] Peter Kolchin, *American Slavery, 1619–1877* (New York: Hill and Wang, 1993), 21.

[16] Richard S. Dunn, *Sugar and Slaves: The Rise of the Planter Class in the West Indies, 1624–1713* (New York: Norton, 1973), 45.

[17] James Horn, "Adapting to a New World: A Comparative Study of Local Society in England and Maryland, 1650–1700," in Lois Green Carr, et al., eds., *Colonial Chesapeake Society* (Chapel Hill: University of North Carolina Press, 1988), 133.

[18] John Demos, *The Unredeemed Captive: A Family Story from Early America* (New York: Knopf, 1994), 11.

[19] Laurel Thatcher Ulrich, *A Midwife's Tale: The Life of Martha Ballard, Based on Her Diary, 1785–1812* (New York: Knopf, 1990), 182–183.

[20] Peter H. Wood, *Black Majority: Negroes in Colonial South Carolina from 1670 Through the Stono Rebellion* (New York: Norton, 1975), 45–46.

[21] Ibid., 131.

[22] E. H. Carr, *What Is History?* (New York: Random, 1967), 32–33.

3: Evidence of the Past: Primary Sources

The Colonial Period

There is an old Japanese tale about a warrior and his wife who are attacked in the woods by a bandit. No one questions the end result: the husband is killed, the wife abused, and the bandit captured, but when the magistrates try to find out what happened, they get conflicting stories. The bandit boasts of his bravery; the wife calls him and her husband cowards and clowns; and the ghost of the husband protests that his conduct was honorable. Finally, a woodsman appears who saw the whole affair from a hiding place in the bushes. He contradicts all the other stories, and the magistrates believe him. But unbeknownst to the magistrates, the woodsman too had a reason to lie: he had found and kept the warrior's beautiful knife. Everyone had a different perspective on what happened and, perhaps, a reason to lie as strong as any reason to tell the truth.

Like the magistrates in the Japanese story, the historian begins with evidence. The evidence may be oral or written. Eyewitnesses may be lying or trying to tell the truth. Even a witness who wants to see everything and tell all is handicapped by the limitations of being human. A favorite trick of professors who teach criminal law is to stage a crime in class and then have all the students write down what they saw. Invariably, no two accounts are exactly alike.

How is the historian to piece together a reasonable account of past events based on such fallible and incomplete evidence? Daunted by the prospect, some cynical observers conclude that history is not worth studying—and then cite historical examples to prove the truth of their claim! Other, more extreme, critics of history even argue that there is no past—only the present. We need only turn to the bedrock of historical evidence—the primary source—to prove that it is possible to know something about the past.

Survivals from the Past

The pieces of original evidence that the historian finds and weighs to build facts are called the primary sources of history. A *primary source* is material—a document or other evidence—that was created during the period or the event that the historian is studying. As long as the piece of evidence was produced during the time under investigation, it is a primary source.

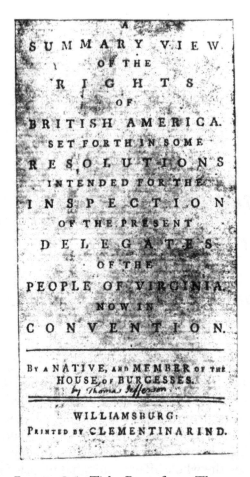

FIGURE 3.1 *Title Page from Thomas Jefferson's Pamphlet "Summary View"*

Primary sources come in many shapes and sizes. Some may be written documents—for example, newspapers, legislative records, or a court's opinions. Last wills and testaments penned in spidery-thin and shaky handwriting are just as much primary sources as leather- and gold-bound first editions of famous books. A primary source can be private—for example, a diary or a letter from a parent to a child—or public, such as an act of Congress or a presidential address. Finally, a primary source can be a physical artifact, such as a piece of furniture, a building, or a painting.

Some primary sources were meant to be private but became public, and their publication changed the course of events. One such source was a secret letter from the royal governor of the colony of Massachusetts, Thomas Hutchinson, to his friends in London, warning them that the Sons of Liberty in Boston were planning riots to oppose English rule. Nothing came of Hutchinson's warning—until Benjamin Franklin came upon the private letter and arranged to publish it in a Boston newspaper. When people in Massachusetts read the letter, they were outraged. Protests erupted, and Hutchinson's warnings came true.

Sometimes the public, official world and the private, domestic world come together in primary sources. The documents shown in Figures 3.1 and 3.2—a title page of one of the most famous pamphlets urging American colonists to resist Parliament on the eve of the Revolution, and the Declaration of Independence itself—were both private and public. Neither was the work of a government, yet both led to the creation of the most powerful state

FIGURE 3.2 *Engrossed (final handwritten) copy of the Declaration of Independence*
Courtesy of the Library of Congress

on the face of the earth. Notice that the pamphlet was printed and the Declaration was handwritten. Both are primary sources for our study of the revolutionary movement.

Primary sources for American history can be understood and enjoyed for themselves. You can get a good deal of pleasure and instruction from reading the essays of Franklin, for example, or wandering the grounds of the great Virginia plantations of the eighteenth century. But as a student of history, you must do much more with primary sources; you must use them to understand the people who created them. Primary sources are original evidence, and evidence must be examined critically. You cannot just believe the woodcutter's tale.

The first section of this chapter will introduce you to two types of primary sources: textual and visual. The chapter will then discuss common problems in verifying and interpreting primary sources.

The tangible, physical remains of primary sources for the study of early American history are all around you. The charter that King Charles of England granted to the Massachusetts Bay Company—the legal basis for the Puritan settlements in the New World—is preserved with loving care in the Massachusetts state house. The weathered clapboard family house of Rebecca Nurse, one of the victims of the Salem witchcraft trials of 1692, still stands on a grassy hill in the modern town of Danvers, Massachusetts. The problem is that these primary sources no longer really fit in with their surroundings. The old charter is protected from thieves by a glass display case unlike any that the Puritans possessed, and at the Peabody Museum and Essex Institute gift shops in Salem, Massachusetts, you can purchase T-shirts depicting the Nurse family homestead. Given this mixture of old and new, how do you pick out a primary source from its modern surroundings?

Exercise 1: Identifying Primary Sources

Following are two sets of documents, each set containing a primary source and a later historian's account of a contemporaneous event. As you decide which is which, think about the definition of primary sources. What clues can you gain from the passage to help you decide?

A Roger Williams was a Puritan minister whose spiritual strength and magnetic personality won him a great following when he came to Massachusetts in 1631. His opinions on religious conformity, particularly his unwillingness to let the colony's government in Boston tell him and his parishioners what to believe and how to worship, threatened political order in the colony and induced Governor John Winthrop of Massachusetts to warn Williams against further protests. Williams continued to battle for the rights of conscience, forgave Winthrop, fled Massachusetts, and set about making Providence Plantation (the Rhode Island colony) a haven for victims of religious persecution. Although Williams and Winthrop were antagonists throughout this episode, the two men genuinely admired and liked each other, and each hoped that the other could be persuaded of the error of his ways.

1. To Winthrop this [religious] liberalism [of Williams's] was . . . ridiculous . . . Williams's views on civil government had degraded the holy purpose of the state; now [Williams] degraded the still holier purpose of the church, welcoming the mixed multitude [to services] . . . To Winthrop and to other New England Puritans of the 1630s such was the counsel not of wisdom but of despair and defeat, the very thing to be expected from a man like Williams, who leaped always from one extreme to another.[1]

2. To Every courteous reader: While I plead the cause of truth and innocencie against the bloody doctrine of persecution for cause of conscience, I judge it not unfit to give alarme to my selfe, and all men to prepare to be persecuted or hunted for cause of conscience . . . Who can now but expect that after so many scores of years preaching and professing of more truth, and amongst so many great contentions amongst the very best of Protestants, a fierie furnace should be heat[ed], and who sees not now the fires kindling?[2]

Which of these two passages is the primary source? _____ Why do you think so?_____

_____

_____

B Williams and Winthrop agreed on one fact—there was a Devil and he had the power to intrude into people's affairs. He could cause disease and disruption in a household and in an entire colony. He could possess people, and only a true faith and a willing spirit could hold him at bay. Throughout the seventeenth century, the New England colonies of Massachusetts and Connecticut experienced periodic outbreaks of suspected witchcraft, and everyone believed the Devil was behind the troubles.

1. In their front-line struggle against the Devil and his legions, New Englanders labored under severe handicaps. Theirs was a supremely difficult task because the enemy was so devious, so shrewd, so resourceful in his methods of attack. His strategy was endlessly varied and surprising; he missed no opportunity for destructive intervention in human affairs. He possessed, moreover, the great advantage of being *invisible* to those whom he strove to subdue. The term most frequently applied to him, "Prince of Darkness," served to characterize both his ends and his means.[3]

2. Thursday night, being the 27th day of November [1679], we heard a great noise without against the house; whereupon myself and wife looked out and saw nobody . . . but we had

stones and sticks thrown at us [so] that we were forced to retire into the house . . . [four days later] in the afternoon pots hanging over the fire did dash so vehemently one against the other [that] we set down one that they might not dash to pieces. I saw the andiron leap into the pot and dance and leap out, and again leap in and dance and leap out again . . . [We saw] a tub . . . fly off of itself, and the tub turn over and nobody near it.[4]

Which passage is the primary source? _____ Why do you think so?_____

_____

_____

The Variety of Primary Sources

The variety of primary sources provides much of the joy of studying history. There is something for everyone's taste. Primary sources describe war and peace, leisure and work, the intimacy of family life, and the bustle of strange, crowded meeting places. In short, primary sources are as varied as the people who created them. The more you know about the time and the people from which the primary sources come, the better you can understand the sources, but written sources often have a charm or compelling power that seems to span time itself.

Exercise 2: Documentary Evidence of Private Life

The following three passages are primary sources about the lives of people in the eighteenth-century English North American colonies. These readings appeal to us because we share the joy, wonder, and humor of the author. Read each passage carefully. What do the passages tell you about the activities and attitudes of their authors? Beneath each passage, write two observations of your own about these authors' worlds based on information you have taken from the passages.

A The author of the first passage was an eleven-year-old girl from a very well-to-do New England family. Her name was Anna Green Winslow, and when her father, mother, and brother left her in the care of a Boston aunt to finish her schooling, Anna began a diary. In it, she recorded the hopes and fears of a girl about to enter a world that subordinated women to men. Anna died of tuberculosis in 1779, at the age of nineteen.

Feb. 9th, 1772. . . . My honored Mamma will be so good as to excuse my using the pen of my old friend just here, because I am disabled by a [sore] on my fourth finger and something like one on my middle finger, from using my own pen; but altho my right hand is in bondage, my left is free; and my aunt says, it will be a nice opportunity if I do but improve [on] it, to perfect myself in learning to spin flax. . . . My fingers are not the only part of me that has suffered with sores within this fortnight, for I have had a great ugly boil upon my right hip and about a dozen small ones . . . I am at present swathed hip and thigh, as Samson smote the Philistines, but my soreness is near over . . . I have to read my Bible to my aunt this morning (as is the daily custom) and sometimes I read other books to her. So you may perceive, I have the use of my tongue and I tell her it is a good thing to have the use of my tongue.[5]

Observation 1:_____

Observation 2:_____

B The second passage comes from the hand of Philip Vickers Fithian, a New Jersey college student who secured a place as a tutor to the children of one of Virginia's richest planters, Landon Carter. Fithian was bemused, delighted, appalled, and kept on his toes not only by his young students but by the master of the house as well.

> Rose by seven, sent for [the] barber and was drest for breakfast—we went to breakfast at ten—I confess I have been seldom more dashed than when I entered the dining-room, for I must of necessity be interrogated [by Carter] . . . about my [health] . . . After breakfast we all retired into the dancing-room, and after the [students] had their lesson . . . there were several minuets danced with great ease and propriety; after which the whole company joined in country-dances, and it was indeed beautiful to . . . see such a number of young persons, set off by dress to the best advantage, moving easily, to the sound of well performed music, and with perfect regularity, tho' apparently in the utmost disorder.[6]

Observation 1:_____

Observation 2:_____

C The third primary source is an old Puritan minister's recollection of his school days. John Barnard, like every New England Puritan boy, was expected to study hard, behave well, and go to church. In the following episode he recounts how he found a way to bend the rules to his advantage.

> Though my [school-] master advanced me . . . yet I was a very naughty boy, much given to play, insomuch that he at length openly declared, ". . . I know you can do well enough if you will; but you are so full of play that you hinder your classmates from getting their lessons [done]; and therefore, if any of them cannot perform their duty, I shall correct you for it." One unlucky day one of my classmates did not look into his book and therefore could not say his lesson, though I called upon him once and again to mind his book; upon which our master beat me. . . . The boy was pleased with my being corrected, and persisted in his neglect, for which I was still corrected, and that for several days. I thought, in justice, I ought to correct the boy, and compel him to a better temper; and therefore, after school was done, I went up to him, and told him I had been beaten several times for his neglect, and since master would not correct him I would . . . and then drubbed him heartily.[7]

Observation 1:_____

Observation 2:_____

Seeing the Past

To some extent, written primary sources seem to speak for themselves. You might assume that visual primary sources would be even easier to understand than letters and diaries, but maps, pictures, and material remains (buildings, home and workplace furnishings, tools, and other artifacts) are actually more difficult to use as primary sources than are documents. Visual sources can be rich repositories of past customs and attitudes, but you must look hard to see deeply into them.

The creators of visual primary sources were expressing their own views, communicating a message to persuade or entertain an audience or capture an idea. Pictures of old buildings, roads, and fields reveal not untouched nature but an artificial human ordering of objects in space. Settlers chose sites for houses not only with wood, water, and food supply in mind, but also to impose a human plan on the natural world. The first European villages in the New World were invariably surrounded by wooden walls or earthen embankments—barriers to keep unwanted visitors out. Later, wealthy colonists built big houses in plain sight of their poorer neighbors (unlike modern mansions deliberately constructed in secluded places) for a reason. John Hancock, the richest man in colonial Massachusetts, and George Washington, the richest man in colonial Virginia, both erected their houses on hills, not just to enjoy the view but to demonstrate their status and authority to everyone else in their communities.

Exercise 3: Visualizing Life in and Around the Big House

The two illustrations in this exercise depict great plantation houses in tidewater (coastal) Virginia. Not many planters could afford to build on such a scale, but all aspired to live in grand style. The living spaces and workplaces of many of the wealthy planters of the colonial South were both functional and symbolic. The great planters were a small minority of the free population of the southern tidewater, but they were the leaders of that society. They built near the water in order to ship their tobacco crops directly to English and Scottish ports. The size and geometric regularity of their homes were intended to give visual proof of their right to rule. The visual impact of their houses reinforced the planters' status in society.

The large plantation was a village in itself, with smokehouses, storerooms, blacksmith's and carpenter's shops, and rows of wooden cabins for slaves. Day laborers and tenants did not live on the grounds of the great house but had their own cabins on the plantation. Authority on the plantation descended from the big house to all corners of the planter's domain. The common folk mingled with the gentry in market towns and in churches, taverns, and courthouses, but the focal point of society was the great house.

Figure 3.3 is a sample of folk art, a homemade painting dating from the start of the nineteenth century. Figure 3.4 is a modern photograph of a restored plantation house, Westover. Both concern the same object but convey the importance of the big house in different ways. Examine these visual primary sources, and answer the questions following each.

At the top of the painting in Figure 3.3 is the great house, and along the hillsides are the outbuildings including slave quarters. What does this arrangement seem to say about the relationship between the master and the servants and slaves?

_____

_____

_____

In the painting, the entire hill seems to rest on water—at its bottom is a river wide and deep enough to support a three-masted sailing ship. Next to the ship is a tobacco warehouse. What does the arrangement of these objects suggest about the source of the planter's wealth?

_____

_____

_____

The William Byrd family house is a three-story, red-brick mansion, built on the same ground on which Byrd's father constructed a frame house, the banks of the James River. The younger Byrd pursued political power and wealth avidly, and though he never became the English nobleman he dreamed of being, he did achieve prominence in Virginia politics.

FIGURE 3.3 *"The Plantation" (1825)*
Courtesy of the Metropolitan Museum of Art.

FIGURE 3.4 *Westover, Home of the William Byrd Family*
Courtesy of the Library of Congress

Imagine that you are approaching the front door. What impressions would you have?

How did his new residence symbolize his importance? (Hint: think about the number of windows and floors, and the cost of bricks.) _____

_____

Evaluating Primary Sources

The textual and visual primary sources you encountered in the previous pages seem authentic, but there is always the possibility that they are not genuine. Some famous forgeries still haunt historians. Not so long ago one of the most respected of English historians tried to authenticate Adolf Hitler's "diaries." These diaries supposedly proved that Hitler never intended to commit genocide. A few weeks later, when the forger was revealed, this historian issued a qualified apology.

Forgers have faked letters from Jefferson, Lincoln, and Washington. Sets of documents have been forged as well, as in the notorious case of the *Horn Papers*. The three volumes of *Horn Papers*, describing explorations in western Pennsylvania from 1765 to 1795, were not what they appeared to be. In 1945, a year after their publication, Julian P. Boyd, a historian, charged that they were composed of fictitious letters, journals, and maps. He was correct. The forger, never identified, had fooled everyone else but not Boyd. Later, scholars concluded that "it is apparent that the creator of the diaries and the maps carefully worked over the modern geological survey maps and may even have traced portions of them."[8]

Mistakes in recreating the past from primary materials may not be the result of intentional forgeries. In the late 1920s, preservationists, historians, and architects, under the leadership of the Rockefeller family, were hard at work restoring the colonial grandeur of Williamsburg, Virginia. It had been a colonial capital with wide spaces and five notable multistory brick buildings—the governor's "palace," the "Capitol" where the government met, and the College of William and Mary. The first two buildings had been lost to fire long before. Their restoration was conjectural. The foundations had been uncovered, but there was no visual representation of the exteriors. The architects were already making mistakes—adding porches and leaving out roof dormers—when by chance an engraved copper plate of the eighteenth-century structures was discovered at the Bodley Library of Oxford University. Using the images (reproduced in Figure 3.5), the restorers retraced their steps and produced the wonders of Colonial Williamsburg enjoyed now by millions of visitors.

The first clues to a source's authenticity are physical characteristics. Is the document or artifact old enough to be dated from the period it supposedly came from? Was it found in an appropriate place? Does it use the language of the times, or was it the product of tools used in that period? Is the handwriting genuine? A good way to authenticate a primary source is to compare it with similar sources that have already been authenticated, although the most interesting forgeries are those that materially add to or contradict existing sources. Another conventional way to test the legitimacy of a primary source is to find references to it in other, well-established sources. The new source then fills a gap in the chain of evidence. Keep in mind, though, that such gaps can be invitations to forgers.

Point of View

The vast majority of surviving primary sources are genuine, but every primary source reveals its own point of view. Whether or not the author of a document sought to gain some advantage or mislead someone else, like the woodcutter in the story at the beginning of this chapter, a particular perspective and position in life colors everyone's observations and expressions. Sometimes a primary source is obviously colored by the prejudices of its author;

FIGURE 3.5 *The "Bodleian Plate" (about 1740)*
Courtesy of the Colonial Williamsburg Foundation

at other times the source's originator may have been badly positioned to see and describe an event.

Although every primary source has a point of view, reading it critically enables you to recognize and avoid the most common pitfalls. The basic principles of source criticism can be reduced to the following seven questions you can ask about every primary source you encounter:

1. Was the person who created the source well positioned to know what was happening? Was he or she well acquainted with the people and places described? Was the author one of the group at the center of the event or a mere observer? Did he or she have access to other documents and other observers?

2. Have other documents or letters written by that person proved to be accurate? Some famous men and women have proved to be notorious liars, and the number of primary materials that include gossip or outright fantasy is immense.

3. Did the author have a personal interest in what he or she was describing that would color the account (or lead to a lie)? Even if the author intended to be objective, such interests would influence what the author thought he or she heard and saw and would undermine the reliability of even a firsthand account.

4. What sort of language does the author of a written account employ? Is it hysterical or calm, angry or sympathetic? If the source is an example of a particular literary genre, such as a novel or a poem, the author has probably rearranged facts—people and settings —for literary effect. (Even a work of fiction can be a primary source of attitudes or literary conventions.) If the work is a picture, how much has the artist's style altered reality? Have dramatic conventions replaced facts?

5. Was the source created immediately, within a short span of time, or many years after the event it describes? (Many primary accounts are recollections by participants or observers in their old age, and psychological studies have shown that we often lose 70 percent of our memory of a particular event within the first 24 hours after seeing or hearing it.)

6. To whom is the account or visual depiction addressed? What was the intended or expected audience? Many documents are written to persuade or reassure a particular audience. For example, although his quarrel was with ministers in neighboring Massachusetts, Roger Williams sent many of his sermons and letters to England to be published so that influential Puritans there might understand why he defended freedom of worship.

7. Finally, what impact did the words or pictures have on their actual audience? Historians have become very sensitive to the changing meaning of common words. Books and pamphlets written in English more than 300 years ago do not always use words in the same way that we use them today. For example, to the seventeenth-century American colonists the word *constitution* was the body of English and American law; today it means a written foundation of government. We retain the earlier meaning when we talk about a person having "a sound constitution."

Exercise 4: Point of View and Reliability

This exercise asks you to assess the reliability of one of the most famous primary sources depicting the struggle between the British and the French for control of North America. Figure 3.6 shows Benjamin West's deeply moving and justly famous painting *The Death of*

FIGURE 3.6 Benjamin West, *The Death of General Wolfe (1770)*
Courtesy of the National Gallery of Canada, Ottawa

General Wolfe (1770), painted eleven years after Wolfe died leading his troops against the French in Canada. Wolfe, dying in the center foreground, is surrounded by his generals and illuminated by a streak of sunlight piercing an otherwise gray and forbidding sky. Beyond him the battle rages. In the foreground a Native American contemplates the scene.

Comment on the impression the picture makes.

1. What emotion does it evoke in you? _____

_____

_____

2. What impression do you gain of Wolfe? _____

_____

_____

3. Of his officers' feeling for him? _____

_____

_____

Benjamin West was not present when the battle he depicted took place, but he might have gathered the details of Wolfe's death from those who were at the scene. The crowds that gathered to view the painting at the Royal Academy exhibition room in England on April 29, 1771, thought West's work brilliant. West, a Pennsylvanian who had come to England to learn to paint and who had gained the support of King George III, had used every artistic convention he could to heighten the drama of Wolfe's dying moments. With this information in mind, answer the next set of questions.

1. For what audience did West paint? Did West intend his work to have any particular impact on that audience?_____

_____

2. What stylistic or other artistic conventions did West employ to heighten the impact of the painting? _____

_____

_____

3. All things considered, how reliable do you find West's depiction of the death of Wolfe?

_____

_____

West's Wolfe was a hero, dying a hero's death, and that assuaged the gnawing doubts that many British leaders had about the appalling expense of the French and Indian War. Britain still staggered under the debt and looked to the American colonists to pay off part of it. What is more, until Wolfe's near miraculous victory, symbolized in the painting by the heavenly light shining on the dying general, British armies in the American wilderness had not fought well. In effect, West's painting offered a history of the war that justified Britain's sacrifices to drive the French from North America.

But was West's history reliable? Certain facts regarding the war are indisputable. On the Plains of Abraham above the French colonial citadel of Quebec a battle was fought that determined the fate of both the French and the English empires in North America. The French and Indian War had already dragged on for four years, with early French successes giving way to a bloody stalemate, when, in 1758, the English thrust at the French colony of

Canada, sealing it off from the French homeland. Rugged French-Canadian farmers, woodsmen, and their Indian allies, along with a handful of regular French troops, continued to defend Montreal and Quebec, however.

The next year, after a spring and summer of fruitless attempts to lure French general Montcalm out of the fortress of Quebec, English commander James Wolfe boldly sailed his expeditionary force down the St. Lawrence River past the city. During the night his rangers and Highlander (Scottish) troops scaled a 200-foot cliff to attack the city from above. The French charged out of their fortifications at dawn on September 13, 1759, but the British held their ground and were victorious. Wolfe, along with his great adversary Montcalm, died in the fighting.

From firsthand accounts, historian Simon Schama has pieced together a composite of the actual circumstances of Wolfe's death, as voiced by a soldier:

> Then up comes the captain and tells me to take a message to the general [Wolfe] to say our line had held and the enemy was put to flight. And I had rather it had been another man; I was tired at all we had done last night and this morning. But I obeyed and ran over the field stepping through blood and faces upturned in death and a few horses, poor beasts their bellies all spilld open . . . when suddenly I saw him, lying on a mound beside a sorry little bush attended by just two men, one leaning over and supporting Wolfe with his arm. . . . I approached Wolfe and saw his face had gone stiff and greenish and his red hair glistened with sun and sweat. Blood had matted his belly where another ball had struck him. . . . seeing he would not live I told him our news and in a groaning gurgling sort of way I could hear him praise God for it.[9]

In life Wolfe had been unsuccessful in most of what he did. Though still in his thirties when he died, he had never won a great battle. Gawky (he resembled the Washington Irving character Ichabod Crane), melancholic, and plagued by stomach ailments, he had a premonition that he would never return from Canada to his beloved England. When the news of the battle reached Britain and its colonies, Wolfe in death became what he never was in life—a hero.

Look again at Figure 3.6. Notice how it differs from the account that Schama presents.

1. In what details does Schama's account differ from West's painting? _____

_____

2. Which of the two do you find more convincing? _____

_____

Point in Time

The seven rules of source criticism and Exercise 4 raise the issue of the context of primary sources. A historically minded reader or viewer of a primary source tries to imagine how it appeared in its original surroundings. This historical setting is the context of the source. For example, you gain a deeper understanding of the Salem witch trials by standing in the restored houses and churches of Danvers, Massachusetts. There, amid the dark-timbered, low-ceiling homes of the Puritans, you can see how closely people lived to one another and how resentments and rivalries could turn into accusations of witchcraft.

The most obvious context of a primary source is the point in time at which the author of the source created it. The actual period of time in which that person lived, as you learned in Chapter 1, influenced what he or she had to say about any subject. Examples of such time spans are centuries, decades, and years. Historians take these actual spans of time and turn them into historical periods—a process called **periodization.** Historical periods provide a way to divide time into segments, in order to group distinct events and ideas together and separate them from other, different groups of events and ideas. For example, historians use centuries as a shorthand way to distinguish periods of human conduct and ideas. The fixed period of time—the century—becomes a symbol of critical changes or innovations in human thought. Thus historians speak of "seventeenth-century rationality," which refers to the movement by some philosophers, scientists, and teachers of the period to replace religious faith with scientific experiment as the highest form of mental activity.

Historians also separate centuries into decades and try to characterize each decade with a central theme. The 1930s becomes the Great Depression decade, the 1960s the decade of protest movements, and the 1980s the "me first" decade. Historians may turn the actual span of time in office of kings or presidents into a historical period, presuming that the political leader created or captured the mood of the era. For example, historians use the phrase "Jacksonian era" to denote the period when Andrew Jackson dominated American politics. The "Reagan era" is synonymous with the period 1981–1988. Historians also divide time into "ages" and "eras" characterized by important events and movements. Examples of such periodization are "the space age" and "the Cold War era."

To begin re-creating the context of a primary source, you must "date" it, but there are many ways to periodize any source. Although centuries, decades, and years may seem to be objective or neutral names for time spans, the symbolic impact of phrases like "the Age of Discovery" goes beyond mere chronology to imply a substantive unity to a period of time. "The Age of Discovery" refers to the era during which European explorers reached the coasts of the Americas, Africa, and Asia. For Europeans, the news that the world could be circumnavigated was a great discovery, but for modern historians to say that "Columbus discovered America" is to ignore the 10 million Native Americans who lived and flourished in what is now North and South America *before* Columbus pridefully claimed any of their lands for the king of Spain.

The power that historians have to place events into periods—like a mail carrier putting letters into pigeonholes—is not without dangers. A common abuse of the power of periodization occurs when a historian gives to the name of the period a concreteness that name should not have. Jerome Frank, a famous American jurist who was an acute observer of historical writing, singled out this mistake in a 1948 essay entitled "Twistory":

> As a matter of convenience, historians usually employ vague words like the "medieval" period, "feudalism," the "Renaissance," "capitalism." Each of those words covers a multitude of varying and relatively little known facts spread over a long period of years. Having given some of those facts a label, some—but not all—historians assume that the label actually represents a thing with a life of its own—a birth, an adolescence, a maturity, an old age, and a death.[10]

Judge Frank's point is well taken, but we cannot write history without periodization. Indeed, the power to periodize enables us to fit particular facts into larger and more significant patterns. At the same time, we have to be aware that by varying the historical period into which we place any primary source, we vary the group of events, lives, and ideas that surround the source—in effect we alter its context. In so doing, we can change the shades of meaning the primary source exhibits. For example, if we place the Declaration of Independence in the "Age of Revolution," we link it to the French Revolution, which occurred in 1789. The Declaration thus becomes the model for the radical French Declaration of the Rights of Man. If, instead, we decide that the Declaration was the closing chapter of "the Colonial era," we root it in 200 years of English colonial history and cut it off from later European radicalism.

Exercise 5: Periodization

Despite the dangers of too grand or too narrow periodization, historians must place primary sources in some chronological context, some period. For this exercise, look through the early American chapters of your textbook and find three examples of periodization. Summarize them below.

1. _____

_____

2. _____

_____

3. _____

_____

Imagining Absent Sources

For every primary source that survives the ravages of time, an incalculable number are lost. War, fire, rain, insects, and rodents are great ravagers of original evidence. Just as you throw out old newspapers and magazines when you clean your room, so people in the past threw out documents that would fascinate modern historians and students. In the end, only a tiny portion of all that people have used and created survives.

Think about how certain types of primary sources seem to survive, while others vanish. Official documents tend to survive because governments make an effort to preserve items such as tax lists, laws and court decisions, and administrative memoranda. These public records are often kept in safe places and watched by specially appointed guardians, while private documents—letters from one family member to another, for example—often survive only by chance.

There are even deeper patterns of human relationships that explain the existence—and absence—of certain kinds of primary sources. Wealth, education, and power directly influence the likelihood that a primary source will survive. Poor people in early history were almost always illiterate. They could not keep diaries, write letters, or prepare inventories of their few possessions. Women, often denied educational opportunities, also left relatively little evidence of their thoughts and feelings. Racial minorities in early America—Native Americans, African-Americans, Asian-Americans—developed rich and varied oral cultures, but their words do not survive as do many official documents or the correspondence of the wealthy and powerful. Historians interested in the everyday lives of the poor, women, and racial minorities must dig into church registers, tax rolls, and militia lists—places where many did leave their mark.

Absent sources are also hidden sources—hidden by layers of later human activity and by even thicker layers of subsequent local lore. For example, the Five Points area of lower Manhattan was a lively place in the early nineteenth-century—thickly populated, full of life, noisy, and dangerous. For much of the twentieth century, however, Five Points was literally covered over by courthouses and office buildings. The neighborhood seemed almost eerie in its silence when evening came. In the 1980s, renovators tore down a block of the twentieth-century buildings and came upon the remains of the early-nineteenth-century settlement. The foundations of old houses and bits of glassware, pottery, furniture, and ironwork revealed a world long thought lost—a world in which poor people lived, worked, and died.

When lost sources are ignored in the stories that local residents tell, it is even harder for the historian to reconstruct the past. In 1985, Timothy H. Breen, a leading colonial historian, was invited to serve as a resident researcher at the East Hampton (New York) Historical Society. East Hampton is a rapidly changing township on the southeastern end of Long Island. Founded in the 1650s as a fishing and farming village by Puritans from New England, it has become a fashionable resort for the rich and famous. Defenders of its old ways wanted Professor Breen to recover a purer, simpler past, but instead he found many layers of self-deception that obscured, rather than revealed, the history of the first town. East Hampton's modern residents had come to believe that the town had been a backwater—a stable, close-knit, farming community of English men and women. Breen found that they were wrong. The community in fact had been multiracial—Native Americans and African-Americans had lived among the New England settlers—but local historians had bit by bit forgotten about the minorities. In addition, colonial East Hampton was not a backwater but part of a commercial network stretching across the Atlantic Ocean. By the end of the colonial era, its fishermen had literally decimated the herds of right whales that migrated along its shores to supply Europe with candle wax and other commodities. Breen concluded that his sources were not only buried in the sands and woods but concealed under layers of local tradition:

> In early East Hampton the process [of people telling stories about themselves] probably involved a kind of informal oral history. People shared remembered traditions [of the founders of the village] . . . At some point local historians began to put the stories into written form, and, as they did so, they often organized the facts in new ways. . . . Over time interpretations . . . were amalgamated into a popular understanding of the [harmonious], communal past, and it eventually became impossible to distinguish the actual past from stories that local historians had written about the past. And slowly, almost imperceptibly, the accretion of interpretation gave birth to mythology.[11]

The relative paucity of sources about the lives of the great majority of people in the past is a serious problem for any student of history. Wealthy planters and merchants kept diaries and ledger books, corresponded with each other, and served in government posts. They wrote laws and edited newspapers. The vast majority of colonists, however, were hard-working farmers, housewives, day laborers, craftspeople, servants, slaves, and children. They did not leave as many diaries or letters. But sometimes they left behind estates (personal property) and the inventories of these estates prepared by court-appointed executors can tell us about how ordinary people lived and what kinds of property they valued.

Exercise 6: Primary Sources Speak

The following inventory comes from the estate of Henry Van Dyck, an inhabitant of Albany, New York. It appears on-line in the Colonial Albany Social History Project web site, www.nysm.nysed.gov/albany/wills. Read it carefully, then answer the questions below.

Done by Barent Bleecker and Leonard Gansevoort, Junior, values in pounds, shillings, and pence

A book case containing 13.0.0.

A number of medical and chirurgical books, a few theological books, and some Moral ones.

A close fire stove 3.4.0.

A Franklin fire stove 7.0.0.

Two common andirons with shovels and tongs 1.4.0.

One iron coffee mill 0.16.0.

One iron ash pan 0.8.0.

A quantity of black bottles 3.0.0.

One wood saw 0.10.0.

One Carpenter's saw 0.6.0.

Two dozen knives & forks 0.16.0.

Three teakettles 2.0.0.

Six brass kittles 3.10.0.

One brass pie pan 0.10.0.

Three brass skimmers 1.4.0.

Five irons pot 3.4.0.

Two waffles iron 0.18.0.

Seven smoothing irons 0.15.0.

One hozer or sprinkler 0.8.0.

One maeking iron 0.6.0.

Four large mahoganies table 12.0.0.

One mahogany tea table 1.12.0.

One round mahogany table 1.4.0.

Seven small round tables 2.16.0.

One small mahogany table with a looking glass and stand 3.0.0.

Seven washing table stands 0.6.0.

Eight mahogany chairs 6.8.0.

One small Mahogany square table 1.0.0.

12 chairs with black leather 7.4.0.

Four Windsor chairs 1.4.0.

Four red chairs 1.0.0.

One large tea cannister 0.6.0.

One tin canister 0.10.0.

One large chest 0.12.0.

Two small trunks 1.4.0.

One large trunk 0.16.0.

One small trunk 0.10.0.

One large black leather trunk 0.12.0.

One small looking glass 1.0.0.

Two large looking glasses 20.0.0.

A small sewing plate 0.3.0.

A steel snuffer and stand 0.8.0.

Six brass candlesticks 1.10.0.

One leaden tobacco vessel 0.4.0.

One pair brass scales 1.0.0.

One pair tin scales 0.8.0.

One iron mortar and pestle 1.12.0.

One marble mortar and glass pestle 2.12.0.

A quantity of medicines and chirurgical instruments 70.0.0.

One large chest containing Gallipots Phials, etc. 4.0.0.

One tin instrument for distilling 1.10.0.

Two small red curtains 0.8.0.

Two sets window curtains 3.0.0.

Two old fashioned hases with tablecloths, linen apparels 40.0.0.

Four China puddings bowl 3.4.0.

One dozen China plates 1.16.0.

Three China pudding dishes 1.0.0.

Two dozen China cups & saucers 1.0.0.

13 China coffee cups 0.12.0.

12 chocolate cups 0.16.0.

Two silver tankards 36.0.0.

Two silver mugs 6.8.0.

Two silver sauce boats 9.0.0.

One silver tea pot 12.0.0.

One silver salver 5.0.0.

One silver sugar cup 3.4.0.

One silver sugar sprinkler 3.4.0.

One silver pepper box 1.0.0.

Two silver salt cellars 0.16.0.

One silver punch strainer 0.16.0.

One silver milk pot 0.16.0.

One silver grill cup 1.0.0.

One silver ladle 4.0.0.

One silver porringer 2.0.0.

14 silver table spoons 12.12.0.

12 silver tea spoons 2.8.0.

Eight Earthen dishes 0.4.0.

Four dozen Earthen plates 0.14.0.

One dozen earthen soup plates 0.4.0.

One Terreen 0.12.0.

One umbrella 0.18.0.

One fusee 1.0.0.

One long Holland gun 3.0.0.

Two cradles 5.0.0.

Three bedsteads with bedding 40.0.0

Three slaabanks with bedding 12.0.0.

One picture of George 3d 3.0.0.

Seven large old-fashioned pictures 2.16.0.
One old fashioned picture 0.8.0.
Two fruit pictures 2.0.0.
Two small pictures 0.8.0.
One block 7 tackle 3.0.0.
Two small coffee mills 0.10.0.
One oil cloth 3.0.0.
One hat case 0.8.0.
One Osnabrig shade for a shop 2.16.0.
One clock 18.0.0.
Two brass branches 2.0.0.
Two blinds 0.8.0.
One cruet stand 0.16.0.
Three decanters 0.18.0.
Two water bottles 0.16.0.
One dozen wineglasses 0.16.0.
One glass oil bottle 0.2.0.
One vinegar bottle 0.2.0.
Two glass plates 0.8.0.
One glass server 0.4.0.
Four glass salt cellers 0.6.0.
Three large tubs 0.15.0.
Six pails 0.18.0.
One gallon measure 0.10.0.
1/2 gallon measure 0.5.0.
One quart measure 0.2.6.
One pint measure 0.1.3.
Three funnels 0.4.6.
One sieve 0.2.6.
One saddle and bridle 1.18.0.
One spinning wheel 0.15.0.
One map of North America 1.4.0.
One silver watch 5.0.0.

1. What was Van Dyck's profession? _____

_____

2. What does the inventory tell us about his home life? _____

_____

_____

3. What does the inventory tell us about his intellectual life?_____

_____

_____

Historians and students of history rely on primary sources to understand and retell the story of how people lived long ago. Such stories are not themselves primary sources. They are "secondary sources" and we learn more about them in the next chapter.

Notes

[1] Edmund S. Morgan, *The Puritan Dilemma: The Story of John Winthrop* (Boston: Little, Brown, 1958),132.

[2] Roger Williams, *The Bloudy Tenent of Persecution* [1643], reprinted in Perry Miller and Thomas H. Johnson, eds., *The Puritans* (New York: Harper & Row, 1963), 1:216.

[3] John P. Demos, *Entertaining Satan: Witchcraft and the Culture of Early New England* (New York: Oxford University Press, 1982), 97.

[4] Quoted ibid., 132–133.

[5] *Diary of Anna Green Winslow: A Boston School Girl of 1771*, ed. Alice Morse Earle (Boston: Houghton Mifflin, 1985), 20–21.

[6] Philip Vickers Fithian, *Journal and Letters of Philip Vickers Fithian* [1773–1774], ed. H. D. Farrish (Charlottesville: University Press of Virginia, 1957), 33.

[7] "Autobiography of the Rev. John Barnard," *Collections of the Massachusetts Historical Society*, 3rd ser. 5 (1836), 178–219.

[8] Douglass Adair and Arthur Pierce Middleton, "The Mystery of the Horn Papers," *William and Mary Quarterly*, 3rd ser. 4 (1947), 445.

[9] Simon Schama, *Dead Certainties* (New York: Knopf, 1991), 68–69.

[10] Jerome Frank, *Fate and Freedom* (New York: Scribner, 1948), 26.

[11] Timothy H. Breen, *Imagining the Past: East Hampton Histories* (Reading, Mass.: Addison-Wesley, 1989), 39.

4: The Historian's Work: Secondary Sources

Causes and Consequences of the American Revolution

———•—————•————•———

Thomas Jefferson played a leading role in the American and French revolutions—two upheavals that gave birth to the modern world—ran a large business, designed the campus for the University of Virginia, supervised a thoroughgoing revision of the laws of his state, kept extensive astronomical and botanical notebooks, reared two daughters after his wife died, served as president of the United States of America, and still found time to be a historian. Understandably, Jefferson insisted that only those who had taken part in important events should write history. His rule would bar most modern historians from practicing their craft. Fortunately for today's historians, Jefferson's premise—that only those close to power can know how power is used—is out of date. In our own day, when the world is no farther from us than our televisions, computers, radios, and newspapers, all of us have the chance to eavesdrop on the secrets of the mighty and sympathize with the sufferings of the many.

The books, articles, and lectures that historians write and deliver are the secondary sources of history. To the original evidence, the primary sources, the historian brings specialized training, craftsmanship, and intellect. The writing of secondary sources is simultaneously painstaking and exciting, arduous and engrossing. There are moments when every historian shares Simon Schama's near despair that "we are doomed to be forever hailing someone who has just gone around the corner and out of earshot."[1] Yet there are other moments that reward our labor, when we are seized by what Timothy Breen recently termed "a nervous inspiration" and grasp, in a blinding flash of light, the connection between past and present.[2]

The Variety of Secondary Sources

Jefferson had faith that the study of history was a vital part of every political leader's education. For him, history taught imperishable truths about human motivation and the fate of nations. After he left the office of president of the United States in 1809, he dedicated himself to the study of history and urged young people to do likewise, arguing that history was the great storehouse of human experience.

Because he believed that people could and should learn from history, Jefferson admonished historians to do more than simply tell a story. They must also explain the meaning of that story. Jefferson's rule is still binding: the historian is duty-bound to explore the causes and consequences of human action.

Causation: The Parent of Historical Theory

All historians approach their study of the primary sources with some notion of how those sources fit together. In the past, some historians believed that important events always fit into an all-embracing, prearranged pattern. For example, medieval European historians saw the causes and consequences of human actions as evidence of the grand design of Divine Providence. For these chroniclers, history was God's plan for the world. Kings and princes won battles because God willed their success. More recently, some nineteenth-century American historians argued that our acquisition of a western empire was proof that God favored the expansion of the American republic. Their histories confidently offered this all-encompassing theory to explain why Native Americans had to bow before the might of European-Americans.

Most modern historians do not bind themselves in this way to an overarching, single-minded theory of causation, but content themselves with more modest conclusions about cause and effect in history. The professional historian forms hypotheses about causes and tests these against the evidence. Even the most cautious and sophisticated modern historian must ponder the connections among the groups of events and decide how these events are related.

We can classify the most common theories about causation into two large, opposite categories: materialistic theories and nonmaterialistic theories. **Materialistic theories** presume that the causes of human behavior over time are rooted in the material world—work, environment, natural resources, markets, nutrition, climate, and geography, for example. Most materialistic theories are *deterministic*—that is, their adherents argue that individuals' particular choices cannot influence or alter the grand pattern of history.

The best known of these deterministic, materialistic theories is Scientific Marxism, first articulated by Karl Marx, a nineteenth-century economist and political theorist. Marx was appalled by the conditions of working people in industrial Germany and Britain and predicted the triumph of communism. He fully believed that the working people would gain control of the factories. He also wrote a number of historical essays to elaborate his theory of dialectical materialism. According to this theory, the course of human history is determined by a struggle among different classes for control of the means of production of wealth. This struggle takes different forms as peoples pass through an inevitable sequence of historical stages: primitivism, feudalism, capitalism, and the revolution of the working people overthrowing their oppressors, finally arriving at a classless society. Marx and those who adopted his theories considered cultures and religions to be superstructures built on the solid economic foundation of history, and they believed that individual choices within a culture cannot change the overall course of history. Some modern Marxist historians—sometimes called Social Marxians—are not so rigid in their determinism and do not dismiss the importance of literature, religion, education, and culture as readily as do the Scientific Marxists.

Nonmaterialistic theories of history focus on chance rather than on predetermined laws of history, stress human motives and interactions, and view change as a product of contingency (accident), human design, or irony (the unintended results of human design). One controversial recent variety of nonmaterialistic historical theory is *psychohistory*, an attempt to explain individual behavior by applying the various theories of psychology. Psychohistory emphasizes personality and personal choices as the prime causes of behavior; it has breathed new life into biographical writing (the subject of Chapter 9).

Exercise 1: Finding Causal Statements in Your Textbook

You already have a secondary source in your book bag—your textbook. Good textbooks heed Jefferson's command to both tell and explain our past. Find the chapter in your textbook that discusses the American Revolution. Read the section that offers explanations for the outbreak of the Revolution. In the space below, using your own words, report three of the causes your textbook's authors give for the Revolution. Decide whether each is materialistic or non-materialistic, and report your reasons below.

1. _____
   _____
   _____

2. _____
   _____
   _____

3. _____
   _____
   _____

Types of History

Jefferson also believed that political history was the most important variety of history. Modern historical writing is no longer limited to political subjects, however. Historians today are interested in studying all manner of human experience. As a result, the secondary sources of history are far more varied now than in Jefferson's time.

Historians writing different types of history select different kinds of evidence. If an author is crafting political history, he or she will be very interested in election results, voting patterns in a legislature, and politicians' speeches, as opposed to the average age at which women gave birth for the first time. By contrast, a historian studying the changing American family will focus on childbirth and marriage statistics, and pay far less attention to what politicians did or said. The types of history flow from the types of evidence the author has chosen, and the author chooses types of evidence that fit his or her subject. Examples of some types of history and possible subjects are the following:

> *Political history:* the story of government, political leaders, electoral activities, the making of policy, and the interaction of branches of government
> *Military history:* the study of the conduct of war, the training and behavior of armies, individual soldiers, tactics and strategy, and weapons
> *Diplomatic history:* the examination of the relations between nations, diplomats, and ideas of diplomacy
> *Social history:* the rediscovery of ways and customs, family size, daily life, education, children, and demography (population change)
> *Cultural history:* the consideration of language and its uses, the arts and literature, and sport and entertainment

Intellectual history: the probing of ideas and great thinkers, and of religion, philosophy, and the sciences

Economic history: the recapitulation of how an entire system (or any of its parts) of production and consumption works, and of markets, industry, credit, and working people at all levels of the system

Exercise 2: Identifying Types of History

The categories of history listed above are neither airtight compartments nor exhaustive. Where does a history of newspapers fit, for example—is it social, economic, or cultural? A history of the founding and early years of Harvard College may be political as well as social and cultural. The following brief passages exemplify types of history. In the space provided, indicate the type that you think best fits the passage. Use *P* for political, *M* for military, *D* for diplomatic, *S* for social, *C* for cultural, *I* for Intellectual, and *E* for economic. Briefly explain your choices.

A The American Revolution worked its greatest changes in the constitutional framework of state government. Republics had replaced royal colonies. Checks and balances ensured that the power of any one political official could be curbed by other officials. Regular elections upon a very broad franchise (for that day and age) guaranteed that the people retained their sovereignty. It only remained to be seen whether thirteen small republics could find a way to become one great nation.

Type: _____ Why? _____

_____

B In the revolutionary era, print culture came into its own. More people than ever before began to read newspapers, pamphlets, magazines, and books. Almanacs, always bestsellers, were joined by all manner of cheaply produced and widely distributed forms of popular literature.

Type: _____ Why? _____

_____

C The Revolution seemed to work a fundamental change in the position and power of women. With their male kin away, women assumed responsibility for farm and family, business and trade. Although women proposed that they be given full legal rights, in fact, women did not gain such rights. Instead, they became the "angels" of the home—models of domestic virtue whose right to property was still circumscribed and whose role in public affairs was curtailed.

Type: _____ Why? _____

_____

D Often, Benjamin Franklin would despair of the innocence and the arrogance of the men the Continental Congress sent to help him guide American interests through the shark-infested waters of European power politics during the Revolutionary War. Franklin charmed the French, carried on secret negotiations with the British, wooed the Spanish, and ensnared the Dutch in his efforts to aid his beleaguered countrymen. He did not need John Adams, fretting and complaining, at his side, and was pleased when Adams left for the Netherlands. While the pedantic New Englander and the plodding Dutch butted heads, Franklin returned to his more subtle tasks.

Type: _____ Why? _____

_____

E No sooner had the Revolutionary War ended than Americans indulged in an orgy of consumerism. They bought luxury items from all over Europe and resumed purchasing goods from England as though the war had never happened. The only difference was that the English and Scottish merchants no longer extended generous credit terms; after all, the Americans were no longer part of the empire. The result was a catastrophic depression that, coupled with the devastation wrought by the war, made many revolutionary leaders doubt that the new American nation could survive.

Type: _____ Why? _____

_____

F George Washington lost most of the battles that he commanded but still is rightly judged one of America's greatest wartime generals. He not only kept an army in being when desertion and disease could easily have destroyed it but gave a moral tone to the Revolutionary War effort. Far more than a general, Washington was what a general should be in the eyes of his officers and his men. His grave face, tall, strong body, and willingness to undergo hardship made him an inspiration to others. His combination of patience and self-discipline worked a tonic upon younger officers. He became for them a symbol of republican virtue, a symbol that would last for him and them after the guns were quiet.

Type: _____ Why? _____

_____

G Thomas Jefferson and Alexander Hamilton were both students of Enlightenment philosophy, but Jefferson believed that men were naturally equal, while Hamilton thought that men were by nature unequal. This difference in their view of human nature would lead to their quarrels over a wide range of political and economic issues.

Type: _____ Why? _____

_____

Thesis in Secondary Sources

A thesis, or theme, in a secondary source is the historian's argument—the point that he or she is trying to make. Historical writing is filled with theses. The mere compilation of evidence explains nothing, for by itself a piece of evidence is not "a hard, cold something with a clear outline, and measurable pressure, like a brick."[3] Primary sources are like clay on a potter's wheel; they take shape only under the pressure of the historian's trained hands. The historian's thesis is what he or she makes out of the evidence.

Exercise 3: Identifying Historians' Theses

Look again at the short passages in the previous exercise. On the lines below, in your own words, write what you think is each author's main point, or thesis.

A _____

_____

_____

B _____

_____

_____

C _____

_____

_____

D _____

_____

_____

E _____

_____

_____

F _____

_____

_____

G _____

_____

_____

When Historians Disagree

You may have noted that at times your instructor has disagreed with portions of the textbook. Such disagreements are normal and remind you that no matter how skilled the authors or how comprehensive the coverage in the textbook, there are many other ways the authors could have told their story than the way they chose. The authors know that many subjects in American history are controversial and that historians may not agree about what happened or why it happened. When your professor and your textbook differ, they merely reflect larger differences of opinion within the community of scholars.

Disagreement among historians is like a brush fire in an overgrown woods; it makes room for new growth—new books and articles. Nevertheless, the perpetually unsettled state of historical scholarship can be disquieting. It is a rare event when historians agree that one of their number has written a definitive account. Indeed, accounts that one generation of historians regard as final are often completely revised by a new generation of historians.

With this fact in mind, some historians believe that it is impossible for historical accounts to be objective or neutral. These "relativists" argue that historians are just as much influenced by their time and place as are the people they study. All secondary sources, relativists insist, are subjective accounts colored by the historian's own bias and background. Ironically, such committed relativists still aspire to write persuasive, assured, and reliable books and articles themselves. The relativists may be right, but their claims do not mean that historians should indulge their prejudices. Every historian can afford to be, in the words of intellectual historian Peter Novick, more "self-conscious about the nature of our activity."[4]

Without taking a position in the quarrel between relativists and their critics, we can state that a good deal of the disagreement among American historians seems to be inter-generational. Each generation of historians seems determined to dispute what previous generations of historians have written. We can gain some perspective on these disagreements by thinking about secondary sources as though they were primary sources. For example, a textbook on early American history written in 1980 can be regarded as a primary source for historians' attitudes in 1980 as well as a secondary source on the colonists' attitudes in 1774. We can then uncover patterns of disagreement among historians by asking the same question about secondary sources that we learned to ask about primary sources: how does the author's work fit into his or her own time and place?

Historians are human and are as influenced by their times as anyone else. Most modern historians are trained in universities to be professional scholars. Part of this training includes recognizing and countering their own prejudices. In earlier periods of our history, historians were not so constrained, and they expressed their points of view more openly. Today, historians still have points of view, and although their differences are muted by professional rules for scholarship, a variety of interpretation is inevitable.

A fairly extended example of historiography—the study of historical writing—may serve to illustrate how historians are historical actors whose view of the world is influenced by the times in which they live. In broad terms, it is possible to group succeeding generations of historians into "schools" of like-minded individuals who lived and worked in the same era of history.

Leading historians of the **romantic school** wrote in the mid-nineteenth century, an age when history was considered a branch of "letters," or literature. They believed that the United States was unique and special, and they described how men and women in America carried out a mission to bring democracy to the wilderness. These histories feature much the same dramatic plots and florid language that characterized the fictional literature of the age. Although the romantic historians visited collections of primary sources in the United States and in Europe, these writers were more concerned with sweeping storytelling than with precise documentation. In this sense, the members of the romantic school were amateur historians. They did not teach history nor did they have advanced degrees from universities. Most of them came from solid middle-class merchant or ministerial backgrounds, and they saw the country's history mirroring the story of their own families.

Despite their popularity, the authority of the romantic historical writers was challenged by a new school of professional historians in the last decades of the nineteenth century. These younger scholars, trained in German and American universities, drafted long and copiously documented dissertations to obtain doctor of philosophy degrees (Ph.D.s) in history, and they progressed to careers as professors. Influenced by the rise of the physical sciences in Germany, England, and the United States, they regarded history as a science, capable of exacting standards of proof, rather than as a branch of literature. They and their students shared a faith that history could be truly objective. This doctrine is not widely accepted today, but the educational standard that this **scientific school** fashioned for history graduate students entrenched itself in the universities: to become a professional historian, one still has to go to graduate school, obtain a graduate degree, and write a dissertation based on exhaustive research in primary materials.

Despite their foreign travel, historians in the scientific school had a very nationalistic view of history and wrote about the rise and progress of the United States as though the "nation" were a natural, inevitable, and desirable product of every people's historical development. Each nation supposedly was different, and its history reflected the traits of its people. Within this nationalism flourished racist and sexist biases that induced some scientific historians to join the movement to restrict eastern European and Asian immigration to the United States.

When the nationalistic doctrine of historical development fed into the fires of World War I, a number of younger historians broke from the scientific school's creed and sought other explanations for Americans' conduct and beliefs. These founders of the **progressive school** announced that they had discovered the wellsprings of human motivation in economic self-interest. This group of historians committed themselves to political and economic reform as well as reform of historical ideas, and their views dominated the scholarly writing of the 1920s and 1930s.

With the approach of World War II, the cynical and dispassionate analyses of the progressive school came under attack. Some politically conservative critics of the progressive historians claimed that their writings undermined American morale by denying the virtue of the founders of the nation, a particularly damaging charge as the nation geared itself for struggle against dictatorships in Europe and Asia. During and immediately after the war, a younger generation of historians proclaimed that American history was not a tale of many warring economic interests, each seeking only its own benefit, but a story of many groups merging into one nation bound by common ideals and opportunities. These historians stressed the ways in which American consensus built a great nation, and thus they have been called the **consensus school.** Although progressive ideas continued to infuse the work of some young historians in the 1940s and 1950s, consensus history dominated these decades.

The rise of the civil-rights movement and increasingly bitter domestic protest against the Vietnam War in the 1960s influenced yet another generation of historians to seek its own theoretical orientation. In reexamining American history, these scholars found that the travails of many Americans—immigrants, women, African-Americans, Native Americans, and the very poor—were minimized in the consensus version of history. The younger historians argued that disfavored groups were the victims of dominant elites, abused in the factories and denied equal treatment in the public arena. The historical writing of this **New Left school** (the Old Left was a handful of radical writers in the previous generation) retains its vitality, and many of the central ideas of the New Left, particularly the need to include minority and women's history in textbooks, have enriched every history survey course.

In recent years, the self-critical momentum of the historical profession has been maintained by historians calling on the profession to recognize the contributions and the separate needs of women throughout American history, as well as the importance of gender relations. In the **feminist school,** contemporary politics and professionalism have once again combined to invigorate historical writing and to prove that historians are historical actors.

The most recent generation of historians does not show the dominance of any one doctrine, however. Indeed, older scholars have recently complained that the historical writing of younger scholars is too fragmented and diverse. One characteristic does shine through this diversity: an attraction to methodological rigor and innovation. Younger historians have embraced interdisciplinary studies and boldly borrow concepts from economics, sociology, anthropology, and literary criticism. Computer printouts of data figure prominently in their work. One might call the proponents of this kind of history a **technocratic school** because its leaders are so concerned with getting the methods and the definitions of the methods right. They do not have an overarching theory of American history; in fact, they attack the very notion of such a theory. Of course, if history is any guide, the next generation of historians will cast aside the technocrats' assumptions and proclaim its own vision of the past.

None of the "schools" of history described here is really as uniform or as narrow-minded as we have suggested. In fact, most historians in the United States are unwilling to classify themselves or to label their work, much less admit that they belong to a particular school of thought. It is only through the fine-grained textures of their arguments that we can even attempt to categorize the writing of a particular historian as belonging to a distinct school.

Exercise 4: Historians' Points of View

Following are seven short paragraphs describing some event in the American Revolution, each representing a version of one of the seven schools described earlier. From the argument in the paragraph, identify the school to which the author belongs—romantic, scientific, progressive, consensus, New Left, feminist, or technocratic. In the space provided, explain your reasoning.

A The American Revolution left in its wake two sets of losers—the Tories, who had kept faith with the Empire, and the wives, mothers, sisters, and daughters who joined in the revolutionary movement. These women had contributed to the victory in many ways, running farms and businesses, rearing children, tending the wounded, and even bearing arms. When the war ended, their claims for equality were brushed aside abruptly.

Type: *Feminist* Why? *Speaks of womens contribution to society*

B By plotting the profitability curve of American exports against the growing indebtedness of Americans on the eve of the Revolution, one can easily explain the motives of many revolutionaries. The data are quite complex, but sophisticated computer simulations of various possible courses of action indicate that the revolutionaries made a sensible choice when they severed the tie with Britain.

Type: *Technocratic* Why?

C Behind the revolutionary leaders' high-toned language was a propaganda machine unparalleled in its effectiveness. Stretching from Boston to Charleston, a network of revolutionary agitators, writers, and strong-arm men worked day and night to rouse the mass of colonists to the cause of resistance, a cause that benefited no one more than the men of wealth and influence who oiled the whole apparatus.

Type: _____ Why? _____

_____

D The revolutionary movement brought together men and women from all walks of life in a common cause. They shared a set of ideas about good government and a fear of luxury, corruption, and conspiracy in high places. These shared understandings motivated them to protest and, when that protest was ignored, spurred them to rebellion.

Type: **New Left School** Why? _____

_____

E Throughout the American Revolution ran a spirit of patriotism and heroism, the mark of a people unparalleled in history. In their sacrifices and achievements the revolutionaries startled the European world, bringing fear into the hearts of its selfish princes and hope into the minds of its huddled masses.

Type: _____ Why? _____

_____

F The germ of the notion of a great nation in the wilderness lay in the special racial characteristics of the American settlers. Theirs was the blood of hardy Anglo-Saxons, whose love of personal liberty and sense of communal responsibility went all the way back to their first settlements in the forests of northern Europe.

Type: _____ Why? _____

_____

G The untold story of the American Revolution took place in the streets of cities like New York, Boston, and Philadelphia. There, workingmen and women banded together to assert their rights not only against the Crown, but against local elites as well. The Revolution was thus a radical event, opening doors for the poor to see a glimpse of the power they might wield.

Type: _____ Why? _____

_____

Logical Fallacies in History

Even when historians have tried to avoid capture by any one school of historical thought and successfully avoid the most obvious bias or impartiality in their work, they may still slip into mistakes of logic. The best historians are fallible. Some of these fallacies have been collected by David Hackett Fischer in *Historians' Fallacies: Toward a Logic of Historical Thought* (1970). Fischer's book created a sensation when it was published, not because his readers were surprised by his charges, but because he had caught so many famous historians committing logical bloopers. He cataloged hundreds of different mistakes in using evidence and setting out arguments, a few of which are so common that you should become acquainted with them:

1. the *"Baconian" fallacy*, named after Francis Bacon, a seventeenth-century English philosopher, of assuming that enough facts piled upon each other, without some preconceived hypothesis or theory to explain them, will explain themselves; and its opposite fallacy.

2. the *fallacy of the lone fact*, in which broad statements about important events or ideas are based on a single fact or on too few facts;

3. the *fallacy of tunnel history*, which isolates the historian's subject from everything going on around it and thereby ignores the complexity of a historical subject; and its opposite,

4. the *fallacy of indiscriminate pluralism*, which takes a problem, event, or subject and broadens it beyond reason, leaving the reader confused about the scope of the historian's work;

5. the *moralistic fallacy*, in which the historian admits only those facts that uplift his or her audience and sanitize his or her account or serve some other moral purpose, and censors all other facts;

6. the *presentist fallacy*, a distant cousin to the moralistic fallacy, in which the historian is interested only in those facts that lead up to the present and thus leaves out of the account dead ends, losers in war and politics, and ideas that did not prove themselves;

7. the *holistic fallacy*, in which the historian does nothing and says nothing until he or she knows everything, a species of perfectionism that is a bad example for students who have a deadline for their papers.

Exercise 5: Identifying Historians' Fallacies

The following brief selections illustrate some of these fallacies. Can you match the examples with the preceding list? Write the number of the fallacy in the space provided.

A It is impossible to know what motivated King George III to reject American compromise proposals until we know everything about his personality and the motives of his many advisers and sycophants. _____

B The federal Constitution was a product of hundreds of years of thinking about how governments should be run and thousands of years of experience with the failure of governments. One must add to these ideas the political compromises, economic deals, or social pressures of the men who wrote it to understand the meaning of the words "We the people" in the Preamble. _____

C Without Virginia's assent to the new federal Constitution, there could be no federal government. This single event made all the difference both before Virginia voted to ratify and after the state ratified the federal Constitution. Before its delegates voted, the nation had no future, after the vote, the nation's destiny was determined. _____

D The framers of the Constitution anticipated many modern problems, and it was their ability to anticipate these problems that made the Constitution so successful. _____

E Alexander Hamilton's marital infidelity; James Wilson's frantic speculation in western lands; Thomas Jefferson's barely concealed radicalism; John Adams's contempt for all moral weakness: these are the endearments of bad biography, not the stuff of good history. _____

F If we could be the fly on the wall at the dinner party Alexander Hamilton gave in New York City, hear him persuade Madison to compromise over the Funding and Assumption Act for the national debt, watch the reactions of the people in the room—had we all these firsthand facts, we could explain everything about the origin of the first two-party system. There is no need for theory; simple facts tracing the breakup of a great friendship are all we need to tell the story. _____

G When the delegates to the Philadelphia Convention met to write a constitution for the new nation, they left behind them all local biases, personal prejudices, and selfish interests. They were motivated only by the desperate straits that America faced. All else paled by comparison. _____

Historians make mistakes, historians are products of their times; historians are capable of bias, narrow-mindedness, and logical errors. All this notwithstanding, every society owes a great debt to its historians. They are the keepers of communal memory. As Carl Becker reminded us long ago, "History [is] the artificial extension of the social memory . . . [it] is an art of long standing, necessarily so since it springs instinctively from the impulse to enlarge the range of human experience."[5]

To most of us, the historian's craft appears a sedentary vocation, in which historians glide almost effortlessly about the archive or the library in search of primary sources, then sit down to write their accounts. But historians are sometimes more than guardians of our past. When tyrants or mobs suppress free expression and disinterested scholarship or demand that history lie or keep silent, then historians can be heroes. In helping all of us to remember a past at odds with the present, historians defend our liberty.

Shortly before the Nazis executed French historian Marc Bloch for his part in the resistance against them, he wrote:

> It is in time and, therefore, in history that the great drama of Sin and Redemption . . . is unfolded. Our art, our literary monuments, resound with echoes of the past. Our men of action have its real or pretended lessons incessantly on their lips. . . . It is not in itself inconceivable that our [civilization] may, one day, turn away from [its] history, and historians would do well to reflect upon this possibility . . . should we come to this, it would be at the cost of a serious rupture with our most unvarying intellectual traditions.[6]

Hiding from the Nazis while writing his last book, *The Historian's Craft*, Bloch lamented that he could not get to a library to check his facts. You have the opportunity that misfortune denied him, and in the next chapter you will find why Bloch, like all historians, regarded libraries as indispensable.

Notes

[1] Simon Schama, *Dead Certainties* (New York: Knopf, 1991), 320.

[2] Timothy H. Breen, *Imagining the Past: East Hampton Histories* (Reading, Mass.: Addison-Wesley, 1989), 295.

[3] Carl Becker, "What Are Historical Facts?" in Phil L. Snyder, ed., *Detachment and the Writing of History: Essays and Letters of Carl L. Becker* (Ithaca: Cornell University Press, 1958), 45.

[4] Peter Novick, *That Noble Dream: The "Objectivity Question" and the American Historical Profession* (Cambridge: Cambridge University Press, 1988), 628.

[5] Carl L. Becker, "Everyman His Own Historian," *American Historical Review* 37 (1932), 236.

[6] Marc Bloch, *The Historian's Craft*, trans. Peter Putnam (1942; reprint, New York: Vintage, 1953), 5.

5: Hunting For Evidence: Library and Web Skills

The Revolutionary Generation

———— •———•———• ————

Historians are investigators looking for clues to understand what happened in the past. As the English historian Robin Winks has written,

> The routine [of investigation] must be pursued or the clue may be missed; the apparently false trail must be followed in order to be certain that it is false; the mute witnesses must be asked the reasons for their silence, for the piece of evidence that is missing from where one might reasonably expect to find it is, after all, a form of evidence in itself.[1]

Where do historians locate this evidence? Sometimes they travel all over the world seeking primary sources, but there is much to find closer to home, in the library and on the Web. Students as well as historians can use college or local libraries and web sites to uncover and check on sources.

We live in revolutionary times—the era of the "information revolution." One easy way to cope with the information revolution is to master basic library and internet skills. The techniques discussed in this chapter are transsubstantive—that is, you can use them to investigate topics in the humanities and social sciences as well as those assigned for this course.

Libraries have always been the great repositories of human learning and aspiration. Indeed, they are synonymous with civilization, for all great civilizations have stored their wisdom in libraries. Among the greatest tragedies in history have been the destruction or desecration of these storehouses of literature and science.

Not all libraries are comprehensive in their holdings. Some, like the Library of Congress in Washington, D.C., the New York Public Library in New York City, or the British Library in London, England, have nearly complete collections of all books and journals ever published. Some university libraries—for example, the library system of Harvard University—have collections that are nearly as extensive as the national libraries of the United States and the United Kingdom. Many smaller university, college, and regional libraries throughout the country offer excellent, if more selective, collections of books, magazines and journals, newspapers, and research aids. The descriptions and exercises that follow are based on the resources of a wide variety of college libraries visited over the past six years. If your college library does not have the particular reference books or research aids we mention, the reference librarian will help you to substitute appropriate materials. With the limitations of smaller libraries in mind, we have provided alternative selections for some exercises.

Libraries and the Web

Many libraries list their resources—their collections of materials—and allow access to their catalogues through their web sites.

The most voluminous of the libraries whose catalogues are available on line is the Library of Congress, at *www.loc.gov*. The opening (or "home" or gateway) page of the web site is reproduced below.

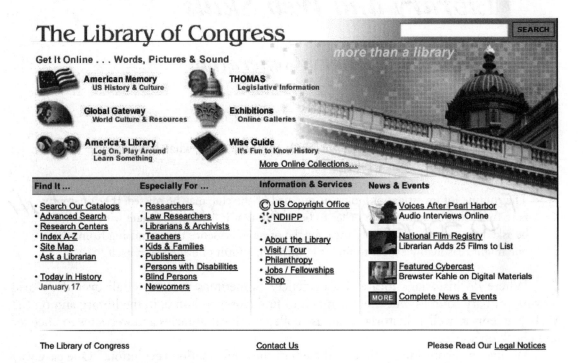

FIGURE 5.1

As you can see, there is a lot more here than just a catalogue of books and other print resources. The library offered many "links" to exhibitions, collections, and announcements. Some of these are "icons" or pictures. Others are words or phrases, usually underlined. When you move your mouse cursor to them, the arrow turns into a hand. That means you can click the left button or panel on the mouse and take yourself to a new page. As the LOC homepage reminds us, the LOC is "more than just a library." But the LOC is not the only government depository that is open to on-line inquiries and searches. The National Archives is another remarkable web source. Try *www.archives.gov.*

FIGURE 5.2

More specialized libraries also offer web pages with connecting links. For information, sources, and links on the founding generation of the new nation, one may try the Omohundro Institute of Early American History and Culture, *www.wm.edu/oieahc.*

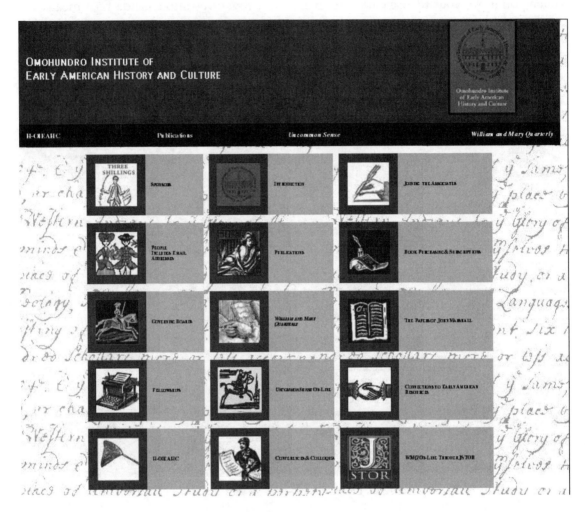

FIGURE 5.3

This web page has many useful links, including connections to the early American History "list serve" (a subscription service for scholars to ask and answer questions and engage in conversations—a kind of early American history chat room). We will have more to say about these list serves in a moment.

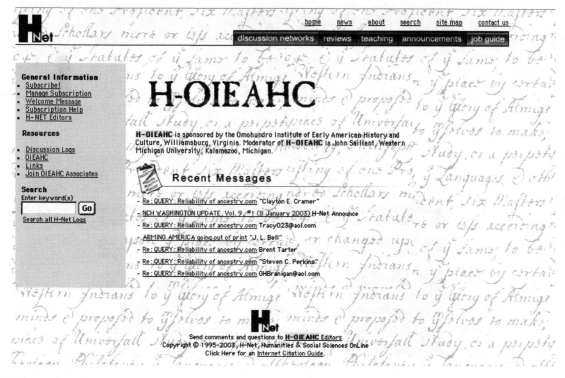

FIGURE 5.4

Other often consulted libraries with web sites are the American Antiquarian Society in Worcester, Massachusetts (*www.americanantiquarian.org*), the Library Company of Philadelphia (*www.librarycompany.org*), The Newberry Library in Chicago (*www.newberry.org*) and the David Library of the American Revolution in Washington Crossing, Pennsylvania (*www.dlar.org*).

FIGURE 5.5

| Home | WolfPAC | Online Store | Events | Fellowships | Economy Program | Exhibits | About LCP | Print Dept | Rights & Repros |

THE LIBRARY COMPANY
of philadelphia

The McLean Conservation Dept.

The Library Company of Philadelphia is a non-profit independent research library with collections documenting every aspect of the history and background of American culture from the colonial period to the end of the nineteenth century. A collection of national importance, its holdings number approximately half a million printed volumes in a wide variety of formats; 75,000 graphics; 160,000 manuscripts; and a small, distinguished collection of early American art and artifacts.

Golden WebAward
>> 2002-2003 Winner

Search our Website [   ] [GO] [sitemap] For Books and Graphics Search WolfPAC

The Library Company of Philadelphia, 1314 Locust Street, Philadelphia, Pennsylvania 19107 (215) 546-3181
Questions or Comments Contact the Website Coordinator nscalessa@librarycompany.org

FIGURE 5.6

The David Library
of the
American Revolution

David Library of the American Revolution
1201 River Road Box 748
Washington Crossing, PA 18977
215-493-6776; Fax: 215-493-9276
General Information E-Mail: dlar@dlar.org
Research E-Mail: research@dlar.org

Go to Overview
Go to Hours, Access, and Location
Go to Description of Collections
Go to Online Guides to Microfilm and Searchable CD-ROM Holdings
Go to Research Fellowships
Go to List of Current David Library Fellows
Go to Lecture program
Go to Exhibitions

FIGURE 5.7

Exercise 1. Browsing and Searching

Every one of these excellent on-line historical resources offers us two options. We can browse or we can search. Actually, both of these are "commands" to the web site to do what we ask of it. To browse, we click on one of the icons or links. This will open up a new page. Sometimes it has information, on other occasions it is a gateway to additional pages. On the LOC homepage, you will find an icon labeled "American Memory: U.S. History and Culture." Move your cursor to it and open it. Find the link labeled "today in history" and open it. In the space below, summarize one of the events the librarians have chosen to describe for this day.

_____

_____

_____

Note that at the bottom of this page are more links (underlined texts). Open one of them that relates to the event you selected and describe below what you have found.

_____

_____

_____

The search command is more specific than the browse command. You can tell the web site what to look for in its stored data by filling a blank field (usually a long empty rectangle) with a search request. This can be a word or a phrase. We are going to do some searching for information on one of the greatest and certainly the best known members of the revolutionary generation—George Washington. In youth a surveyor and planter, Washington became a famous officer during the French and Indian War, joined the protest against Parliament in the 1760s, and became the commander in chief of the Continental Army in 1775. After leading it to victory over the British, he laid down his command and returned to his plantation in 1783. Called back to public service to chair the federal Constitutional convention in 1787, he was unanimously chosen the first president of the federal government in 1788 and served two terms. Then he retired once again, setting a pattern that would last until 1940. His willingness to set aside private interests to serve the public good combined with his rejection of the temptations of great power made him the perfect symbol of republican virtue and the first "father" of his country.

Go back to the American Memory homepage and click on the link labeled "search" the collections in the American Memory data base. This sends us to a new screen with a series of search fields we can fill by moving the cursor to the box and keying in our request. Scroll down to the collection called "Washington, George–Papers–1741–1799." This is a digitalized (computer accessible) assemblage of our first president's letters, diaries, speeches, and public papers. Click on it.

Find the "search by keyword" link and click on it. As an optional exercise, find in your textbook any quotation from Washington (a phrase will do) and type it *exactly* into the big field labeled "Search descriptive information and/or full text." Go down to the first "menu" box below the empty field where the default entry is "match any of these words" and select instead (by clicking on the down arrow next to the box and then clicking on the menu offering) "match all of these words." When you click on the search box to the left of the field, you will get every document in the collection that has the exact wording of the phrase you chose. Hint: many textbooks have a short quotation from either Washington's farewell

FIGURE 5.8

address to his troops in 1783, the Neutrality proclamation of 1793, or his Farewell Address to the nation. Describe below what you find.

_____

_____

A Tour of the Library

A typical college library includes the following locations:

1. Card catalog and/or computer terminals
2. Circulation desk—where books are checked out
3. Reference desk and reference room or area
4. Reserve desk or room
5. Periodicals room or section
6. Stacks or shelves where most books are located
7. Government-documents room or area
8. Rooms housing "special collections" of primary sources
9. Interlibrary loan department
10. Microfilm and microforms reading area

Many libraries provide written guides or pamphlets for users that include a map showing rooms and areas of interest. Almost all college libraries will arrange tours for students.

Primary Sources in the Library

Libraries contain primary sources of history in many forms. Some libraries have "special collections" of original historical documents deposited by the descendants of the authors of these documents. Almost all libraries have government-documents rooms or areas. Federal- and state-government reports, records of legislative debates, copies of the acts of legislatures and the opinions of courts, and published transcripts of the hearings of committees are examples of government documents and are primary sources. The library also has newspapers, magazines, and books published in the past—primary sources for the study of the periods in which these printed materials were written.

Exercise 2: On-line Search

Your next exercise utilizes the card catalog or the computer-assisted search terminal to track down books in the stacks or shelving area of the library. In many college and university libraries, card catalogs are no longer used. Instead, entries on all new acquisitions are placed in a computer memory. You can access this information by following a series of instructions on screens that the computer terminal displays. Most library computer systems are menu driven, with a list of possible commands offered on screen. The GIL system at the University of Georgia Library is one such facility. For purposes of explanations let us use this computer cataloging system to find information about George Washington. The first screen is a home page, welcoming us and inviting us to begin our search.

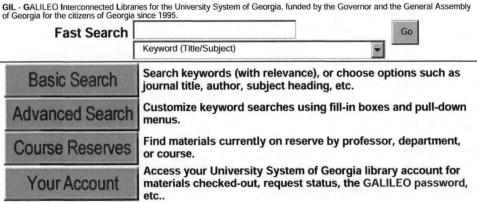

FIGURE 5.9

To familiarize yourself with the opportunities and the obstacles in a guided on-line library search, we have prepared the following exercise on one—arguably the greatest and certainly the best known—member of the revolutionary generation: George Washington. Assume you want to know about him as a commander of the Continental Army in the revolutionary war. Let's begin with a basic search. You have to enter the key words for your search in the empty box (the "field") and then select what kind of search—for a title, a subject, an author, and so on—from the menu box to the right.

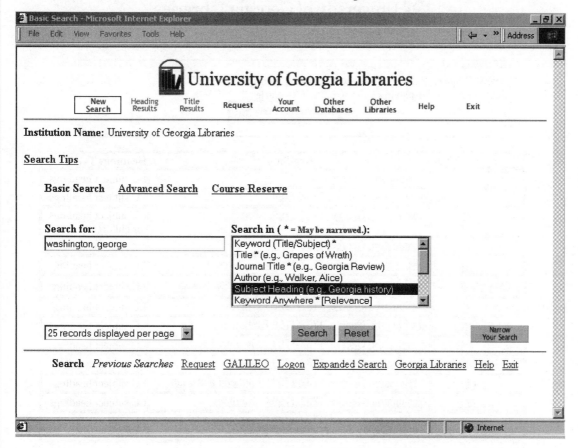

FIGURE 5.10

Note that we have put in the name as George Washington because we are searching for him as the subject of books. If we wanted to find out what he had written, we would put in the name Washington, George in the empty box and then select "author" from the menu. If you enter the name George Washington in the empty box or field—and indicate that he is the subject of your search in the "search in" menu box, you will get the following screen:

University of Georgia Libraries

New Search	Heading Results	Title Results	Previous Search	Request	Your Account	Other Databases	Other Libraries	Help	Exit

Institution Name: University of Georgia Libraries
Search Request: Subject Browse = washington, george
Search Results: Displaying 1 through 25 of 25 entries.

◀ previous | next ▶

#	Titles	Headings	Headings Type
1	1	Washington, George.	LC subject headings
2	603	Washington, George, 1732-1799	LC subject headings
3	7	Washington, George, 1732-1799.	LC subject headings for children
4	3	Washington, George, 1732-1799	not applicable
5	1	Washington, George, 1732-1799 Anecdotes.	LC subject headings
See also 6	25	Washington, George, 1732-1799 Anniversaries, etc.	LC subject headings
7	5	Washington, George, 1732-1799 Archives	LC subject headings
8	5	Washington, George, 1732-1799 Bibliography.	LC subject headings
9	1	Washington, George, 1732-1799 Biography Psychology.	LC subject headings
10	2	Washington, George, 1732-1799 Birthplace.	LC subject headings
11	1	Washington, George, 1732-1799 Childhood and youth.	LC subject headings
12	1	Washington, George, 1732-1799 Chronology.	LC subject headings
13	1	Washington, George, 1732-1799 Contributions in architecture.	LC subject headings
14	1	Washington, George, 1732-1799 Contributions in gardening.	LC subject headings
15	1	Washington, George, 1732-1799 Contributions in nationalism.	LC subject headings
16	5	Washington, George, 1732-1799 Correspondence.	LC subject headings
17	14	Washington, George, 1732-1799 Death and burial.	LC subject headings
18	1	Washington, George, 1732-1799 Death and burial Poetry.	LC subject headings
19	3	Washington, George, 1732-1799 Death and burial Sermons.	LC subject headings
20	1	Washington, George, 1732-1799 Diaries.	LC subject headings
21	24	Washington, George, 1732-1799 Drama.	LC subject headings
22	1	Washington, George, 1732-1799 Dwellings.	LC subject headings

FIGURE 5.11

We want to find out about the man, and there are, as we put this work text in print, 603 works in print about him. Let's look at the first few of these.

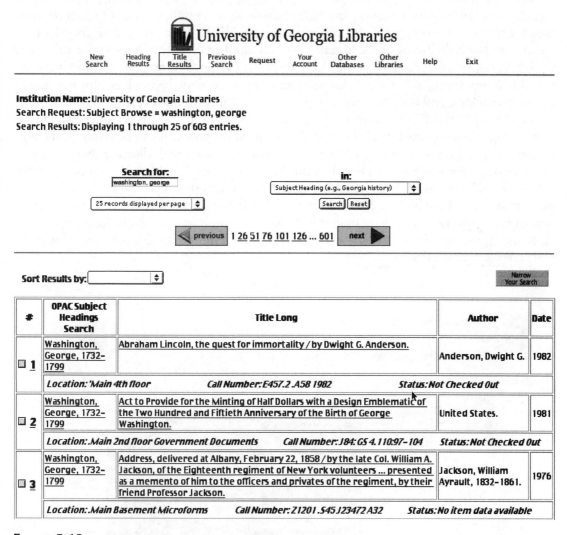

FIGURE 5.12

As you can see, the search not only reveals the titles, authors, and dates of the books, the screen tells us where in the library to look for the volume. Some are simply addresses or sermons published under "separate covers." That is, they are not magazine or newspaper articles, or scholarly journal essays, but have been published on their own. The first is a book about President Lincoln that also has material on Washington. It can be found in the "stacks" or book shelf area of the library. The call number, E457.2.A58 1982 is a Library of Congress call number. Some libraries have their own systems of numbering, and some use the old Dewey Decimal System. This call number tells us that the book is with the American history books, and is shelved with other books on Lincoln. Books about Washington are usually found in the E312's, however. The second entry on our list is a Congressional Act celebrating Washington's birthday by minting coins in his honor. It can be found in the government documents section of the library and has a J call number, indicating that it is a government or political science subject. The third entry is a speech published as a book in 1858. It has a Z call number, and can be found in the microforms (the microcard, microfiche, and microfilm) area of the library. Although it was a book, the library owns it as part of a collection of early American books on microfilm. Other entries have an HS call number, and can be found in the rare book room. At the University of Georgia, rare books are kept at the Hargrett Rare Book Room.

University of Georgia Libraries

HARGRETT
RARE BOOK & MANUSCRIPT LIBRARY

Site Contents

- New World
- Colonial America
- Revolutionary America
- Revolutionary Georgia
- Union & Expansion
- American Civil War
- Frontier to New South
- Savannah & the Coast
- Transportation

Trouble Printing?

Imaging Services

Publishing Information

Rare Map Reference Questions

Rare Map Collection

- Collection Information
- Information about the map images on the site
- Links to other helpful sites

The Hargrett Rare Book and Manuscript Library at the University of Georgia maintains a collection of more than 800 historic maps spanning nearly 500 years, from the sixteenth century through the early twentieth century. The collection provides a graphic resource upon which scholars can draw in re-discovering the minds and movements of early American explorers, revolutionary statesmen, cultural figures and politicians represented by the library's book and manuscript collections.

Although not limited to a single geographic subject, the collection heavily emphasizes the State of Georgia and the surrounding region. To locate maps of geographic regions or time periods not represented on this web site, please visit one of the sites listed below.

Here the researcher will find an America drawn by cartographers who imagined the New World based upon the earliest explorations of the Eastern coastline, as well as the geographically maturing images of mapmakers whose creations reflect an increasing European expedition into the American continent. A colonial presence manifested itself in forts, then settlements, and then as a nation conceived of thirteen revolutionary colonies.

The largest of these colonies to break from the English crown, revolutionary Georgia, closes the eigtheenth century as a staging-area or battleground in the struggle for independence. In the next century, while the country as a whole undergoes union and expansion and a bloody civil war, the state wrestles with questions of property and political boundaries, transforming itself from frontier to New South.

Finally, the Hargrett collection recognizes the early strategic importance of Savannah and the coast in Georgia's development. A group of maps of this area complements those which acknowledge the role of transportation -- by rail and then highway -- in getting the crops to the market, Sherman to the sea, and, nowadays, everybody to Disney World.

FIGURE 5.13

Well, by now you may be getting concerned that you will never find the kind of book you want. Don't be discouraged. You need to narrow your search. Let's use the "advanced search" capabilities of the on-line catalogue. The advanced search allows you to combine search commands using "Boolean logic." The key is the employment of connectives like "and," "or," and "not."

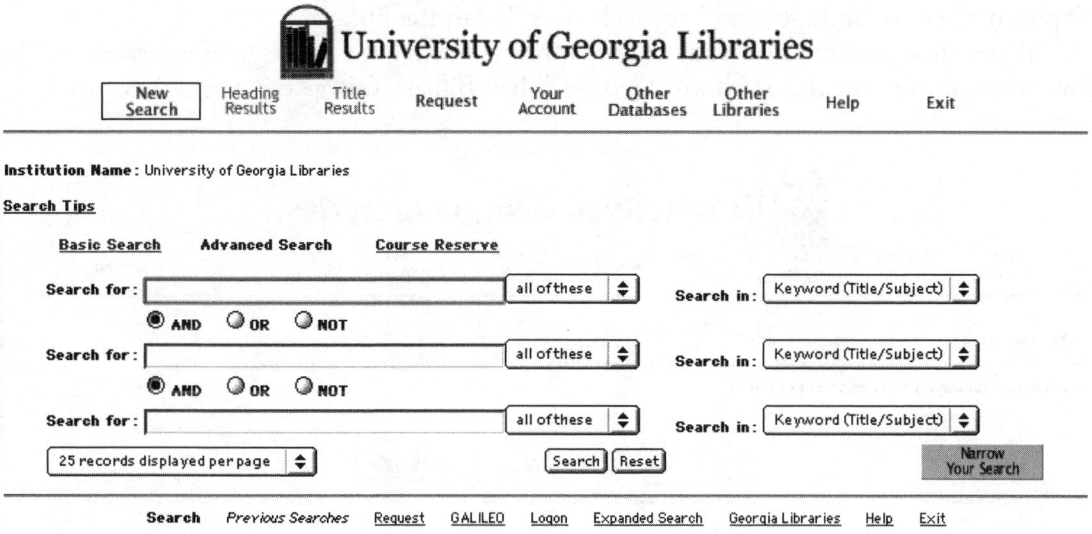

FIGURE 5.14

The big empty box is for a word or phrase. The drop-down menu in the middle allows you to specify how much of the phrase has to appear in the search. The final menu, on the right, is the choice of topic, again "keyword in the title or subject" the author, etc. We'll limit our search by adding the word "army" to the second line and label it as a subject. Now we are looking for books that have Washington *and* army as subjects. The resulting list has only 134 entries, and they are sorted by relevance. Note that they tend to be much more recent books and are available on the shelves in the stacks. Sometimes older books are sent to the "repository" or to "storage" and have to be recalled to the library.

If you click your mouse on any of the entries you will get a full page of information. We have selected from the list one book, George Athan Billias's *George Washington's Generals*.

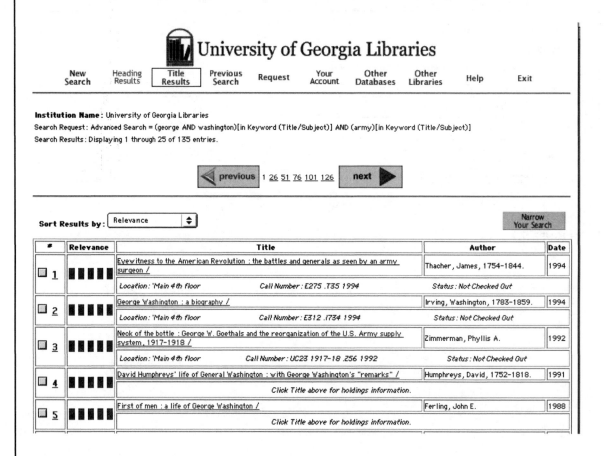

FIGURE 5.15

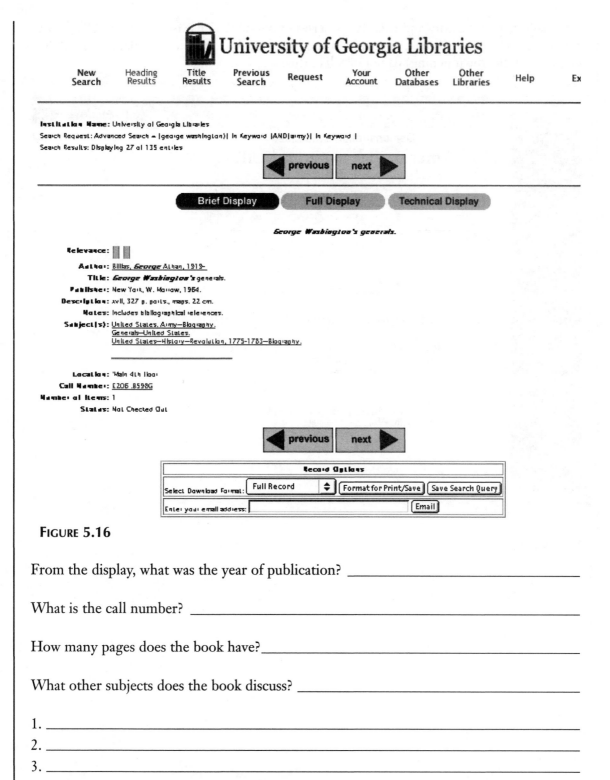

FIGURE 5.16

From the display, what was the year of publication? _____

What is the call number? _____

How many pages does the book have?_____

What other subjects does the book discuss? _____

1. _____
2. _____
3. _____

Books are not the only sources of information at the library. Another major scholarly source is the periodical. These may be scholarly journals, topical magazines, or specialized collections. They are called periodicals because they are published at regular intervals or periods, sometimes once a month, sometimes four times a year (quarterlies), sometimes twice a year, sometimes once a year. They may be called abstracts. One way to search them is to use America: History and Life. It is a series of bound volumes or a group of CDs in the reference room of the library, and can also be found on-line. On line, available from ABC-CLIO, its welcome (opening) page looks like this:

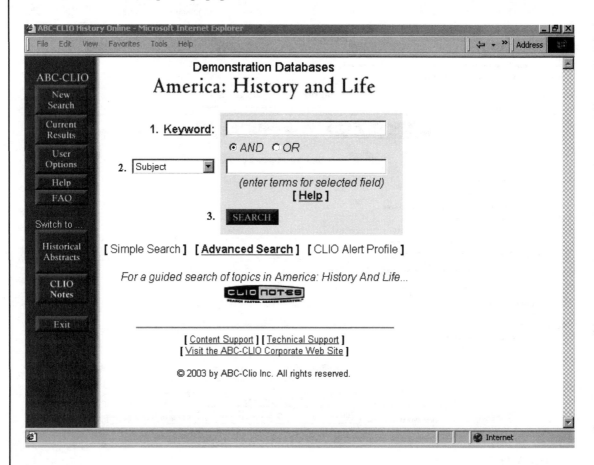

FIGURE 5.17

If you asked for George Washington in the first field and army in the second, indicating that both were subjects, you would get a series of displays like those below. In fact there are 18 from this search.

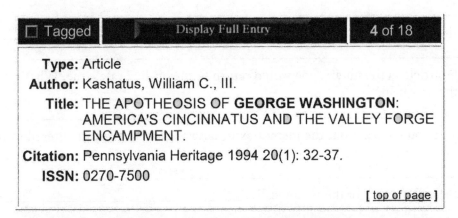

☐ Tagged	Display Full Entry	**4** of 18

Type: Article
Author: Kashatus, William C., III.
Title: THE APOTHEOSIS OF **GEORGE WASHINGTON**: AMERICA'S CINCINNATUS AND THE VALLEY FORGE ENCAMPMENT.
Citation: Pennsylvania Heritage 1994 20(1): 32-37.
ISSN: 0270-7500

[top of page]

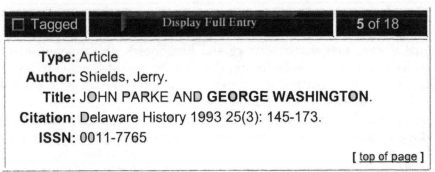

☐ Tagged	Display Full Entry	**5** of 18

Type: Article
Author: Shields, Jerry.
Title: JOHN PARKE AND **GEORGE WASHINGTON**.
Citation: Delaware History 1993 25(3): 145-173.
ISSN: 0011-7765

[top of page]

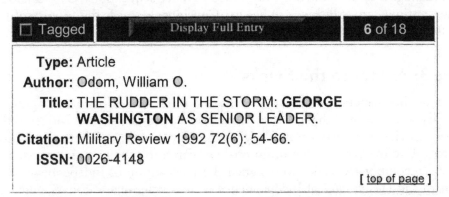

☐ Tagged	Display Full Entry	**6** of 18

Type: Article
Author: Odom, William O.
Title: THE RUDDER IN THE STORM: **GEORGE WASHINGTON** AS SENIOR LEADER.
Citation: Military Review 1992 72(6): 54-66.
ISSN: 0026-4148

[top of page]

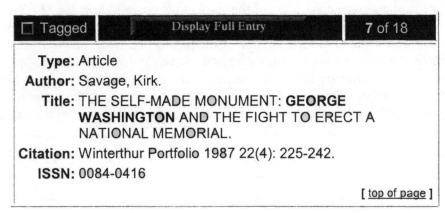

☐ Tagged	Display Full Entry	**7** of 18

Type: Article
Author: Savage, Kirk.
Title: THE SELF-MADE MONUMENT: **GEORGE WASHINGTON** AND THE FIGHT TO ERECT A NATIONAL MEMORIAL.
Citation: Winterthur Portfolio 1987 22(4): 225-242.
ISSN: 0084-0416

[top of page]

Looking at the four displays, what is the name of the author of the first article?

_____

What is name of the journal in which the article appears?

_____

What is the year, the volume number, and the page numbers of the article? _____

_____

To find the article in the library, you would return to the on-line catalogue. What would you enter in the first field? _____

_____

What would you choose from the menu box to describe the words you entered in the first field? _____

_____

What is the call number of the periodical? _____

_____

Another way to find articles is to use the library's on-line resources. Both JSTOR (the on-line journal storage site) at *www.jstor.org* and Ebscohost's electronic journals service at *www.ebsco.com* have search engines (software) that can use guided searches to find articles by author, topic, and title for many history journals. Sometimes you can get the full text of the journal, on other occasions only the citation of the article.

Commercial search engines like Google™, Alta Vista™, and Yahoo™ are not as helpful for searching for articles or books, but often can get you to a site that has a summary of the topic.

Card catalogs may offer the only way to access older acquisitions. Card catalog entries, though now antique, are still things of beauty. Consider the cards the Library of Congress prepared for *The Papers of George Washington* (Figure 5.18).

Exercise 3: A Trip to the Stacks

Collections of the "papers"—letters, speeches, and writings—of historical figures contain many primary sources, for each letter and document is a primary source. Modern editions of these papers provide extensive commentary on the events and people mentioned in the primary sources. Use the card catalog or an on-line search to find a volume of the papers or writings of a revolutionary leader who signed the Declaration of Independence. (*Hint:* All the signers of the Declaration of Independence were revolutionary leaders, and most textbooks include in their appendixes a list of the signers.) Prepare a short list of revolutionary leaders, and look in the card catalog's subject section or search your library's terminal by subject (remember, last name first) for a volume of the papers of anyone on your list. With the catalog card or the result of your terminal search as your guide, write in the space below the name of your revolutionary figure, the names of the editor of his papers, the full title of the book or the series of volumes, the city in which it was published, the name of the publisher, the year of publication, the number of volumes in the collection, and the call number.

_____

_____

_____

_____

Card #1

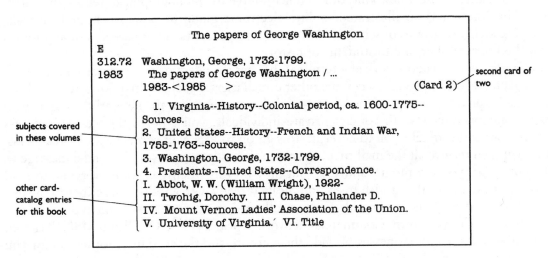

call number — where book can be found on the shelves

editors and/or authors

date(s) of publication

International Standard Book Number

identification of the library from which the card was taken (GU = University of Georgia)

The Papers of George Washington

E
312.72   Washington, George, 1732-1799.
1983   The Papers of George Washington /
           W. W. Abbot, editor, Dorothy Twohig, associate editor,
           Philander D. Chase, Beverly H. Runge, and Frederick Hall
           Schmidt, assistant editors. --
           Charlottesville : University Press of Virginia,
           1983-<1985   >
             <v. A, 1-4; B, 1; in 5   >: ill. ; 25 cm.
           "Sponsored by the Mount Vernon Ladies' Association of the
           Union and the University of Virginia with the support of the
           National Endowment for the Humanities".
           Includes bibliography and indexes.
           ISBN 0-813-9-0912-0 (Colonial ser. : v. 1)
GU

author
title
publisher and place of publication
height of the book
sponsors of publication
additional features
number of volumes in library so far

Card #2

The papers of George Washington

E
312.72   Washington, George, 1732-1799.
1983   The papers of George Washington / ...
           1983-<1985   >   (Card 2)

subjects covered in these volumes

other card-catalog entries for this book

           1. Virginia--History--Colonial period, ca. 1600-1775--
           Sources.
           2. United States--History--French and Indian War,
           1755-1763--Sources.
           3. Washington, George, 1732-1799.
           4. Presidents--United States--Correspondence.
           I. Abbot, W. W. (William Wright), 1922-
           II. Twohig, Dorothy.   III. Chase, Philander D.
           IV. Mount Vernon Ladies' Association of the Union.
           V. University of Virginia.´ VI. Title

second card of two

FIGURE 5.18 *Cards from the Card Catalog*
Reprinted courtesy of University of Georgia Library

In the stacks, library books are shelved according to various numbering systems. The Dewey Decimal system is common in most local libraries. College librarians prefer the Library of Congress system, which combines letters and numbers. Widener Library at Harvard University developed its own cataloging system, but it has given way to the Library of Congress system.

In the stacks, find the volume you described in Exercise 3. Remove the volume from the shelves, and photocopy one of the letters in it. This letter is a primary source. Review Exercise 3 "Discovering Differences," in Chapter 1, and describe two ways in which the habits, ideas, or behavior portrayed in the primary source that you copied contrast with modern customs and conduct.

1. _____

2. _____

Getting into History on the Internet

Historians already use a new kind of reference source for bibliographical items—the Internet. The Internet is an illustrated, online electronic guide to newspapers and journals, libraries, archives, groups of scholars, and even other students. There are a number of ways that the Internet offers aid to students of history.

E-mail allows you to work at a terminal that has a modem or is otherwise connected to the telephone lines and directly contact other e-mail users. Much of what flows over the lines in e-mail is private correspondence, but e-mail also connects you to "networks" of users who have common interests. To contact private individuals, you type in their e-mail address where your software tells you to enter it. To sign on to lists, you contact a sign-on address. You will then receive all the mail that anyone on the address receives. To send a message to the entire list, you use the list address—but only do this when you want everyone to read what you have to say. If you wish to communicate directly with another subscriber to the list, you should use only his or her address. You will need an account to sign on and an address to receive mail of your own. Commercial network providers like AOL™ and MSN™ as well as various schools and businesses provide the software and the account information for you to begin to use e-mail.

The exchanges of opinion on the history lists are fun to follow and the lists also are sounding boards for new ideas, places to go when you have a specific inquiry, and even offer up-to-the-minute book reviews. Some of the lists have dozens of pieces of mail posted each day which will end up in your mailbox, so you need to be circumspect about the number of lists to which you subscribe. Two or three is best. The software will tell you how to dump and save mail. Some of the history lists on the "H-Net," founded by professor Richard Jensen at the University of Illinois, Chicago, among others, follow.

You can get into history on the Internet. The H-Net is an umbrella organization for a wide variety of specialized history networks. The H-Net welcome page is *www2.h-net.msu.edu/contact*. The affiliates of the list can be contacted directly, or through the web site *www2.h-net.msu.edu/about/affiliates.html*. The list appears below. Click on any of these from the H-List homepage and you will get information on how to join the list.

For students particularly interested in the revolutionary generation and the Revolution, the Omohundro Institute offers a series of relevant web links on its page. Go to *www2.h-net.msu.edu/~ieahcweb/links*. You'll find libraries, class resources, organizations, museums, on-line exhibits, and documents there.

H-Net Affiliates

scholarly organizations

INDEX · A | B | C | E | G | H | I | J | K | M | N | O | P | S | T | U | W

A

African Literature Association - ALA is an independent non-profit professional society open to scholars, teachers and writers from every country. It exists primarily to facilitate the attempts of a world-wide audience to appreciate the efforts of African writers and artists.

African Political Science Association

African Studies Association - open to all individuals and institutions interested in African affairs. Its mission is to bring together people with a scholarly and professional interest in Africa.

American Association for the Advancement of Slavic Studies - The American Association for the Advancement of Slavic Studies (AAASS) is a nonprofit, nonpolitical, scholarly society which is the leading private organization dedicated to the advancement of knowledge about Russia, Central Eurasia, and Eastern and Central Europe.

American Association for Study of Hungarian History - The American Association for the Study of Hungarian History was founded in 1970 for the purpose of furthering interest in Hungarian history and to encourage research in this field. The association also aims to cooperate with scholars and institutions with similar interests in Hungary and elsewhere in the world.

American Historical Association - The American Historical Association (AHA) is a nonprofit membership organization founded in 1884 and incorporated by Congress in 1889 for the promotion of historical studies, the collection and preservation of historical documents and artifacts, and the dissemination of historical research.

American Italian Historical Association - Our Association is devoted to the interdisciplinary study of the culture, history, literature, sociology, demography, folklore, and politics of Italians in America.

American Political Science Association - With more than 13,500 members residing in over 70 countries worldwide, the American Political Science Association is the world's largest professional organization for the study of politics.

American Society for Environmental History (ASEH) - ASEH seeks understanding of the human experience of the environment. Emphasis is on the perspectives of history and the liberal arts and sciences. The Society encourages dialogue among the disciplines on every aspect of the present and past relationship of humankind to the natural environment.

American Society for Legal History - The American Society for Legal History is a nonprofit membership organization dedicated to fostering scholarship, teaching, and study concerning the law and institutions of all legal systems, both Anglo-American and international.

Arts Council of African Studies Association (ACASA) - The organization exists to facilitate communication among scholars, teachers, artists, museum specialists and all others interested in the arts of Africa and the African Diaspora.

Association for History and Computing (AHC) - The Association for History and Computing exists to encourage and maintain interest in the use of computers in all types of historical studies at all levels, in both teaching and research.

Association for Women in Slavic Studies (AWSS) - Promotion of the interests of women in the field, and of the study of women, family, and gender in the cultures and languages of Central and Eastern Europe and the Soviet successor states.

Australian History Association

B

Business History Conference - "...keeping our members in touch with each other and with what is going on in the business history profession."

C

California Studies Association

Canadian Committee on History and Computing - The Canadian Committee on History and Computing (CCHC) is a committee of the Canadian Historical Association (CHA) and is the Canadian section of the Association for History and Computing. The mandate of the CCHC is "to encourage and sustain interest in Canada in the use of computers in all types of historical studies at all levels, in both teaching and research."

Center for Austrian Studies - The Center for Austrian Studies was founded in 1977 to serve as a catalyst for interdisciplinary scholarship and to provide fresh perspectives on Austria and Central Europe.

Center for Global Partnerships at the Japan Foundation of Tokyo - CGP was established in 1991 to help achieve closer relations between Japan and the United States, and to contribute to a better world through the cooperative efforts of both countries.

Cervantes Society of America - The Society's purpose is to advance the study of the life and works of Miguel de Cervantes.

Chicago Historical Society - The Chicago Historical Society is a privately endowed, independent institution devoted to collecting, interpreting, and presenting the rich multicultural history of Chicago and Illinois, as well as selected areas of American history, to the public through exhibitions, programs, research collections, and publications.

The Cliometric Society - The Cliometric Society is an academic organization of individuals interested in using economic theory and statistical techniques to study economic history.

Conference on Latin American History - The Conference on Latin American History (CLAH) is a professional association devoted to encourage the diffusion of knowledge about Latin America through fostering the study and improving the teaching of Latin American history.

E

Economic History Association - Its purpose is to encourage and promote teaching, research, and publication on every phase of economic history, and to encourage and assist in the preservation and administration of the materials for research in the field.

Economic History Society of Australia and New Zealand (OZNZ) - The aim of the EHSANZ is to promote the teaching, study and understanding of Economic History; to disseminate knowledge in the field of Economic History; to hold conferences and to participate in other relevant meetings which encourage the conservation of historical materials and artifacts.

G

German Studies Association - The German Studies Association is the multi- and interdisciplinary association of scholars in German, Austrian, and Swiss history, literature, culture studies, political science, and economics.

Grand Rapids Area Council for the Humanities - The Grand Rapids Area Council for the Humanities is the first grass-roots organization in the nation dedicated to promoting the humanities at the community level.

H

Historians of Islamic Art (HIA)

History and Macintosh Society (HMS)

History News Service (HNS) - HNS is an informal syndicate of professional historians who seek to improve the public's understanding of current events by setting these events in their historical contexts.

History of Economics Society, The - The History Economics Society is an international organization of scholars in the history of economics.

Humanities Council of West Central Michigan - Regional council of the Michigan Humanities Council and offers humanities programs in Lake, Mason, Mecosta, Newaygo, Osceola and surrounding counties. The goal of this nonprofit organization is to help residents of those rural counties understand the humanities and know how they apply to their lives.

I

The International Association for the History of Crime and Criminal Justice - The study of the history of crime and criminal justice in the widest sense.

Indiana Historical Society - The Indiana Historical Society works to collect, preserve, interpret and share information about the unique heritage of Indiana.

Institut fur Geschchtswissen schaften of Humbolt-Universitat zu Berlin

International Commission on Historical Demography

J

Japan-American Student Conference (JASC)

Jhistory - Jhistory, founded in August, 1994, has been a forum for many fascinating discussions, with professors, graduate students and professionals debating and exploring journalism history topics.

K

Kansai Institute of Asian-Pacific Studies (KIAPS)

M

Michigan Archival Association - the Michigan Archival Association has evolved into the primary organization devoted to the archival community in Michigan.

Michigan Council for Arts and Cultural Affairs - The Michigan Council for Arts and Cultural Affairs serves to encourage, develop and facilitate an enriched environment of artistic, creative, cultural activity in Michigan.

Michigan Humanities Council - The Michigan Humanities Council is an independent, nonprofit organization which encourages and supports a variety of activities which bring humanities scholars and the public together in promoting understanding and appreciation of the humanities.

Middle East Medievalists (MEM)

Middle East Studies Association of North America (MESA) - Middle East Medievalists (MEM) is a professional non-profit association of scholars interested in the study of the Islamic lands of the Middle East during the medieval period (defined roughly as 500-1500 C.E.)

MINERVA: The MINERVA Center for Women and the Military - A Nonprofit Educational Foundation Supporting Study of Women in War & Women and the Military.

N

National Coalition of Independent Scholars (NCIS) - The National Coalition of Independent Scholars is a nonprofit (501(c)3) organization created in 1989 to facilitate the work of independent scholars.

National Coordinating Committee for the Promotion of History (NCC) - H-NCC is the official electronic voice of The National Coordinating Committee for the Promotion of History.

Nature in Legend and Story (NILAS) - NILAS is a non-profit, tax-exempt organization, devoted to exploration of relationships between human beings and the natural world, reflected in folklore, literature and other cultural activities.

New York Humanities Council - The New York Council for the Humanities devotes itself to insuring the presence of the humanities in the state's cultural and intellectual life and to guaranteeing the future of the humanities among young people.

O

Omohundro Institute of Early American History and Culture (OIEAHC) - OIEAHC is the only organization in the United States exclusively dedicated to the advancement of study, research, and publications bearing on the history and culture of early America to approximately 1815.

Oral History Association - The Oral History Association, established in 1966, seeks to bring together all persons interested in oral history as a way of collecting human memories.

P

Political Methodology Society

Popular Culture Association and American Culture Association (PCA/ACA) - H-PCAACA encourages scholarly discussion of popular culture. This Web site, affiliated with The Popular Culture Association and American Culture Association, makes available diverse bibliographical, research and teaching aids.

S

Society for Anthropology of Europe (SAE) - SAE provides a forum for debate and discussion about European societies and cultures, as well as an arena within which to examine the foundations, contemporary relevance, and future of anthropology as an academic discipline.

Society for Austrian and Habsburg History - The purpose of the Society for Austrian and Habsburg History is to encourage, support, and further the study of Austrian history and the history of the Habsburg Monarchy and of its successor states.

Society for History of the Early American Republic (SHEAR) - H-SHEAR provides an interactive network/forum for scholars of the History of the Early American Republic.

Society for History of the Gilded Age and Progressive Era (SHGAPE) - SHGAPE encourages scholarly discussion of US Gilded Age & Progressive Era. makes available diverse bibliographical, research and teaching aids.

Society for Shaykhi, Babi and Bah'i Studies, The - H-Bahai encourages scholarly discussion of the culture and history of millenarian and/or esoteric religious traditions originating in modern Iran, such as Shaykhism, Babism and the Baha'i faith, and makes available diverse bibliographical, research, and teaching aids.

South African Historical Association - H-SAfrica is an international electronic discussion group dedicated to the promotion of all aspects of South and Southern Africa history and culture, and Southern African studies in general.

South African Political Science Association - SAPSA promotes knowledge and understanding of national and international political affairs through teaching, workshops, discussion and study groups, seminars, congresses, publications and research.

Southern Association for Women Historians (SAWH) - H-SAWH is free and open to everyone with an interest in the history of women and gender in the U.S. South.

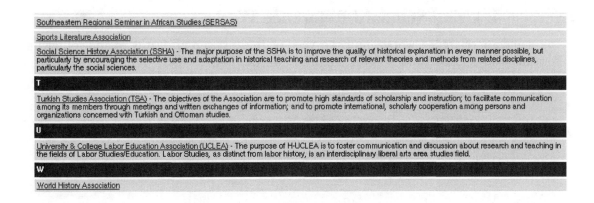

FIGURE 5.19

Finally, the major historical associations have their own web sites with links to more exciting historical sources. See, for example, The American Historical Association (*www.theaha.org*) and the Organization of American Historians (*www.oah.org*) web homepages.

Remember that the Web, like all electronic finders, is very unforgiving of typos. If you mistype a single punctuation mark or put in a space by mistake you will not be connected. Also bear in mind that the Web, like e-mail, may be busy when you sign on, and you may have to wait a long time to connect with your source. Finally, the electronic source moves with the speed of your modem and not one step faster. If your modem has a fast baud rate, you will get your information quickly. If it is slow, your information will take longer to reach you. If you are trying to bring up pictures on your screen and have a slower modem, you may still be waiting for your data an hour later. Lists, internet access providers, and Web page addresses are constantly changing. You can keep up with the changes by using the techniques you have learned here.

The Reference Desk

The reference desk is the most important help station in the library. At or near the reference desk are collections of indispensable research aids—encyclopedias, glossaries, and other reference works. There are also historical reference works that list other historical reference works: Helen J. Poulton, *The Historian's Handbook: A Descriptive Guide to Reference Works* (1972); Eugene Sheehy, *Guide to Reference Works* (8th ed., 1976); and Carl M. White, *Sources of Information in the Social Sciences* (1973). For a place or date in American history, you can use Thomas H. Johnson, *The Oxford Companion to American History* (1966); Louise Ketz, ed., *Dictionary of American History*, 8 vols. (rev. ed., 1976); or Richard B. Morris, *The Encyclopedia of American History* (16th ed., 1982). Brief biographies of leading Americans appear in the many volumes of *The Dictionary of American Biography*, the more recent *American National Biography*, and the four volumes of *Notable American Women*. The Hammond *United States History Atlas* is one of many sources for historical maps.

Locating the exact research aid you need is the first step in using the reference area of the library. Almost all libraries group reference works by subject and shelve them accordingly. You can find these works by looking them up at the terminal or in the catalog by title or author and then using the call number to track down the shelf location. The reference librarian will assist you in this task, as well as in deciding which research aid to use.

Exercise 4: Using Standard Reference Works

Using standard reference works, find the year of the births and deaths of the following Americans who became famous in the era of the Revolution.

Abigail Adams   born _____ died _____

Tecumseh   born _____ died _____

Benjamin Rush   born _____ died _____

Martha Washington   born _____ died _____

Phillis Wheatly   born _____ died _____

Today, birth dates are common pieces of information, and most of us celebrate birthdays. In the eighteenth century, many Americans did not know their exact birth date or even their exact age. Scholars may not agree about the birth dates of famous people who lived long ago. For example, historians still debate whether Alexander Hamilton was born in 1755 or 1757.

Even when a subject's exact birth and death dates can be offered with confidence, scholars who write biographical essays for standard encyclopedias and directories may vary in their emphases and assessments of the same subject. This is particularly likely when scholarly treatments of an individual, movement, or period of history have changed markedly over time. To continue Exercise 4, read the biographical entry on Tecumseh in the *Dictionary of American Biography*. This entry was written in the 1930s. Next read the entry on Tecumseh in Magill's *Great Lives from History, American Series*, published in 1987, or any other encyclopedia or biographical dictionary published after 1970. Do you find differences in tone and emphasis? In particular, are Native Americans viewed differently in the two essays? Why might this be so?

_____

_____

_____

_____

Exercise 5: Using Reference Guides to Find Old Books

In addition to basic reference works, the reference area has many highly specialized guides and research aids for locating old books on particular subjects. This exercise asks you to track down a particular book that was written between 1800 and 1815 and published in the United States. In those years, there was a veritable explosion of what scholars now call "print literacy." Cultural leaders in the new nation were eager to prove that Americans were capable of preserving their liberty, and widespread literacy was seen as an important part of this project. Towns and churches were expanding their support for elementary schools, and publishing firms were springing up all over the country. Peddlers carried books along with pots and tools up and down frontier trails.

One of the bestsellers in this new market for American books was a biography of George Washington written by an American shortly after Washington died in 1799. Many editions followed the first, with some variation of title. Using these clues, and the information that follows, find the author's name, the title, and date and place of publication of any edition of the book, and write this information in the space provided. What famous story about young Washington originated in this book?

_____

_____

_____

If your library has it, Charles Evans, *American Bibliography: A Chronological Dictionary of All Books . . . Printed in the United States of America . . . 1639–1820* (1903; reprinted 1941) will give you immediate help. Not every library has the Evans Index or the short-title Evans Index. Your library may have Joseph Sabin, *Bibliotheca Americana: A Dictionary of Books Relating to America from Its Discovery to the Present Time* (1936). The twenty-nine volumes of this dictionary are arranged alphabetically, not by date, so you will have to trudge through it looking for publication dates. You can also use the on-line catalog to find your book.

Secondary Sources in the Library

Good secondary sources help you understand times and places unlike your own. They put primary sources into context, the larger picture of the people and places in which the primary source originated. The best secondary sources are also how-to manuals and models for students. You can agree with or take issue with any individual author's arguments, but able scholarship always helps you to frame your thinking. Secondary sources are an essential part of any study of history.

The Shapes of Secondary Sources

Secondary sources come in many forms. They can be books, articles, parts of encyclopedias, or annotated bibliographies. They can be old or new. Sometimes a scholarly book or article published many years ago stands the test of time. Succeeding generations of scholars continue to find it provocative and instructive. Just as Beethoven's symphonies and the Beatles' "Norwegian Wood" have retained their power to entertain us, so these classics of historical writing continue to enlighten us. Nevertheless, the number of secondary sources in history is increasing at an exponential rate. To find the classics and keep track of the latest literature on any topic, you need to know where to look. As with your search for primary sources, help is at hand in the library.

Professional historians and historical editors prepare most secondary sources in history, edit and (if necessary) translate primary sources, review each other's work, direct the preservation of historical sites, manage archives and collections of historical materials, serve on local and national advisory committees, and most important of all, teach history. Historians have no monopoly on producing secondary sources, however. Journalists, political scientists, economists, anthropologists, and sociologists have all written excellent histories.

Some nonhistorians research and write for specialized audiences. For example, genealogists are researchers who receive fees to help individuals prepare genealogies, sometimes called family trees. Ancient Roman families called on genealogists to perform this service, and medieval European monks furnished genealogies for noble families. (Often the results were highly fanciful.) Modern genealogical techniques were first introduced by William Dugdale (1605–1686) of England. He insisted that every birth and death be fully authenticated and supported by scholarly references.

Local and community histories are another common secondary source. Today the curators or staff of local historical societies research and write these accounts of the origins and development of towns, counties, and regions, but in the past commercial firms specializing in such publications sold them directly to families whose names were mentioned or businesses whose buildings were pictured.

Finding the Best Secondary Sources

You can find secondary sources on historical topics in a number of ways. Once you have found one, it will lead to others. For example, at the end of each chapter of your textbook you will see suggestions for further reading in other secondary sources. In the bibliographies of each of those books you will discover still more secondary sources on the same topic.

There are three other ways to begin a broad search for secondary sources on any topic:

1. You can use the card catalog subject index or the computer terminal subject search to look for a topic. For example, if you are looking for books on urbanization, you can also look for books on cities or, a little more imaginatively, books on particular cities. Once you have decided on a series of keywords (for example, the names of particular cities), you can switch over to the title index in the card catalog or to the title search in the computer terminal. Likewise, if you want to find other books by the same author, you can use the card catalog author index or the computer terminal author search.

2. You can search in the stacks. Once you have found one secondary source, look at the other books around it on the shelf. Books are shelved first according to subject matter and then alphabetically by the author's last name. The books next to your book on the shelf are on the same or closely related topics. Read their bibliographies to trace the books and articles that their authors used. These bibliographies and notes refer to books and articles written before the author wrote her or his book. Not all books on your topic are shelved in the history section of the stacks. For example, you may be interested in books on the history of the first American cities. Some of your secondary sources will be shelved with the books on architecture, others with the books on urban sociology or urban literature.

3. Spadework in the stacks helps you to extend your search for secondary sources back in time. To find the most recent works on your subject, you should refer to reference aids like *America: History and Life*, a comprehensive listing of articles with brief summaries (called abstracts) of contents, and citations of reviews and doctoral dissertations. *America: History and Life* also features comprehensive indexes by author, subject, and title, covering the years 1954 to the present.

Books are not the only secondary sources you may wish to consult. For every history book on any topic there are dozens of scholarly articles in historical journals. The best way to get at recent literature on any historical subject is to use these scholarly journals. Some of them focus on particular topics—for example, *Diplomatic History*, *Feminist Studies*, and *Journal of Southern History*. Others concentrate on a particular state—for example, *Georgia Historical Quarterly* and *Pennsylvania Magazine of History and Biography*. There are journals concerned with the methods that scholars use—for example, *Journal of Interdisciplinary History* and *Social History*. Still other journals reserve their space for a particular period of time—for example, *Civil War History*, *Journal of the Early American Republic*, and *William and Mary Quarterly* (pre-1815 American history and culture). Lists of journals by topic and title are available in your library on microfiche and in the card catalog. Back issues of these journals are bound by volume and kept in the stacks. Current issues are in your library periodical room. Many journals are now on-line as well.

Scholarly journals have three or four articles in each issue. Some journals have yearly indexes, but often you just have to plow through the bound issues to find something on a particular topic. The *Journal of American History* lists articles and dissertations in American history published during that year. When you have found an article on your topic, use the notes in it just as you used the bibliography and notes in the books to widen the search for secondary sources.

Evaluating Secondary Sources

Familiarity with a wide range of secondary sources is the first step in deciding which secondary sources are the most trustworthy guides. Secondary sources vary in their quality. Some books and articles are better researched and more thoughtful than others. How can you tell which secondary source is more convincing? There are *intrinsic* and *extrinsic* measures of quality. Intrinsic gauges of quality appear in the book or article itself. You do not need to go to outside authorities to use these tests. Extrinsic measures of quality require you to refer to book reviews and other published aids to assess the quality of a secondary source.

Intrinsic measures of merit include the following tests:

1. How detailed is the author's account? Does it have enough facts to satisfy an ordinary reader's curiosity? How well did the author convince *you*?

2. Does the author seem familiar with other scholars' arguments? Does he or she recognize and augment or challenge other scholars' conclusions in the text and notes?

3. Does the author use sufficient reference notes? Do the notes cite primary material or merely other secondary sources? Does the author seem to have gone directly to the primary material or relied on others' research? Do the notes seem fresh (that is, has the author made use of the most recent research on his or her topic)?

4. If your secondary source is a book, who published it? A good piece of scholarship will generally find a good publisher—that is, if the book was published by a first-rate press, you can be sure that it received a thorough review before it was accepted. Universities sponsor some of the best scholarly presses. Many leading commercial publishers also have extensive lists of history books.

At the press, editors read manuscripts that prospective authors submit, and if the manuscript passes muster it is sent out to "referees" (reviewers)—well-known and respected scholars working in the same field as the author of the manuscript. The reviewers make comments—sometimes 20 or 30 pages of comments—advising the press about the quality of the manuscript. The editor relays these comments to the author, who emends the manuscript accordingly. If the manuscript is accepted for publication, it undergoes copyediting and proofreading before it becomes a book.

The quality of the journal in which an article is published is a good guide to the quality of the article. The best journals send out article manuscripts to be reviewed. The author works with the journal's editor to produce the final product. A first-rate article will get published in any reputable scholarly journal. You can assess the quality of an individual article by employing the same measures you used to judge the quality of individual books.

Here are some extrinsic guides to quality secondary sources:

1. In every field of historical study there are leading authorities whose work has set the agenda for study or captured the audience in that field. Quite often, these historians will

have written books that bring together the historical writing on a topic or period. Series of such books include the New American Nation Series published by HarperCollins, the American Moment Series published by the Johns Hopkins University Press, and the American History Series published by Harlan Davidson Publishing. All of the books in these series have excellent critical bibliographies that list other books on the subject.

2. As you become familiar with a number of secondary sources on any topic, you will begin to find that some of them are cited widely. By their choice of authorities, the historians themselves are telling you which secondary sources they rate the highest.

3. Book reviews will help you to discover other scholars' evaluation of the history book you have in your hand. The reviewers restate the thesis or theme of a book, report its findings, and then assess the quality of the book and the success of the author in completing the task he or she has set out to accomplish. In your library, you will find reviews of history books in commercial periodicals like *Choice, Current Reviews for College Libraries* and *Library Journal.* These are the publications that help librarians decide which books to order. *Choice* was first published in 1963, and reviews in it can be quite incisive. An older and somewhat blander source of reviews is *Book Review Digest.* The *Digest* goes back to 1910 and, like *Choice,* has been published continuously up to the present. It offers short excerpts of reviews from many publications, including *Choice* and major scholarly journals. Like *Choice,* the *Digest* includes full bibliographical citations for books. The *Book Review Index,* which first appeared in 1965, indicates where book reviews may be found for just about every book published. The abbreviations for these sources are explained at the front of the *Index.*

More extensive reviews of books on American history appear in historical journals. The *Journal of American History* commissions reviews for just about all the serious books on American history. Many American history books are also reviewed in *American Historical Review.* Books on early American history are reviewed in *William and Mary Quarterly.* The essays in *Reviews in American History* are excellent extended assessments of individual books as well as specific areas of research. In addition, reviews in state and regional journals and topical journals cover books in the journal's specialty.

Exercise 6: Evaluating Secondary Sources

This exercise helps you to formulate your own tests for evaluating secondary sources. Find a scholarly book about one of the following individuals from the generation of men and women who left their mark on the literature of the new American nation: Louisa May Alcott, James Fenimore Cooper, Nathaniel Hawthorne, Edgar Allan Poe, Harriet Beecher Stowe, or Noah Webster. Give the full citation of your book in the space provided: author, full title, publisher, place of publication, date of publication, and number of pages.

_____

_____

_____

Read the first chapter of the book and evaluate it using the intrinsic measures you have learned. We summarize them in the following series of questions:

1. Does the author acknowledge other scholars' work? _____

_____

2. Does the author use reference notes? _____

_____

3. Does the author refer to primary sources? _____

_____

_____

4. Do you find the author's work convincing? Why or why not? _____

_____

Continue the exercise by finding two reviews of your book. Indicate where you found each review. Give the reviewer's name, the title of the review, the journal or magazine in which it was published, the month and year of publication, and the page numbers.

1. _____

_____

2. _____

_____

Next, summarize the contents of the reviews. Pay particular attention to any favorable or unfavorable comments by the reviewers.

1. _____

_____

_____

_____

2. _____

_____

_____

_____

How did your intrinsic measures of quality of the work compare with the opinions of the reviewers?

_____

_____

You began this chapter by finding primary sources and continued on to assess the quality of historians' efforts. Criticism of this sort is a necessary part of any student's education. Thus far you have been asked to find and read text. Another source of historical information that you can use in the library is maps, the subject of the next chapter.

Note

[1] Robin Winks, ed., *The Historian as Detective: Essays on Evidence* (New York: Harper & Row, 1968), xvii.

6: *Reading Historical Maps and Interpreting Visual Data*

Country and City in the New Nation

Though still in his twenties, Meriwether Lewis was not surprised when President Thomas Jefferson asked him to serve as a private secretary. Lewis had no formal education, but he was a bright, hard-working, and able officer in the army, a neighbor of Jefferson, and soon the older statesman's confidant. Jefferson had dreamed of a great American empire stretching from the Atlantic to the Pacific, watered by the great rivers of the Northwest, and Lewis shared the dream. Even before Jefferson had arranged to purchase the vast tract known as the Louisiana Territory from France in 1803, he turned to Lewis and asked him to lead an expedition across the territory to the Pacific, mapping the features of the land. Lewis, a man of mercurial moods but vast self-confidence and great determination, leapt at the chance.

The Louisiana Purchase from France doubled the size of the United States, but few Americans had visited its endless grasslands, climbed its towering mountain ranges, or canoed along its twisting rivers. The Spanish, the French, and the British had some idea of its riches, but their maps were faulty and Jefferson knew that Americans would have to traverse the land in order to secure legal rights to the entire territory. Jefferson told Lewis that his mission was diplomatic as well as exploratory. Lewis was to negotiate with all Native Americans and Europeans he found along the way, for Jefferson had a not-so-secret goal—to ensure that the Louisiana Territory included the Pacific coast.

Lewis had seen much of the eastern United States and was a bold spirit, but he could not undertake the trip alone. He asked William Clark, the younger brother of the famous soldier and explorer George Rogers Clark, to join the expedition. Clark was a red-haired six-footer with an easygoing disposition. He could handle a boat, ride, shoot, draw a good map, and was willing to be Lewis's subordinate, though the two men agreed that the soldiers, trappers, and translators they recruited for the "voyage of discovery" were not to know about the difference in rank. Congress provided funds; Lewis spent nearly a year purchasing equipment, Clark the same time selecting the men; and after a winter of training, their long journey began in the spring of 1804.

The Lewis and Clark expedition up the Missouri, across the Continental Divide in the Rocky Mountains, and down the Columbia River to the Pacific Ocean was as epic an adventure as any Americans had ever undertaken. The explorers discovered two dozen Native

American tribes and hundreds of species of birds, mammals, and flowers that no easterner had previously seen. They sent back samples of the animals and plants to Philadelphia, where painter Charles Willson Peale exhibited them in his new museum. Meanwhile, Lewis and Clark and their men (and one woman, the sixteen-year-old Shoshone Indian, Sacagawea) discovered that the Rocky Mountains were a formidable obstacle between the high prairies of the eastern plains and the lush greenery of the Pacific slope. Their expedition destroyed forever the aspiration that a water passage could be found from the Mississippi to the Pacific, for the upper reaches of the Missouri were barely navigable, and the explorers had to ride across the mountains on horseback.

Their journals describing the two years of travel were condensed and published in 1814, but the many scientific discoveries that Lewis made in botany and zoology were not published for nearly eighty years. Always moody and sometimes morose, Lewis convinced himself that hidden enemies were plotting against him. In 1809 he committed suicide. Clark distinguished himself as Indian commissioner, and his many rough drafts of maps of the northwestern parts of the Louisiana Purchase, printed with the journal of the expedition, radically altered Americans' thinking about the Far West. When Jefferson saw them, he was delighted. Lewis and Clark had done what he had asked, and the maps proved it: they had staked the United States' claim to the Pacific shore.

Exercise 1: Mapping a Wilderness

Spanish, French, and British explorers, traders, missionaries, and soldiers had passed through portions of the Louisiana Territory and had published their maps. Jefferson read them and so did Lewis. Shown in Figure 6.1 is the last of these maps to appear before Lewis and Clark sailed their barge up the Missouri. This map was prepared by an American map-maker, Nicholas King of Philadelphia. King was no explorer, but his map reflected the state of knowledge about the Northwest in 1803. Compare King's map with one showing the modern United States or North America in your textbook, and list the key features of the Far West that King omitted. (Hint: one is a river, one is a lake, and one is a mountain range.)

_____

_____

_____

Figure 6.2 is a reproduction of Clark's map, published in 1814. Clark had redrawn many of the sketches he had made on the expedition, put them together, and incorporated the discoveries made by trapper Zebulon Pike's expedition into the Rockies during 1806 and 1807. What are two striking differences between Clark's map and King's?

1. _____

_____

2. _____

_____

FIGURE 6.1 *Nicholas King's 1803 Map of the Western Part of North America*
Courtesy of the Library of Congress

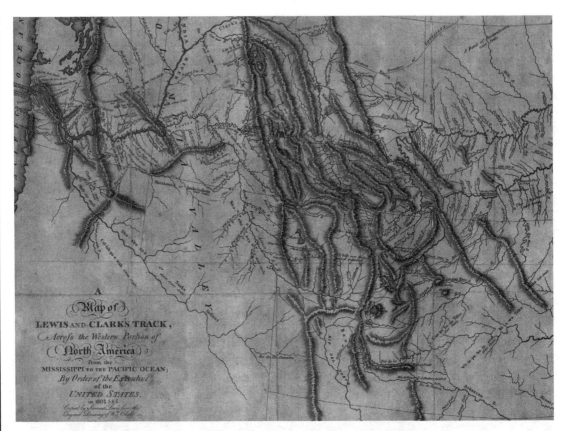

FIGURE 6.2 *Samuel Lewis's Copy of Clark's 1810 Manuscript (Detail)*
Courtesy of the Library of Congress

The Functions of Maps: Possession, Information, and Memory

Historically, maps perform one or more functions. The first is to claim possession of land. The second is to give directions, to guide, and incidentally or purposely to advertise places. Maps also capture a moment in time, a visual memory of where people lived, roads and rivers passed, and natural geographic features once stood.

Maps defined the land grants that European kings gave to proprietors in the New World. Mapmakers guessed at distances and the shapes of coastlines. Explorers, traders, and settlers made their own rough maps of the edges of the North American continent. Columbus was an amateur mapmaker and used a compass and other tools to map Hispaniola and the other islands of the West Indies that he visited between 1492 and 1502. His maps, as much as the rare ores and the Native American captives he carried back with him, substantiated Spain's claims to the New World.

For the settlers themselves, maps of towns and the surrounding countryside were a visual record of who owned what piece of land. No sooner were the first British immigrants in the New World finished with their house building than they took out their surveyor's tools—compasses, tripods and rods for measuring, and ruled paper—and began to lay out plats of their property. George Washington was a trained surveyor and never lost his skill; it helped him decide which parcels of land to buy for his plantation in Virginia. During the Revolutionary War he complained to the Continental Congress that he could not fight the British without better maps.

Colonial officials commissioned surveyors like Washington to make maps of the dividing lines between colonies. William Byrd of Virginia, who served on the commission that surveyed the line between North Carolina and Virginia, left two journals of his experiences. The official journal contained a map. The unofficial journal featured riotously funny gossip about the other commissioners and a thoroughly nasty description of the "lubbers" of North Carolina. When the proprietors of Pennsylvania and Maryland could not determine the boundary line between their colonies, they sent to England for surveyors. Charles Mason and Jeremiah Dixon arrived in 1763 and spent the next four years laying out the dividing line between Pennsylvania and Maryland. Preceded by axemen to clear their field of vision and friendly Indians to give warning of raids by less-well-disposed Native Americans, the two Englishmen took measurements so precise that their accuracy has been confirmed by modern technology. In 1807 Congress established a federal program to map the coastlines, but not until 1879 did the U.S. Geological Survey begin to make official maps of the western lands.

Clark mapped the land to lay claim to the Pacific coast in the same way that Christopher Columbus had drawn a map to claim the Caribbean islands for the king of Spain. Both men gave new names to the places they drew on their maps, ignoring many Native American names, just as they ignored most Native Americans' rights to the land. Native Americans fought over territory but did not believe that any tribe could claim absolute control over land. Jefferson and Congress, following the European legal tradition, assumed that real estate belonged to its purchaser, and the United States had paid millions of dollars to France for the Louisiana Territory.

Lewis and Clark's map did more than authenticate the new nation's right to part of the Pacific coastline. Clark's many detailed drawings indicated how Americans could go west from the Mississippi and arrive at the great Columbia River emptying into the Pacific Ocean. Later maps would fill in the details that Clark had sketched. Read alongside their extensive journals, Clark's map told fur trappers, explorers, and settlers what to expect. Indeed, on their way back from the Rockies in 1806, Lewis and Clark met the first boatloads of American fur trappers and hunters eager to follow in the expeditionaries' footsteps. In effect, the map advertised a region, opening it for enterprise—and for despoliation as well.

Finally, the Clark map captured a moment in time. It showed how the Far West appeared before the settlers came. The accompanying journals and drawings gave texture to that picture. Lewis was filled with wonder at "the immense herds of Buffaloe, deer Elk and Antelopes" that fed upon the rich grasslands. He soon learned that the game was seasonal, for his men gorged themselves when the salmon ran or when the elk herds migrated nearby, but had to survive on roots and berries when game was scarce. Maps are repositories of memory, primary sources that capture in lines and shading the way places looked in the past.

Lewis and Clark's survey had preserved a moment of time in the lives of the surveyors, the Native Americans they visited, and the animals and plants they encountered. At the same time, the Lewis and Clark mission permanently changed the high plains. No sooner had the explorers left the lower reaches of the Missouri to return to the east coast than some Native Americans began to fall ill from diseases Lewis and Clark's men had carried with them into the mountains. The trading goods the expedition distributed altered Native American ways of hunting and dressing, particularly on the western slopes of the Rockies, the inhabitants of which had not been drawn into the European market system. The delicate balance among the tribes was permanently shifted, just as the first French explorers in Canada had shifted the balance of power between the Algonquin- and Iroquois-speaking peoples of the Northeast. The Lewis and Clark notebooks and maps became a reminder of a lost world.

Maps as Primary Sources

In all three ways—as forms of legal documents, as guides for travelers, and as records of a moment in time—maps can be vital primary sources for historians. If a map is an original or a copy of an original, like the Clark map, it is a primary source about the ideas of mapmakers at the time and place when it was drawn. Such maps may reveal relationships among people and places that may not be so easily seen in surviving textual materials.

Historians have found maps and plans to be extraordinarily exciting primary sources. For example, when Professors Paul Boyer and Stephen Nissenbaum were preparing materials to teach their students about the Salem witchcraft episode, they found a town map of Salem. The map, published in 1867, told them where the accusers and the accused lived. The two historians rediscovered what contemporaries no doubt knew but historians had overlooked: there was a distinct geographical grouping of accusers in the western end of the farming community of Salem Village, while the accused resided at the eastern edge of the settlement, close to Salem Town. Intrigued by the map, Boyer and Nissenbaum launched an investigation that unearthed the bitter antagonism between people in the Village whose wealth and status were on the decline and people whose ties to the Town had helped them rise up in the world. Increasingly, the Village was becoming an agricultural backwater, economically languishing and politically dependent, while the Town next to it was becoming a flourishing port. The authors concluded that jealousies and resentments originally having nothing to do with witchery fed into the terrible tragedy of the Salem witchcraft trials—a marvelous example of historical detection that began with a map.

An old map or plan must be treated like any other primary source. A map or plan reflects the state of knowledge and the value system of the person who drew it. It has a point of view and transmits a message, which the modern map reader must decode.

Exercise 2: Maps as Original Evidence

The Pennsylvania colony was a gift from King Charles II to William Penn, the son of one of Charles's loyal supporters. Penn had converted to Quakerism, a religion persecuted in England, but he was allowed to recruit fellow Quakers as settlers for his colony. Penn knew that in order to thrive the colony needed the labor of immigrants; his problem was how to induce men and women to go to the American wilderness. They needed not only directions to their new homes but a reason for leaving old, familiar people and places behind.

One of the tools Penn used to advertise the colony to prospective purchasers was a map of the land between the Delaware and the Schuylkill Rivers. There he proposed to build a "green country town." To these "first purchasers" Penn offered large tracts of land. He also granted to them more self-government, political rights, and civil liberties than anyone enjoyed in the mother country.

As you look at the maps in Figures 6.3, 6.4, 6.5, and 6.7 and read the accompanying descriptions, think about the three functions of maps: to show how land is distributed and who owns it, to guide people to and advertise places, and to capture the relationships between humans and natural features of the land. All four maps exhibit these three functions. Headnotes describe each map and specific study questions follow. Answer them in the space provided.

A Penn had given serious attention to the design of the town of Philadelphia. He was much impressed by plans for a renovation of London after the Great Fire of 1666. The London City Council did not adopt any of these plans, but Penn did. He decided that his new town would not resemble a typical English town, with its winding streets and its haphazard development, nor would it be a teeming, crowded metropolis like London. Instead, Penn opted for geometrical symmetry and equality. His town would be laid out in a grid of square blocks with streets crossing each other at right angles from the Delaware River in the east to the Schuylkill River in the west. In Penn's plan shown in Figure 6.3, each square represented a block of land that could accommodate four or five two- or three-story houses. At the back of each row of houses there was an alley, bisecting the square. Penn drew large gardenlike squares to bring trees and greenery into the town and prevent the spread of fires like that which consumed much of London.

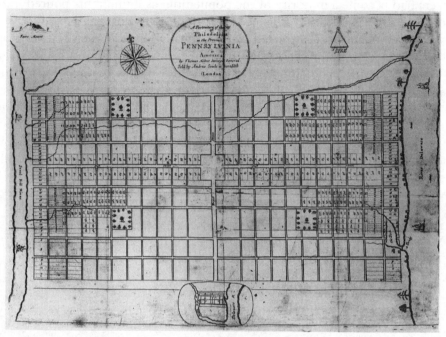

FIGURE 6.3 *William Penn's "Plan of Pennsylvania" (Philadelphia)*
Courtesy of the Library of Congress

1. Look at Penn's plan closely. What was the overall geometric shape of Philadelphia?

_____

_____

2. How did that shape reinforce Penn's design of the block system of lots? _____

_____

_____

3. Would this design facilitate the selling of lots by land speculators? (*Hint:* A square contains more area than any other geometric shape with the same perimeter.) _____

_____

_____

4. What were the main streets? _____

_____

5. Why might a lot facing on the main street be more valuable than one facing on a side street? _____

_____

6. The Quakers were often good businessmen and businesswomen. How well was the city placed for commerce? _____

_____

B Over the years between its founding in 1682 and the outbreak of the American Revolution, the country town of Philadelphia became a city whose warehouses overflowed with goods and whose streets overflowed with people from all over the British Empire. Devastated by the Revolutionary War, Philadelphia recovered, and its ships soon plied the oceans in search of profits for its enterprising merchants.

By the 1790s, maps of the city displayed how far Philadelphia had diverged from Penn's original design. The "green country town" had become a beehive of commercial activity. The Quakers had become a minority of the population, as immigrants poured into the city from all over the British Isles and Europe. Most were poor working people—tailors, shoemakers, weavers, and laborers—attracted by dreams of improving their station in life.

In 1796 Philadelphia was the capital of a new nation stretching from Maine to the northern edge of Florida. The city itself had become wealthy, powerful, and proud. John Hills, a surveyor as well as a draftsman, needed more than a square yard of paper to complete his detailed enumeration of the public buildings and major businesses of the Center City bounded by the Delaware and the Schuylkill Rivers on the east and west, and by Cedar and Vine Streets on the south and north. In 1796, he dedicated the map, shown in Figure 6.4, to the mayor and aldermen of the city and sold engraved copies to the general public.

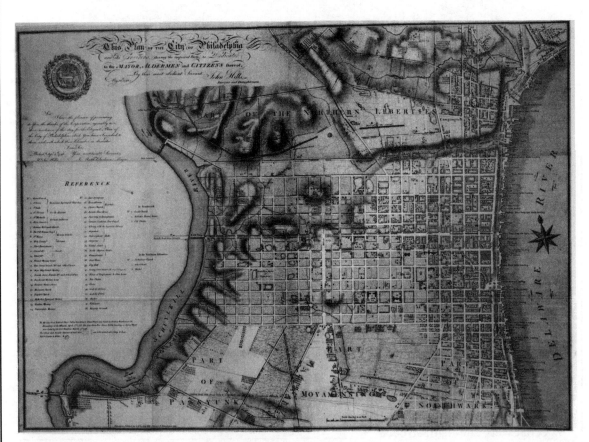

FIGURE 6.4 *John Hill's "Plan of the City of Philadelphia," 1796*
Courtesy of the Library Company of Philadelphia

1. What had happened to the Penn design for the city? In particular, were city inhabitants spreading themselves out between the two rivers as Penn envisioned? _____

_____

_____

2. Where in fact were they congregating? _____

_____

3. Why might this pattern of development characterize a port city? _____

_____

_____

    C By 1825 Philadelphia was a thriving city of more than 140,000 people, but its official boundaries were still limited to the original city lines from the Delaware River to the Schuylkill River, and from Cedar Street to Vine Street.

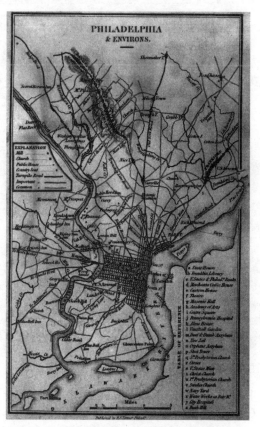

FIGURE 6.5 *"Philadelphia and Environs"*
Courtesy of the Library Company of Philadelphia

1. How is the focus of the map shown in Figure 6.5 different from the Hills map (Figure 6.4)?

_____

_____

2. How does the map shown in Figure 6.5 suggest that Philadelphia had become a commercial center? _____

_____

_____

3. The heavy lines are roads. What does the pattern of roads linking the city to the countryside suggest to you about the relationship between the two?_____

_____

_____

D Figure 6.5 suggests that Philadelphia was extending its tendrils into the countryside, but the distinction between city and countryside is still sharp. You can plainly see where the city ends and the country begins. Ambitious building projects like the new state penitentiary were set in rural surroundings just outside the city. You can find the site marked "Penitentiary" just east of the Schuylkill and north of the city line. A view of the penitentiary (Figure 6.6) drawn in 1833 shows the fields around it. Throughout the eastern seaboard there was a growing fascination with nature, a romantic craze to rediscover the countryside. One element of this cultural movement was criticism of cities as dirty, crime filled, and disease ridden.

FIGURE 6.6 George Lehman, *Eastern Penitentiary of Pennsylvania (1833)*
Courtesy of the Library Company of Philadelphia

1. What is the relationship between the back-to-nature fad and the artist's visualization of the penitentiary? _____

_____

2. What sort of building does the penitentiary resemble? _____

_____

3. What setting has the artist given the building? *(Hint:* What do you see around it?) _____

_____

_____

E There was still a sharp dividing line between city and countryside, as maps of Philadelphia in the early nineteenth century illustrate. In 1825, the city of Philadelphia was still surrounded by many independent townships. This arrangement came to an end in 1854 when the city absorbed or "incorporated" much of the countryside around it. Henceforth, Penn Township, the Northern Liberties, Spring Garden, and villages as far north as Germantown and as far south as the edge of Southwark and Passyunk, would be part of the city. By 1856, greater Philadelphia sprawled for nearly ten miles up and down the Delaware and across the Schuylkill.

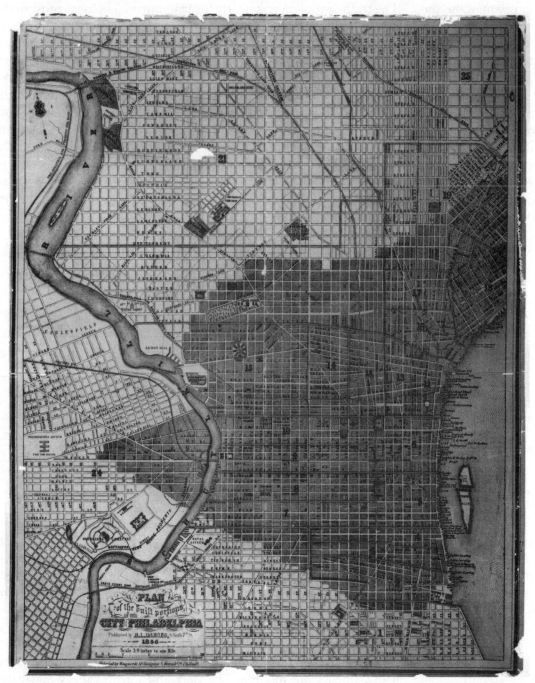

FIGURE 6.7 *1856 Map of Philadelphia*
Courtesy of the Library Company of Philadelphia

The changing physical contours of the city brought new challenges and problems. Historian Sam Bass Warner has observed that "Speed, bigness, newcomers, and money beat upon settled manners with a rain of harassment and opportunity." Old community relationships within the neighborhoods of Philadelphia came apart under the strain of rapid and largely unplanned expansion of people and space. "The grid street, the narrow house lot, the row house, the interior alley, and the rear yard house or shack were endlessly repeated. When so repeated, however, they lost entirely their eighteenth-century character and took on instead that mixture of dreariness and confusion which so characterized nineteenth-century mass building." The traffic problem was nearly insurmountable, because most of the streets were too narrow to accommodate more than one carriage or cart, and the streets in the grid crossed each other too often to allow for smooth traffic flow. Factories, warehouses, and mills were scattered throughout older residential areas, further congesting traffic flow. There were few natural centers for community activities, as in New England towns.[1]

The map shown in Figure 6.7 was drawn in 1856, after the merger of the city and the county of Philadelphia. The townships that bordered the old city had become neighborhoods within it. The new metropolis had become an industrial center, and with industry came railroads. Railroad lines went in and out of the city to the north, south, and west. The railroads carried passengers in addition to freight, and for the first time allowed people to live in the countryside and commute to the city to work. The number of streets had multiplied and with them the complexity of the city. This complexity made getting around more difficult because there were many more streets to navigate.

1. How does your impression of the map in Figure 6.7 differ from your impression of the other maps? _____

_____

2. In what ways does Figure 6.7 resemble a modern street map? _____

_____

3. Is Figure 6.7 an advertisement for the charms of the city, or is it an aid to movement through the maze of the city streets?_____

_____

4. Does there seem to be a plan behind the city's sprawling growth?_____

_____

_____

Maps as Secondary Sources

You may not be accustomed to thinking about maps as secondary sources, but a map drawn by a professional scholar to illustrate an event (a battle, for example), a movement (the westward migration of Americans in the 1840s and 1850s, for example), or a distribution of some sort (a map of the comparative population of various cities, for example) is a form of argument. A modern map illustrating a historical time is a secondary source, a tool prepared by an expert to help you understand the geographic aspects of a historical issue or event.

Secondary-source maps became popular among historians with the rise of historical geography, the study of the effect of terrain and climate on human habitation, at the end of the nineteenth century. Some historical geographers strongly argued that physical setting—resources, land quality, impassable mountain barriers and fertile valleys, navigable rivers, and jagged coastlines—provided challenges that either aided or retarded human achievement.

By the 1910s, historians were beginning to seek the relationships between political voting patterns from place to place and other variables, such as wealth, religious affiliation, and ethnic origin, that could also be mapped. Historian Frederick Jackson Turner was an early proponent of the importance of geography in history and became a prominent advocate of "analytical" mapping. In 1893 he gave a talk at the Columbian Exposition in Chicago arguing that the vast expanse of free land on the American frontier had shaped Americans' unique faith in democracy and individualism. By the 1920s he had brought his commitment to historical geography to the Huntington Library in San Marino, California. There he drew and redrew maps to show the association between politics and economic and cultural life.

A historian who uses maps to present data and explain events is concerned not so much with representing the geographic features—the lay of the land—as with using these features to make a point about how or where people lived. The map is a teaching device, not an exact representation of physical reality. For example, in *Forging Freedom: The Formation of Philadelphia's Black Community, 1720–1840* (1988), Gary Nash presents three maps (see Figures 6.8 to 6.10) of the residential dispersion of African-Americans in Philadelphia between 1800 and 1837 to demonstrate graphically how racial attitudes and economic forces led to the beginnings of a ghetto.

Exercise 3: Maps as Analytical Tools

Slaves were imported into Penn's colony from its inception, and Quaker merchants and landowners not only bought the slaves but financed the slave trade. In the 1750s, however, the grandchildren of these Quakers experienced a crisis of conscience. Along with non-Quaker reformers and evangelical preachers, Quaker leaders began to speak out against slavery. In 1765 there were 100 free Africans and African-Americans in Philadelphia and 1,400 slaves. By 1783 there were 1,000 free African-Americans and 400 slaves. The Revolution did not free African-Americans, despite British promises to emancipate slaves if they deserted their revolutionary masters; but afterward Pennsylvania adopted a law gradually ending slavery. Many owners went further, manumitting (freeing) their slaves immediately.

It remained for the freed men and women and the many other African-Americans migrating to the city to find jobs, begin families, and build a community. The city attracted African-Americans seeking jobs as day laborers, servants, dock workers, street salespeople, and craftworkers. At first, free African-Americans rarely reached above lower-class occupations. Few could read or write, and their fates remained tied to the decisions of white people. But bit by bit, a small number of African-Americans moved into the middle class. They began their own businesses and with African-American ministers provided leadership within the black community.

Meanwhile, Philadelphia had become a haven for runaway slaves from Maryland and Virginia, where slavery had not been abolished. The natural increase of local African-American families also added to Philadelphia's African-American population. As the black community became more visible, white racial attitudes changed and white animosity toward African-Americans grew. Although African-Americans in the city built churches, pursued businesses, and created a thriving community that overlapped the whites' institutions, the prospect of a just multiracial society died in the early nineteenth century. As more blacks arrived, many without the skills to cope with city life, white leaders drew a color line in businesses, schools, churches, and the streets. African-Americans responded by looking within their own ranks for leadership and fashioned a distinct cultural life.

Examine the three maps shown in Figures 6.8, 6.9, and 6.10. For each there are some study questions to ponder and answer.

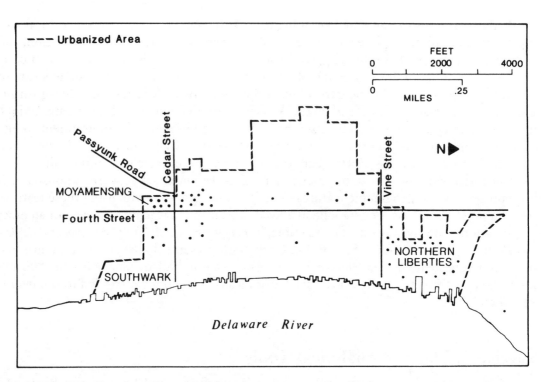

FIGURE 6.8 *Residential Pattern of Black Households in Philadelphia, 1800 (each dot represents 10 households)*
Reproduced from Gary Nash, *Forging Freedom: The Formation of Philadelphia's Black Community, 1720–1840* (Harvard University Press, Cambridge, Mass.: 1988)

1. Using the map legend in Figure 6.8, determine how many African-American households there were in Philadelphia in 1800. _____

_____

_____

2. Assuming that each household contained two parents and two children, how many Philadelphians in 1800 were African-American? _____

_____

_____

3. Using the Hills map in Figure 6.4, describe where these African-American families settled in relation to the central part of the city._____

_____

_____

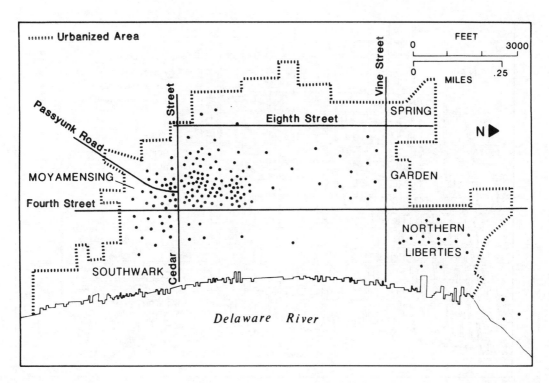

FIGURE 6.9 *Residential Pattern of Black Households in Philadelphia, 1820 (each dot represents 10 households)*
Reproduced from Nash, *Forging Freedom.*

1. What differences or similarities are there between the maps in Figure 6.8 and 6.9 in total African-American population and concentration or density of population? _____
   _____
   _____

2. Did African-Americans distribute themselves more widely over the city between 1800 and 1820? _____
   _____

Professor Nash has concluded that African-Americans were forced by their relative poverty to crowd into cheap tenements in the northern and southern sections of the city. In other words, it was not the racial prejudice of their neighbors so much as economic want that forced African-Americans to live where they did.

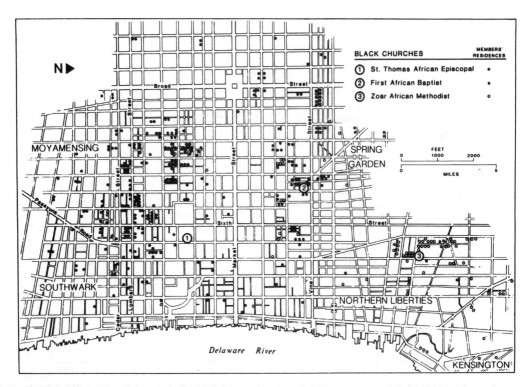

FIGURE 6.10 *Residential Distribution of Three Black Philadelphia Congregations, 1837*
Reproduced from Nash, *Forging Freedom.*

1. From Figure 6.10 can you discern another reason why African-Americans lived where they did? _____
_____

2. What modern residential pattern in American urban life do you see prefigured in the map above? _____
_____

Maps can be dramatic and explicit tools for historians—an example of a picture that is worth many words. Bear in mind that such maps are arguments meant to convince you of the historian's thesis, in much the same way as the passages you read in Chapter 4. Such maps distort physical reality in order to make the author's point. Notice that Professor Nash omitted many details in the first two maps, including streets. He did this deliberately, for such details would obscure his important message—the creation of African-American communities in neighborhood living patterns. In the third map, he included streets in order to show where congregants of the three churches resided.

Even had Nash decided to re-create African-American Philadelphia in a detailed map, he would have faced obstacles. The best mapmakers must deceive us in order to inform us. As geographer Mark Monmonier reminds us, "To portray meaningful relationships for a complex, three-dimensional world on a flat sheet of paper or a video screen, a map must distort reality. . . . the map must offer a selective, incomplete view of reality. There's no escape from the cartographic paradox: to present a useful and truthful picture, an accurate map must tell white lies . . . [for] a single map is but one of an indefinitely large number of maps that might be produced for the same situation or from the same data."[2]

Professor Nash's maps, even examined in isolation, as here, outline salient facts about the experience of African-Americans in a northern city. In his book, the maps are but one part of a larger story filled with sharply etched details and driven by a powerful theme. Nash is a master narrator, a skill to which we now turn.

Notes

[1] Sam Bass Warner, Jr., *The Private City: Philadelphia in Three Periods of Its Growth* (Philadelphia: University of Pennsylvania Press, 1968), 49, 50.

[2] Mark Monmonier, *How to Lie with Maps* (Chicago: University of Chicago Press, 1991),1, 2.

7: *Narrative: Telling the Story*

The Way West

———————— · ♦ · ♦ · ————————

The most popular and compelling historical writing is narrative: the retelling of a story. The secret of historical narration is to capture change over time. Narrative answers the question, What happened next? Historical narrative focuses on the fortunes and misfortunes of people, merging their many stories into a whole. The narrator selects the most striking and representative details, keeping the story flowing and the reader's attention fixed. Because of its subject matter—human action—narrative can be both swift and deep. Good narrative carries us away with its drive yet allows us to identify with individuals' hopes and fears.

Narration can be difficult. According to historian Bernard Bailyn, historians must be "narrators of worlds in motion—worlds as complex, unpredictable, and transient, as our own. The historian must re-tell, with a new richness, the story of . . . the worlds of the past."[1] Recently Bailyn joined other leading historians in a general call for more and better historical narratives.

One of the most popular subjects in American history, westward migration, lends itself to narrative. Continually thrust together in encounters that neither side really planned, with consequences no one fully understood, Native Americans and European-Americans remade the face of the West. Signs of heroism, cowardice, and tragedy marked every trail to Oregon, California, and Texas. Chapter 7 reviews the basic skills of narration and then offers you the opportunity to transform a collection of excerpts from primary and secondary sources into a short narrative of people and places on the way west.

The Parts of a Narrative

The most striking characteristic of well-written narrative is its ability to carry a reader along from beginning to end. The best narrators seem to have taken to heart the advice that the king gave to the white rabbit at the trial of the knave of hearts in *Alice in Wonderland*: "Begin at the beginning," the king said, very gravely, "and go on till you come to the end. Then stop."

The beginning of a story sets the scene; it whets your appetite for what is to come. Instead of merely summarizing the rest of the story, a good beginning gives you a taste of the plot, propounds a problem, sets a scene, or introduces you to a key character. The best beginnings grab your attention; you want to read more.

Good endings satisfy you; they convince you that what you have read was well worth the effort. In historical narrative, a good ending not only brings the story to a close, but reassures you that you have learned something. A good ending is also suspenseful; it should leave you reaching for the telephone, wishing you could call the author and ask for more.

The middle of the story should not just be the link between beginning and end. A good middle envelops you, drawing you into the tale. From the best historical writers you expect a new twist, an exciting episode, a sparkling insight, or a moving characterization on every page.

Exercise 1: Beginning, Middle, and End

The following three passages are taken from historian Paul Horgan's prize-winning *Great River: The Rio Grande in North American History*. Horgan was a superb stylist and a riveting storyteller. The first passage comes from the beginning of his book, the next from the middle, and the last from near the end. Read them and think about why Horgan put them where he did. Also note his use of illustrative detail. Then answer the questions that follow.

A Horgan begins with this description of the sources of the Rio Grande:

> The mountain system of the northern Rio Grande was a vast secret world. Wandering Indians there made shrines of twig and feather and bone, and went their ways. Close to the high clouds that made their rivers, inhuman peaks doubled the roar of thunder, or hissed with sheets of rain, or abided in massive silence. Below them lay every variation of park and meadow and lost lake; gashed canyon and rocky roomlike . . . temples of the high wilderness.[2]

1. How does Horgan's choice of opening fit the subject of his book—the river itself?

_____

_____

2. Does his dramatic depiction of the mountain vastness whet your appetite for more of his story? If so, why? _____

_____

B On the banks of the Rio Grande many peoples found homes, hunted, and made war on each other. Among these the Comanches were much respected and feared. They ride through the middle of Horgan's book, cynical and hardened, pursuing the vanishing buffalo. Compare Horgan's word picture with George Catlin's contemporary drawing (Figure 7.1).

> Superbly mounted, [the Comanches] used cured sheepskins or pieces of buffalo hides to ride on, and their bridles were made of rawhide. They were armed with bows made of [hardwood], metal-tipped arrows, ash-wood lances, shields of buffalo hide edged with turkey feathers, a flint-stone battle axe, and sometimes with rifles, bowie knives, and machetes. . . . In Camp their tepees rose and fell as if by magic—the women were expert at handling the long poles and skins with which the shelters were made. The teepee seemed like a great garment, as it were, drawn about the shoulders of a seated Indian giant.[3]

FIGURE 7.1 *George Catlin,* Comanche Village in Texas *(1834)*
Courtesy of the Smithsonian American Art Museum, Washington, DC/
Art Resource, New York

1. How does Horgan's account of the Comanches' ways capture your imagination?
_____
_____

2. In particular, how does the variety of their weaponry suggest that the Comanches belong in the middle of the story? _____
_____

3. How does Horgan's account foreshadow the life-and-death struggle between the Comanches and the Texans that he would soon describe? _____
_____

   C The end of Horgan's story is poignant. The frontier West gave way to the benefits and costs of settlement. Gone were the vast herds of buffalo and their natural predators:

> On barbed-wire fences, like symbols of the new order of affairs over the controlled range lands, dead, skinned coyotes were impaled in a frieze—twenty or thirty of them at a time. They were stretched in mid-air with a lean, racing look of unearthly nimbleness, running nowhere; and their skulled teeth had the smile of their own ghosts, wits of the plains. . . . The day of unrestrained predators was over.[4]

1. How does this passage make you feel about the end of the frontier?_____
_____
_____

2. What images in particular capture a mood of something passing into memory?
_____
_____

3. How does the imagery fit into the ending of the story? _____
_____

Making Your Point

Narrative must be convincing. Every twist and turn in the narrative should logically persuade a reader to believe the author's reconstruction of events. Narrative is argument, and argument rests on an author's choice of details and arrangement of facts, a series of decisions about what to include and what to omit. Every sentence in a narrative could be made longer by the insertion of more information or cut short. Every paragraph could be extended or pruned in the same way. You have to judge what kinds of information belong together.

Exercise 2: Unnecessary Information in Narrative Paragraphs

In each of the following three passages there is a sentence that should be removed because it is not essential to the narrative or contradicts the other sentences. Underline the sentence that can be omitted. Be prepared to defend your choice.

A Americans yearned for a literature of their own. They wanted to take their place with other "refined" European countries as a producer of literature and art. Much effort went into the search for an author to rival Sir Walter Scott in popularity. For a time James Fenimore Cooper seemed to fill the bill. His novelistic accounts of the frontier became bestsellers. Rampant racism undermined all these literary efforts. Cooper's portrait of the countryside was unrealistic, but catered to Americans' romantic notions of heroic frontiersmen and damsels in distress.

B Southerners like Robert E. Lee and Jefferson Davis began their careers in the military during the Mexican-American war of 1846. In the course of the war, they came to believe that a martial spirit, dash, heroism, and persistence were the keys to victory. The old smooth-bore muskets were rapidly replaced by rifles, giving the soldiers far greater range and accuracy. Lee and Davis were to stress these virtues when they went to war again, this time to defend the Confederacy against federal forces. The result was a theory of war based upon attack rather than defense and, at Gettysburg, the needless sacrifice of thousands of Confederate men and boys.

C As eager as they were to transform wild nature into a landscape of farms and towns, Americans clung to a vision of wilderness as a repository of virtue. They professed their love of undisturbed nature even as they transformed the forests and the prairies into fields and factories. When they depicted railroads belching smoke and flaming coals in valleys that were once quiet and green, they framed the picture with the symbols of untamed nature—rolling wooded hills, bubbling streams, and undisturbed wildlife. There was no limit to some Americans' enthusiasm when it came to reforming their countrymen's bad habits.

Exercise 3: Inference from Narrative

The sequence of argument in a narrative must be logical, and the reader must be able to follow that logic. Every arrangement of facts into arguments requires readers to make logical jumps. Read the following. After each passage you will find four statements. Can they be inferred from the narrative in the passage? If a statement is a logical inference from the narrative, write *true* in the space provided. If a statement is contradicted by the author's account, or cannot be inferred from it, write *false*.

A If many [nineteenth-century European immigrants to the west] at first intended to emulate the [earliest] backwoodsmen . . . whose thrilling exploits they had read in

American works of fiction, the resolve generally faded . . . upon learning that the backwoods lay far from the port . . . [where they landed]. Those who nevertheless pursued their original intention soon regretted their [boldness]. The boundless forest was a disheartening sight, and the American ax a dangerous instrument in the hands of a novice. After the first tree was felled with painful toil, the forest still loomed dense and gloomy; and the knowledge of all the labor that must be expended to clear each acre for corn . . . deepened the feeling of discouragement. The experience was one they shared with the colonists of two centuries before . . . [for among the first backwoodsmen] every third blow of the ax was drowned out by an oath.[5]

1. At first, nineteenth-century immigrants to America lacked the skills necessary to turn forests into farmlands. _____

2. The nineteenth-century immigrants were all from cities in Europe. _____

3. The lesson the nineteenth-century immigrants learned from the forest was to return to towns and cities. _____

4. In their initial experiences with the American wilderness, there was little difference between the nineteenth-century immigrants and the backwoodsmen who preceded them. _____

> **B** Women aged more noticeably on the frontier than did men. Because of constant childbearing and the immensely difficult job of maintaining a home, caring for the children, and working in the fields, a thirty-year-old woman was already old and worn out . . . Because women were at a premium, however [there were so few], they obtained certain advantages not granted their sisters in settled areas. . . . It was Wyoming Territory and Colorado that [first] granted women the vote . . . In order to attract women to the new frontiers, Western territories granted wives the right to hold their land separately from their husbands. In the 1850s, single women in Oregon were given 320 acres if they would migrate there.[6]

1. There were relatively few women in frontier areas. _____

2. Women on the frontier were weaker than frontiersmen. _____

3. Frontierswomen did not stay on the frontier long. _____

4. Without women, life on the frontier would have been far harsher for men. _____

Exercise 4: Using Sources

The time has come for you to craft your own story. We will give you the pieces; you must weave them into a narrative. You choose where to begin, where to end, and how to arrange and embellish your arguments.

The following map, illustrations, and reading selections include primary and secondary sources. Examine each selection. After each, answer the study questions and follow the instructions.

A The emigrants who went west before the Civil War did not have good maps of the terrain they were to cross. They hired guides, sometimes sought the aid of passing Indians, and followed natural landmarks on their way west. The map in Figure 7.2 was drawn for a modern textbook and therefore contains more information than was available to many of the pioneers.

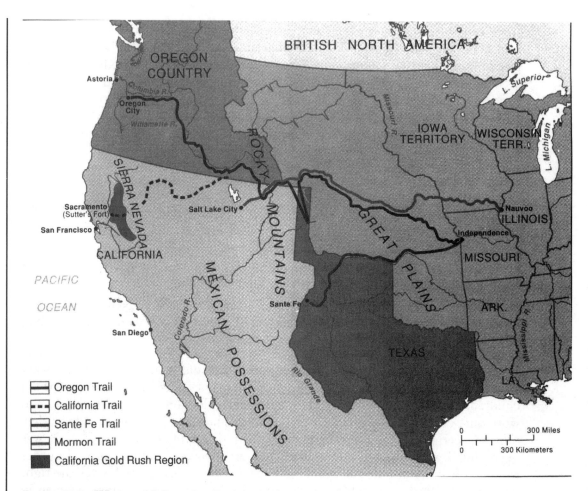

FIGURE 7.2 *Westward Migration Routes, 1850*

1. What were the major trails west? _____

_____

2. Where did they go? _____

_____

3. What obstacles lay between the jumping-off sites and the Pacific shore? _____

_____

_____

4. How many miles separated Nauvoo from Salt Lake City? Independence from Astoria?

_____

_____

B The grassy plains were the home of many Indian tribes. The Arapaho, Comanche, Cheyenne, Lakota (Sioux), Blackfoot, Crow, Snake (Shoshone), and Pawnee had all mastered the horse and vied for control of vast stretches of prairie. Although all the tribes hunted and fished, their main source of sustenance was the vast herds of buffalo that roamed the grasslands. The Indians used every part of the buffalo, eating the meat, wearing the hides, drinking from the hollowed-out horns, and making bowstrings from the sinews and arrowheads and fishing hooks from the bones. In 1837 a twenty-seven-year-old Baltimore artist named Jacob Alfred Miller traveled through the high plains, stopping to make drawings of the Indians. Figure 7.3 shows his later painting of a buffalo hunt.

FIGURE 7.3 Jacob Alfred Miller, *The Buffalo Rift (1867)*
Courtesy of the National Archives of Canada, C-000403. Gift of Mrs. J. B. Jardine

1. From the painting, what can you deduce about the Indians' skill with their horses?

_____

_____

2. What was their attitude toward the hunt?_____

_____

C Midway through his journey, Miller stopped to paint the portrait of a Snake Indian chief, Ma-Wo-Ma (Little Chief). Little Chief, a sturdy six-footer, gave Miller a present of a drawing that the chief had made on a buffalo hide. The exchange of presents was a vital social courtesy among Plains Indians. The drawing (Figure 7.4) strikingly portrays the self-image of a mighty warrior.

FIGURE 7.4 *Buffalo-Hide Drawing: Ma-Wo-Ma (Little Chief) (1837)*
Courtesy of the National Archives of Canada, C-013839. Gift of Mrs. J. B. Jardine

1. Where is Ma-Wo-Ma in the picture? _____
_____

2. What is he doing, and to whom? _____
_____

3. What weapons did he use? _____
_____

4. What do you suppose the fifteen arrows represent? _____
_____

   D Indian artists had no monopoly on symbolic depiction or heroic virtues. The illustration in Figure 7.5 is a painting entitled *American Progress*. Its central figure is Liberty, carrying aloft a symbol of progress, the telegraph lines. She flies above the plains, westward, the Rocky Mountains in front of her and civilization (cities, railroads, farms) behind. Buffalo, Indians, and wild animals flee before her.

FIGURE 7.5 John Gast, *American Progress (1872)*
Courtesy of Christie's Images

1. What can you infer about the artist's attitude toward the Indians? _____
   _____

2. What means of transportation are portrayed? _____
   _____

3. What occupations are represented among the European-Americans at the bottom of the painting? _____
   _____

4. What does the artist suggest will be the outcome of the migration of these men and women? _____
   _____
   _____

5. How might this artist's assumption about progress enter into encounters between European-Americans and Native Americans? _____
   _____

E Before the settlers began to cross the plains and mountains of the American West in great numbers, there came the trappers, explorers, and soldiers. One of the last of these expeditions was led by a bold and ambitious army officer named John C. Frémont. With him rode a bad-tempered and sharp-eyed German engineer and mapmaker, Charles Preuss. The selections below from Preuss's diary of the second expedition to California in 1843 and 1844 give you an idea of how chancy the mountain crossings could be.

December 1
[1843]

Here I am in the mountains, sitting on an old fir trunk, with thin snow around me and a mule beside me, waiting for the caravan. I had to give up my place in the wagon. Frémont said that progress was too slow on the bad roads and gave the wagon away. Yet the cannon causes just as much delay, and unless he presents it to someone as he did the wagon, we shall move ahead slowly. . . .

God only knows what we shall still have to go through on this winter journey. We still have two thousand miles back to the States. . . . Yesterday we made only eight miles, and today it will not be more than five. . . . Our Indian guides gave us to understand that we shall find no grass for two days. Unless that is a lie, I don't see how we can get our wretched animals through. We ourselves are now well provided. Flour, peas, sugar, and coffee were purchased in large quantities at Vancouver. The beef cattle follow the caravan; one was slaughtered and the meat divided for several mules to carry. This California beef is very savory and almost as good as buffalo. Whenever our cook has time to fix a stewed steak in the iron pot, we lead the life of a lord. . . .

December 3

Tonight we are without water and are camping on a slope where the sun has left some snow. I have eaten so much salty food and this tobacco makes one's mouth so dry that I cannot melt enough snow to drink. . . .

January 5, 1844

We've been sitting here for three days, wrapped in fog, on a miserable plateau surrounded by bare hills. The animals are dying, one after the other. Very little grass, snow instead of water. We have turned more to the southwest. We shall probably cross over to California. It appears to be impossible to move with such animals through the plains in winter, almost without grass and water. What a Christmas and New Year we have had this year!

[February 3]

We are getting deeper and deeper into mountains and snow. We pay one roving Indian after the other to guide us across. . . .

The snow is terribly deep, and we can make only a few miles each day. I am almost barefoot. This surpasses every discomfort that I have experienced so far. With the old Prussian surveying office [where Preuss had worked] one often had bad days, but one could expect comfortable quarters in the evening. Here a buffalo hide is spread on the snow—that is the feather bed. . . .

February 24

Finally we are out of the snow. Yesterday was still a bad day: snow, rocks, brush. Terrible march. In nine hours we made three miles, until we came to a place where another fork joins the river. . . . The sun had melted almost all the snow. It was quite steep where we had to go up and down across canyons; in general, however, there was earthy soil under the fir trees, etc.; mighty boulders thrown in between. We made about twelve miles in four hours and found some grass and horsetail for our hungry beasts. We therefore made a halt, for such spots are rather scarce here in the forest.

Another horse was just shot; I hope the eating of horse meat will soon be over. Tomorrow, I think, we should come pretty close to the valley. Then my Polly [Preuss's horse] can recuperate with good grass so that I can ride again, for walking is, after all, a little hard. Horse meat gives no strength, and every student of nature knows that peas contain little nourishment.

The mules grew so hungry that they ate the tail of Fitzpatrick's horse, also parts of saddles, my bridle, etc.[7]

Underline the most striking details in the passage.

1. What features of the land most impressed Preuss? _____

_____

2. What hardships most annoyed or frightened him? _____

_____

F While Preuss and Frémont descended into the Sacramento Valley of California, a young Bostonian named Francis Parkman was setting out on his own journey to Oregon. He had little respect for the migrants who trekked across the great plains in search of new homes. Parkman was there for the adventure, an adventure he later described in his book *The Oregon Trail*. The portion from it reproduced below was originally written at the end of May 1846.

May 28th. Wolves all night. Camped on Little Blue [River]. Saw wolves and two antelopes in the morning. Grave of a child 4 yrs. old—May 1845.

Henry hunted in vain for antelopes. Nooned [spent midday] on Little Blue. Made a very long afternoon march—hour after hour over a perfect level—not very well. Sorel wounded an antelope. After twelve miles riding, approached Little Blue again. Immense masses of blue, lurid clouds in the west shadowed the green prairie, and the sun glared through purple and crimson. As we draw near the valley of the stream, a furious wind, presaging a storm, struck us. We galloped down in the face of it—horses snorting with fear. Rode to the ground—up went the tent and on came the storm.

May 29th. Left camp—saw plenty of antelopes and fired at one across the river. Kept along the Little Blue, and just before nooning had great trouble in crossing a tributary creek [Pawnee Creek?]. As we (we) were dining, Henry brought in a fine antelope—a very welcome acquisition as our bacon is almost gone. Afternoon—more antelope and turkeys. Scenery very beautiful and prairielike. The Capt. very merry, riding off in all directions and running a wolf over the prairie. Bones of game scattered in all directions, indicating a surround. Moved rapidly and merrily—camped on a beautiful plain, hard by the woods that fringe the Little Blue. Flowers—prairie peas—*pommes blanches.*

Mounted guard for the first time last night—three hours. Middle watch to me and Delorier tonight. Delorier is a true Canadian—all his acts and thoughts are subject to the will of his *bourgeois* [boss].

Met yesterday in a rough meadow by the Little Blue [River] two Delaware Inds. returning from a hunt—one of them a remarkably handsome fellow.

May 30th. Made a very hard day's work—came more than thirty miles from the Blue [River] to the Platte [River]. We had all along mistaken our route, thinking that we were less advanced than in fact we were. Soon after leaving the Blue, saw two men, Turner and another, come back from the emigrants [settlers on their way to Oregon or California] in search of an ox. They set us right, telling us we were 26 miles from the river. Just before seeing us, they had met six Pawnees, who wanted to change horses, and laid hand on the bridle of one of them, till threatened with a pistol—the only weapon they had. . . . Camped late—an emigrant came to us, on his way to look for Turner—he told us that Robinson's party were encamped three miles off—that the four waggons that had joined us, and got ahead a few days ago, were in advance—and that a large hunting-party of Pawnees were encamped close to them.

This afternoon, passed a very large Pawnee trail, and a small foot trail recently travelled.

May 31st. Early this morning, the Pawnees, about 30 in number, passed a short distance from our camp—a hunting-party—no women, these being probably planting corn at the village. Rather mean-looking fellows, each with a bow and arrows—led horses, loaded with dry meat. The chief walked behind—I gave him a piece of tobacco, which very much pleased him. . . .

Papin reports that the Mormons are a few miles ahead—that the Pawnees have taken 10 of their horses, and whipped one of their men into camp—that the Sioux have been out in force, and driven off the buffalo—all this alarms the Capt. exceedingly.[8]

Underline the most striking details in Parkman's diary.

1. What did Parkman think of the Pawnees? _____
_____

2. What impression did he have of the scenery? _____
_____

3. What did he expect to happen when the settlers and the Indians got too close to one another? _____
_____

G Women also set out on the way west. Though they walked alongside husbands, fathers, and sons, their story was different from their menfolk's, as John Mack Faragher and Christine Stansell remind you.

The disintegration of the physical base of domesticity [furniture was the first thing dumped when the wagons were too heavy to cross a river] was symptomatic of an even more serious disruption in the female subculture. Because the wagon trains so often broke into smaller units, many women were stranded in parties without other women. Since there were usually two or more men in the same family party, some male friendships and bonds remained intact for the duration of the journey. But by midway in the trip, female companionship, so valued by nineteenth-century women, was unavailable to the solitary wife in a party of hired men, husband, and children that had broken away from a larger train. Emergencies and quarrels, usually between men, broke up the parties. . . . On the day [one family] separated from the others, [a woman] wrote in her journal: "The women came over to bid me goodbye, for we were to go alone, all alone. They said there was no color in my face. I felt as if there was none." She perceived the separation as a banishment, almost a death sentence: "There is something peculiar in such a parting on the Plains, one there realizes what a goodbye is." . . . Uprootedness took its toll in debilitation and numbness. After a hard week, men "lolled around in the tents and on their blankets seeming to realize that the 'Sabbath was made for man,'" resting on the palpable achievements of miles covered and rivers crossed. In contrast, the women "could not fully appreciate physical rest, and were rendered more uneasy by the continual passing of emigrant trains all day long. . . . To me, much of the day was spent in meditating over the past and in forebodings for the future."

The ultimate expression of this alienation was the pressure to turn back, to retrace steps to the old life. Occasionally anxiety or bewilderment erupted into open revolt against going on.

> *This morning our company moved on, except one family. The woman got mad and wouldn't budge or let the children go. He had the cattle hitched on for three hours and coaxed her to go, but she wouldn't stir.*

Short of violent resistance, it was always possible that circumstances would force a family to reconsider and turn back. During a cholera scare in 1852, "women cried, begging their men to take them back." When the men reluctantly relented, the writer observed that "they did the hooking up of their oxen in a spiritless sort of way," while "some of the girls and women were laughing." There was little lost and much regained for women in a decision to abandon the migration.

Both sexes worked, and both sexes suffered. Yet women lacked a sense of inclusion and a cultural rationale to give meaning to the suffering and the work; no augmented sense of self or role emerged from augmented privation. Both women and men also complained, but women expanded their caviling to a generalized critique of the whole enterprise. Margaret Chambers felt "as if we had left all civilization behind us" after crossing the Missouri. . . . Civilization was far more to these women than law, books, and municipal governments; it was pianos, church societies, daguerreotypes, mirrors—in short, their homes. At their most hopeful, the exiles perceived the Trail as a hellish but necessary transition to a land where they could renew their domestic mission: "Each advanced step of the slow, plodding cattle carried us farther and farther from civilization into a desolate, barbarous country. . . . But our new home lay beyond all this and was a shining beacon that beckoned us on, inspiring our hearts with hope and courage."[9]

Underline the most striking details in the passage.

1. What was it like for women traveling west, according to this selection? _____
_____

2. What did women resent most about life on the trail? _____
_____

3. What evidence does the passage offer for this resentment? _____
_____

H Some migrants lost their fortunes, their children, their parents, and finally their own lives as they trekked across the continent. The most infamous of these tragedies involved the Donner party of emigrants from Illinois. At its head were two patriarchs, George and Jacob Donner. With them came their families, their friends, and their servants. Half of them died of hunger in the high passes of the Sierra Nevada, the gateway to California. Their fate has become a symbol of the hardships of the trail, for, trapped in the snow, they resorted to cannibalism.

There is no point in devoting to the Donner party the space it receives in this book except as it provides one of the varieties of frontier experience. It has been a favorite story of historians and novelists because it is concentrated, because the horror composes a drama. But the reader of this book will understand that the disaster which overtook the Donner party was part of the trail's *if*, one factor in the equation of chance under which emigration across the mountains and desert traveled. The fate of the Donners or its equivalent was, as a hazard, part of the equipment packed in every white-top [covered wagon] that pulled up the slope beyond Fort Laramie, this year, the years before it, and for some years still to come. Whether the risk was to be taken successfully or unsuccessfully depended on chance, weather, skill, intelligence, and character—all inscrutable. . . . The Donners were not the only emigrants who disintegrated in panic, and the fact which the public chiefly remembers about them, their cannibalism, was no novelty in the West. It had occurred along the route they traveled, and when, in the last days of 1848, Frémont's fourth expedition stalled in the San Juan snows, Bill Williams' detachment probably killed and certainly ate one of their companions. Kit Carson remarked of Bill Williams that in starving times no man should walk ahead of him on the trail, and old Bill shared that reputation with numerous others. In fact, the last resource of starving men is a commonplace.

It is as the commonplace or typical just distorted that the Donners must be seen. Beyond Fort Laramie every stretch of the trail they traveled, at some time during the history of emigration, saw one or another party just escaping disaster, and a number of stretches saw some parties not altogether escaping it.[10]

Underline the most striking details in the passage.

1. What is the author's main message?_____

_____

2. Was the Donner party's fate unusual? _____

_____

I One member of the Donner party, Patrick Breen, left a diary, and a portion of it serves as the last selection for your narrative writing assignment.

Friday, Nov. 20th 1846 came to this place on the 31st of last month that it snowed we went on to the pass the snow so deep we were unable to find the road, when within 3 miles of the summit then turned back to this shanty on the Lake, [Charles T.] Stanton came one day after we arrived here we again took our teams & waggons & made another unsuccessful attempt to cross in company with Stanton we returned to the shanty it continuing to snow all the time we were here we now have Killed most part of our cattle having to stay here untill next Spring & live on poor beef without bread or salt[.] It snowed during the space of eight days with little intermission, after our arrival here, the remainder of time up to this day was clear & pleasant frezing at night the snow nearly gone from the valleys.

Sat 21st fine morning wind N.W. 22 of our company are about Starting across the mountain this morning including Stanton & his indians, some clouds flying thawed today wind E

Sunday 22nd froze hard last night this a fine clear morning, wind E.S.E. no account from those on the mountains

Monday 23rd same weather wind W the Expedition across the mountains returned after an unsuccesful attempt . . .

Thursday the 26th began to snow yesterday in the evening now rains or sleet the mountaniers dont start today the wind about W, wet & muddy

Friday 27 Continues to snow, the ground not covered, wind W dull prospect for crossing the Mountains . . .

December 1st Tuesday Still Snowing wind W snow about 5½ feet or 6 deep difficult to get wood. no going from the house Completely housed up looks as likely for snow as when it Commenced, our cattle all Killed but three or four of them, the horses & Stantons mules gone & Cattle suppose lost in the Snow no hopes of finding them alive . . .

Frid. 5th [January] snowd. hard all untill 12 O'clock at night wind still continues to blow hard from the S.W. to day pretty clear a few clouds only Peggy very uneasy for fear we shall all perrish with hunger we have but alittle meat left & only part of 3 hides has to support Mrs. Reid, she has nothing left but one hide & it is on Graves shanty Milt. is livi[n]g there & likely will Keep that hide [William M.] Eddys child [Margaret] died last night-

Satd. 6th it snowd. faster last night & to day than it has done this winter & still Continues without an intermission wind S.W. Murphys folks or Keyburgs say they cant eat hides. I wish we had enough of them Mrs [Eleanor] Eddy very weak.

Sund. 7th Ceasd. to snow last after one of the most Severe Storms we Experienced this winter the snow fell about 4 feet deep I had to shovel the snow off our shanty this morning it thaw so fast & thawd. during the whole storm to day it is quite pleasant wind S.W. Milt here today says Mrs. Reid has to get a hide from Mrs. Murphy & McCutchins [William McCutchen's] child [Harriet] died 2nd of this Month

Mond 8th fine clear morning wind S.W. froze hard last [night] Spitzer died last night about 3 Oclock to [day?] we will bury him in the snow Mrs Eddy died on the night of the 7th [*deleted:* Mrs Murp]

Tuesd. 9th Mrs Murphy here this morning [William M.] pikes child [Catherine] all but dead Milt at Murphys not able to get out of bed Keyburg never gets up says he is not able. John went down to day to bury Mrs Eddy & child heard nothing from Graves for 2 or 3 days Mrs Murphy just now going to Graves fine moing wind S.E. froze hard last night begins to thaw in the Sun

Wednd. 10th beautiful morning Wind W. froze hard last night, to day thawing in the Sun Milt Elliot died las night at Murphys Shanty about 9 Oclock P.M. Mrs Reid went there this morning to see after his effects. J Denton trying to borrow meat for Graves had none to give they have nothing but hides all are entirely out of meat but a little we have our hides are nearly all eat up but with Gods help spring will soon smile upon us . . . [11]

Underline the most striking details in the passage.

1. What happened to the Donner party as they reached the high mountain passes?

_____

_____

2. What was their decision in response to this unexpected occurrence? _____

_____

3. What then happened to the emigrants? _____

_____

4. How did they cope with the winter in the mountains? _____

_____

Narrative is fun to read but hard to write. You are now ready to try your hand at it.

Exercise 5: Telling Your Story: The Way West

Using the primary and secondary sources in this chapter, write a historical narrative (third person, please, using the past tense) describing what it was like on the way west before the Civil War. Begin the task by reviewing the readings and illustrations, including your own short answers and the parts you underlined. Write your main ideas here:

_____

_____

_____

_____

Now, write your narrative. Be sure your beginning grabs the reader's interest, your middle is detailed and lively, and your ending provides a satisfying conclusion. Ask yourself whether your ideas flow logically from paragraph to paragraph. Is your style colorful? Does each main point you make have sufficient support? Have you incorporated interesting excerpts from the primary sources? Your choice of a story line makes the narrative your own. Do not be afraid to reach your own conclusions. Originality is an important part of every narrative. Be sure to give citations for all quotations and paraphrases.

_____

_____

_____

_____

_____

_____

_____

_____

_____

_____

_____

_____

_____

_____

_____

_____

_____

_____

_____

_____

_____

_____

Most of the people who traveled on the overland trail were poor farmers or farm laborers. They could read and write, however, and enjoyed reading romances, tales of high adventure, and how-to books. Some of these writings were the work of a small but energetic circle of novelists, poets, essayists, and philosophers who lived in eastern cities. These creators of an American literature are the subject of the next chapter.

Notes

[1] Bernard Bailyn, "The Challenge of Modern Historiography," *American Historical Review* 87 (1982), 24.

[2] Paul Horgan, *Great River: The Rio Grande in North American History* (New York: Funk and Wagnalls, 1968), 2:460.

[3] Ibid., 2:850.

[4] Ibid., 2:886.

[5] Marcus Lee Hansen, *The Immigrant in American History* (1940; reprint, New York: Harper & Row, 1964), 66.

[6] June Sochen, *Herstory: A Woman's View of American History* (New York: Alfred Publishing, 1974),114.

[7] Excerpts from *Exploring with Frémont* by Charles Preuss, translated and edited by Erwin G. and Elizabeth Gudde (Norman: University of Oklahoma Press, 1958), pp. 99–113.

[8] Mason Wade, ed., *The Journals of Francis Parkman* (New York: Harper & Brothers, 1947), 430–433.

[9] Excerpted from Johnny Mack Faragher and Christine Stansell, "Women and Their Families on the Overland Trail to California and Oregon, 1842–1847," *Feminist Studies* 2 (1975), 150–166. Used by permission of the authors.

[10] Bernard De Voto, *The Year of Decision: 1846* (Boston: Houghton Mifflin, 1943), 340–341.

[11] "The Breen Diary," in Dale Morgan, ed., *Overland in 1846: Diaries and Letters of the California-Oregon Trail* (Georgetown, Calif.: Talisman Press, 1963), 306–322.

8: Reading Literary Texts in History

American Literature in the Middle Period

As we have already seen in our work on primary and secondary sources and our narrative exercises in the previous chapter, reading historical sources requires critical thinking skills. We have learned how to read secondary sources for content and argument and primary sources for point of view and accuracy. But certain kinds of historical sources demand a little more from us than sorting through motive and perspective, and spying out forgeries and deliberate lies. Works of literature from the past are also historical documents. Works of literature from the past demonstrate the styles, uses of language, and literary preferences of an age. They also show us how people of especially acute sensitivity viewed their world. In sum, works of literature, or texts as they are often called by literary critics, have both an internal and an external history. As three of the most respected intellectual historians of our time have recently written, "the text itself becomes an object with properties of its own."[1] As historians, we have to learn to interpret and explain them.

Reading Literary Texts

The internal history of a work of literature can be divided into two parts. The first part focuses our attention on the language itself—the words chosen, the figures of speech employed, and the type of work. (Is it poetry or prose? If a poem, what is its meter, rhyme scheme, and form? If a sonnet, is it Shakespearian or Spencerian? And so on). The second part of the internal history of the text is how it reflects or plays off of other texts. This is sometimes called "inter-textuality." Authors of poems often adopt the same metaphors, similes, and other figures of speech from earlier poems. Some works of fiction are out and out tributes to an earlier writer and some authors seem especially fond of direct and indirect references to earlier works. The rules against plagiarism do not seem to apply to certain kinds of literature. (Inter-textuality is not limited to works of literature. For example, judicial opinions borrow authority, arguments, and even particular phrases from prior opinions.)

The external history of the work is a species of biography. It relates the story of how the piece of literature was composed. Critical editions of writers' works often feature more than one version of a poem, essay, or other composition, showing how the author revised it over time, how an editor or publisher changed it before for publication, and how it was received by readers. Literary biography allows us "to view with a biographer's aid, the processes of artistic development and fruition." The biographer of an author puts the author's work into its chronological and intellectual niche. It also leaves authors at the mercy of biographers who are themselves the product of a particular time and place and whose own moral and political views may not be sympathetic to the author's.[2]

For historians, the literary work is a primary source document. We see the poem, essay, short story, novel, and play as a way to understand the aspirations and artistic conventions of a period. We treat an author's work as expressive of their ideas and fold those ideas into a cultural history of the era. Because cultural history looks at the sets of meanings that are common to a people in the past, it is always concerned with the use of language and, it follows, with literature.

Historians and Literary Criticism

Historians share the task of interpretation of texts with literary critics. They ask different questions about the literary piece from those that historians ask, because the literary critic is less interested in using the literature as historical evidence and more interested in assessing its value as art. Some may attempt to measure its contribution to the "canon" of great works that everyone should read, while other critics want to know how the work functions in and of itself. Like the historical profession over the past half century, the variety of literary criticism has grown and diversified. Indeed, in some sense literary criticism itself has a history that "always depended on the *climate of opinion* that prevails in a particular culture during a specific historical period." Within this general climate of opinion, "the prevailing mood of the literati who are concerned with criticism" generates the modes of literary criticism in fashion. In the first half of the nineteenth century, the dominant form of literary criticism may be called "expressive criticism."[3] Its exponents viewed literature as the product of individual genius. Any particular work simply expressed its author's own insights and imagination. Poetry was conceded to be the highest form of literary genius, which explains why so many novelists, essayists, and travel writers also tried their hand at poetry.

Today, there are feminist critics, Marxist critics, Freudian critics, ethno-critics, eroto-critics, and even literary criticism that attacks the entire enterprise of literary criticism. Indeed, the importance of theory in reading literary works has declined as the number of approaches has multiplied.[4] But from the 1930s through the 1960s, the dominant academic theory of literature was the "new criticism." It opposed older historical (or philological) approaches to understanding texts, in favor of a stress on technique and readability. Works of literature, the new critics asserted, are complete in themselves and should not be read as representative of a moment in an author's life or a product of a historical time and place. Instead, the critic should help a reader to see more deeply into the genius of the work and appreciate its merits. The new critics also believed that artistic works reflected fundamental and unchanging human values. Historians might argue that the values the new critics assign to all literature were in fact merely a product of the new critics' own time and place, in particular a longing for something of value in a world turned upside down by the Great Depression, World War II, and the Cold War, but new critics would reply that the historians were trivializing literature.

One successor to New Criticism among academic literary critics calls itself "deconstruction." It originated in France after the liberation from Nazi control and flowered through the 1980s. Its foremost spokesmen had little use for the ideal of universal truth in literature, but like the new critics rejected the biographical approach to literary analysis. The deconstructionists likened literary texts to portions of an ongoing conversation among the authors. They were speaking in their work to one another. Language itself did not reflect anything basic about a culture (it was not a mirror of a culture or people) but instead was a collection of signs that were temporary and constantly changing. The text itself thus had no outside references and should not be read as representative of an outside world. Thus literature was historical (insofar as every text's meaning was generated at a particular time and place) but texts were not historical documents. One should not read them for anything but themselves.

As we can see, both new criticism and deconstruction do not easily lend themselves to the kind of work that historians conventionally do, but an even more recent theory has returned literature to its historical moorings. The "new historicism" sees works of literature as commentaries on the world of the author and reads the work as though it were an attempt to deal with contemporary problems. New historicists find in all literature moral statements about the author's time and place. New historicists see authors as normal human beings with strengths and weaknesses. Indeed, the tendency of many new historicists is to be critical of the work of earlier American authors because it was insensitive to racism, homophobia, and sexism. Thus new historicism is not exactly historically minded in the sense that we have defined that approach to the past.

American Literature in the Middle Period

Whatever the brand of literary criticism one adopts, no devotee of American writing would deny that the middle period (1815–1860) brought a Renaissance in literature to the new nation. Indeed, although they owed much to English literary conventions and European Romantic sentimentality, the leaders of American writing saw themselves as spokesmen and women for their people and a nation. They came to call themselves "Young America." Educators, editors, and orators all welcomed the American age of letters.[5]

The explosion of literature rested in part on technological innovations in printing. The introduction of the rotary press had made newspapers cheaper in the 1820s, and this in turn encouraged editors to print and customers to read serialized versions of short stories and novels. These authors, mixing popular topics like crime, adventure, and sentimentality, with deeper themes of moral depravity and regeneration, found a wide audience among lowbrows and highbrows. At the heart of the new literature was romantic sentimentality, religious uplift, and reform idealism. Cities like Boston, New York, and Philadelphia welcomed the growth of literary communities and became the homes of literary magazines, journals, and publishing houses. Collections of poems, novels, and travelogues became best sellers.

Another focus of the American Renaissance in literature was America itself. Poets like Harvard College professor Henry Wadsworth Longfellow set old Indian tales to rhyme, and his "Song of Hiawatha" and "Evangeline" became instant classics. James Russell Lowell, another Harvard professor, wrote some of his poems in Yankee dialect, and used his poetry and prose to lampoon political corruption. John Greenleaf Whittier, another New England poet, turned to more immediate themes, in particular the injustice of slavery. Novelists like Nathaniel Hawthorne, Edgar Allan Poe, and Herman Melville also manipulated American themes to create masterworks of fiction. Hawthorne was a native of Salem, Massachusetts, whose Puritan ancestry flavored his novels. The best known of them, *The Scarlet Letter* (1850), set a tragedy of secret sinfulness in the historical atmosphere of early Massachusetts. Poe was a Virginian who lived most of his short life in New York City and Baltimore. His journalism, poems, and short stories, particularly the poems "Lenore" and "The Raven," short stories like "The Telltale Heart" and "The Gold Bug," and novellas (short novels) like *The Fall of the House of Usher* relied on American settings to create a sense of mystery, guilt, and lost love. Melville, the most highly regarded of the three today, was then the least known. He served as a sailor before he became a journalist, and his great novel of the American whaling industry, *Moby Dick* (1851), brought together motifs of revenge and adventure.

A final theme in the middle period literature was religious and secular idealism and reformism. The essayist and lecturer Ralph Waldo Emerson and the naturalist writer Henry David Thoreau, among others, believed that people could live close to nature and appreciate its bounty. They also shared a religious faith that men and women were perfectable, in touch with the "oversoul" that was a benevolent and loving God. A younger generation of poets, novelists, and essayists including Walt Whitman, Louisa May Alcott, and Harriet Beecher Stowe drew inspiration from the idealism and the sentimentality of the age. Whitman's collection of poems, *Leaves of Grass* (1855), broke through the traditions of poetry to feature free verse celebrations of manhood and democracy. Alcott's semi-autobiographical *Little Women* (1868) made her the most famous authoress of her day. Stowe's account of the travails of Uncle Tom and little Liza in the early 1850s were the most popular newspaper serials of the time.

Exercise 1: Reading Literary Works for Manifest Content

Reading for manifest content—reading for content that we believe is there—is a technique that we apply to works of literature all the time. That is, although we appreciate the artistic qualities of literary works, in particular the use of language and structure to convey emotion, as historians we are looking in them for evidence of how people thought and expressed themselves in a particular time and place. In this kind of reading we look for indications of time and place.

A It may be argued that the so-called American Renaissance in literature began in Boston, after the War of 1812. There a new generation of college-trained intellectuals and reformers began to think about creating a uniquely American culture. The best known of these thinkers was a teacher, minister, lecturer, essayist, poet, and literary promoter named Ralph Waldo Emerson (1803–1882). He traveled in Europe and appreciated its culture, but wanted Americans to find ways to express the strengths of their own character in fiction, poems, and philosophical works. His first great essay, "The American Scholar," delivered as an oration in 1837 at his alma mater, Harvard College, laid out a program for such a renaissance of American culture. Below are a series of passages from his essay. Read them, and then in the space below summarize his three major points. In particular, how did his arguments reflect the relationship between intellectual activities and character? Between reading and common labor? Between the authority of old books and the authority of creative impulses?

> ... Our day of dependence, our long apprenticeship to the learning of other lands, draws to a close. The millions, that around us are rushing into life, cannot always be fed on the sere remains of foreign harvests. Events, actions arise, that must be sung, that will sing themselves....
>
> In this hope, I accept the topic which not only usage, but the nature of our association, seem to prescribe to this day,—the AMERICAN SCHOLAR. Year by year, we come up hither to read one more chapter of his biography. Let us inquire what light new days and events have thrown on his character, and his hopes....
>
> I. The first in time and the first in importance of the influences upon the mind is that of nature. Every day, the sun; and, after sunset, night and her stars. Ever the winds blow; ever the grass grows. Every day, men and women, conversing, beholding and beholden.

The scholar is he of all men whom this spectacle most engages. He must settle its value in his mind. What is nature to him? There is never a beginning, there is never an end, to the inexplicable continuity of this web of God, but always circular power returning into itself. Therein it resembles his own spirit, whose beginning, whose ending, he never can find,—so entire, so boundless. . . .

[Nature's] beauty is the beauty of his own mind. Its laws are the laws of his own mind. Nature then becomes to him the measure of his attainments. So much of nature as he is ignorant of, so much of his own mind does he not yet possess. And, in fine, the ancient precept, "Know thyself," and the modern precept, "Study nature," become at last one maxim.

II. The next great influence into the spirit of the scholar, is, the mind of the Past,—in whatever form, whether of literature, of art, of institutions, that mind is inscribed. Books are the best type of the influence of the past, and perhaps we shall get at the truth,—learn the amount of this influence more conveniently,—by considering their value alone. . . .

Yet hence arises a grave mischief. The sacredness which attaches to the act of creation,—the act of thought,—is transferred to the record. The poet chanting, was felt to be a divine man: henceforth the chant is divine also. The writer was a just and wise spirit: henceforward it is settled, the book is perfect; as love of the hero corrupts into worship of his statue. Instantly, the book becomes noxious: the guide is a tyrant. The sluggish and perverted mind of the multitude, slow to open to the incursions of Reason, having once so opened, having once received this book, stands upon it, and makes an outcry, if it is disparaged. Colleges are built on it. Books are written on it by thinkers, not by Man Thinking; by men of talent, that is, who start wrong, who set out from accepted dogmas, not from their own sight of principles. Meek young men grow up in libraries, believing it their duty to accept the views, which Cicero, which Locke, which Bacon, have given, forgetful that Cicero, Locke, and Bacon were only young men in libraries, when they wrote these books.

Hence, instead of Man Thinking, we have the bookworm. Hence, the book-learned class, who value books, as such; not as related to nature and the human constitution, but as making a sort of Third Estate with the world and the soul. Hence, the restorers of readings, the emendators, the bibliomaniacs of all degrees. . . .

Undoubtedly there is a right way of reading, so it be sternly subordinated. Man Thinking must not be subdued by his instruments. Books are for the scholar's idle times. When he can read God directly, the hour is too precious to be wasted in other men's transcripts of their readings. . . .

III. There goes in the world a notion, that the scholar should be a recluse, a valetudinarian,—as unfit for any handiwork or public labor, as a penknife for an axe. The so-called 'practical men' sneer at speculative men, as if, because they speculate or see, they could do nothing. I have heard it said that the clergy,—who are always, more universally than any other class, the scholars of their day,—are addressed as women. . . .

The world,—this shadow of the soul, or other me, lies wide around. Its attractions are the keys which unlock my thoughts and make me acquainted with myself. I run eagerly into this resounding tumult. I grasp the hands of those next me, and take my place in the ring to suffer and to work, taught by an instinct, that so shall the dumb abyss be vocal with speech. I pierce its order; I dissipate its fear; I dispose of it within the circuit of my expanding life. So much only of life as I know by experience, so much of the wilderness have I vanquished and planted, or so far have I extended my being, my dominion. I do not see how any man can afford, for the sake of his nerves and his nap, to spare any action in which he can partake. It is pearls and rubies to his discourse. Drudgery, calamity, exasperation, want, are instructers in eloquence and wisdom. The true scholar grudges every opportunity of action past by, as a loss of power. . . .

Of course, he who has put forth his total strength in fit actions, has the richest return of wisdom. I will not shut myself out of this globe of action, and transplant an oak into a flower-pot, there to hunger and pine; nor trust the revenue of some single faculty, and exhaust one vein of thought, much like those Savoyards, who, getting their livelihood by carving shepherds, shepherdesses, and smoking Dutchmen, for all Europe, went out one day to the mountain to find stock, and discovered that they had whittled up the last of their pine-trees. Authors we have, in numbers, who have written out their vein, and who, moved by a commendable prudence, sail for Greece or Palestine, follow the trapper into the prairie, or ramble round Algiers, to replenish their merchantable stock.

If it were only for a vocabulary, the scholar would be covetous of action. Life is our dictionary. Years are well spent in country labors; in town,—in the insight into trades and manufactures; in frank intercourse with many men and women; in science; in art; to the one end of mastering in all their facts a language by which to illustrate and embody our perceptions. I learn immediately from any speaker how much he has already lived, through the poverty or the splendor of his speech. Life lies behind us as the quarry from whence we get tiles and copestones for the masonry of to-day. This is the way to learn grammar. Colleges and books only copy the language which the field and the work-yard made. . . .

I hear therefore with joy whatever is beginning to be said of the dignity and necessity of labor to every citizen. There is virtue yet in the hoe and the spade, for learned as well as for unlearned hands. And labor is everywhere welcome; always we are invited to work; only be this limitation observed, that a man shall not for the sake of wider activity sacrifice any opinion to the popular judgments and modes of action. . . .

These being his functions, it becomes him to feel all confidence in himself, and to defer never to the popular cry. He and he only knows the world. The world of any moment is the merest appearance. Some great decorum, some fetish of a government, some ephemeral trade, or war, or man, is cried up by half mankind and cried down by the other half, as if all depended on this particular up or down. The odds are that the whole question is not worth the poorest thought which the scholar has lost in listening to the controversy. . . .

Men such as they are, very naturally seek money or power; and power because it is as good as money,—the "spoils," so called, "of office." And why not? for they aspire to the highest, and this, in their sleep-walking, they dream is highest. Wake them, and they shall quit the false good, and leap to the true, and leave governments to clerks and desks. This revolution is to be wrought by the gradual domestication of the idea of Culture. . . .[6]

1. _____

_____

_____

2. _____

_____

_____

3. _____

_____

_____

B Henry David Thoreau (1817–1862) was a younger friend of Emerson, also a graduate of Harvard College, and for a time a teacher. Thoreau longed to be a successful writer, and his first great work, *Walden* (1854), a journal of his days living by Walden Pond in eastern Massachusetts, has become a modern classic. He took nine years to finish the work, but in its time it did not sell well. The publisher returned hundreds of copies to Thoreau, in part because its sentiments were too lofty and some of its references too obscure for many readers. In *Walden* he tried to convey his immediate impressions of nature and society in day to day life at the pond. Read the following selections and in the spaces below record what you find to be three major themes. Do you see any similarities to any themes in Emerson's speech? To Emerson's up-beat tone?

I was seated by the shore of a small pond, about a mile and a half south of the village of Concord and somewhat higher than it, in the midst of an extensive wood between that town and Lincoln, and about two miles south of that our only field known to fame, Concord Battle Ground; but I was so low in the woods that the opposite shore, half a mile off, like the rest, covered with wood, was my most distant horizon. For the first week, whenever I looked out on the pond it impressed me like a tarn high up on the side of a mountain, its bottom far above the surface of other lakes, and, as the sun arose, I saw it throwing off its nightly clothing of mist, and here and there, by degrees, its soft ripples or its smooth reflecting surface was revealed, while the mists, like ghosts, were stealthily withdrawing in every direction into the woods, as at the breaking up of some nocturnal conventicle. The very dew seemed to hang upon the trees later into the day than usual, as on the sides of mountains.

This small lake was of most value as a neighbor in the intervals of a gentle rain storm in August, when, both air and water being perfectly still, but the sky overcast, mid-afternoon had all the serenity of evening, and the wood-thrush sang around, and was heard from shore to shore. A lake like this is never smoother than at such a time; and the clear portion of the air above it being shallow and darkened by clouds, the water, full of light and reflections, becomes a lower heaven itself so much the more important. From a hill top near by, where the wood had been recently cut off, there was a pleasing vista southward across the pond, through a wide indentation in the hills which form the shore there, where their opposite sides sloping toward each other suggested a stream flowing out in that direction through a wooded valley, but stream there was none. That way I looked between and over the near green hills to some distant and higher ones in the horizon, tinged with blue. Indeed, by standing on tiptoe I could catch a glimpse of some of the peaks of the still bluer and more distant mountain ranges in the north-west, those true-blue coins from heaven's own mint, and also of some portion of the village. But in other directions, even from this point, I could not see over or beyond the woods which surrounded me. It is well to have some water in your neighborhood, to give buoyancy to and float the earth. One value even of the smallest well is, that when you look into it you see that earth is not continent but insular. This is as important as that it keeps butter cool. When I looked across the pond from this peak toward the Sudbury meadows, which in time of flood I distinguished elevated perhaps by a mirage in their seething valley, like a coin in a basin, all the earth beyond the pond appeared like a thin crust insulated and floated even by this small sheet of intervening water, and I was reminded that this on which I dwelt was but *dry land*.

Though the view from my door was still more contracted, I did not feel crowded or confined in the least. There was pasture enough for my imagination. The low shrub-oak plateau to which the opposite shore arose, stretched away toward the prairies of the West and the steppes of Tartary, affording ample room for all the roving families of men. "There are none happy in the world but beings who enjoy freely a vast horizon,"—said Damodara, when his herds required new and larger pastures. . . .

After a still winter night I awoke with the impression that some question had been put to me, which I had been endeavoring in vain to answer in my sleep, as what—how—when—where? But there was dawning Nature, in whom all creatures live, looking in at my broad windows with serene and satisfied face, and no question on *her* lips. I awoke to an answered question, to Nature and daylight. The snow lying deep on the earth dotted with young pines, and the very slope of the hill on which my house is placed, seemed to say, Forward! Nature puts no question and answers none which we mortals ask. She has long ago taken her resolution. "O Prince, our eyes contemplate with admiration and transmit to the soul the wonderful and varied spectacle of this universe. The night veils without doubt a part of this glorious creation; but day comes to reveal to us this great work, which extends from earth even into the plains of the ether."

Then to my morning work. First I take an axe and pail and go in search of water, if that be not a dream. After a cold and snowy night it needed a divining rod to find it. Every winter the liquid and trembling surface of the pond, which was so sensitive to every breath, and reflected every light and shadow, becomes solid to the depth of a foot or a foot and a half, so that it will support the heaviest teams, and perchance the snow covers it to an equal depth, and it is not to be distinguished from any level field. Like the marmots in the surrounding hills, it closes its eye-lids and becomes dormant for three months or more. Standing on the snow-covered plain, as if in a pasture amid the hills, I cut my way first through a foot of snow, and then a foot of ice, and open a window under my feet, where, kneeling to drink, I look down into the quiet parlor of the fishes, pervaded by a softened light as through a window of ground glass, with its bright sanded floor the same as in summer; there a perennial waveless serenity reigns as in the amber twilight sky, corresponding to the cool and even temperament of the inhabitants. Heaven is under our feet as well as over our heads.[7]

1. _____

_____

_____

2. _____

_____

_____

3. _____

_____

_____

The writings of Emerson and Thoreau fused the natural and the sacred, suggesting that there was divinity in people and nature. This was one of the major themes of the romantic literature of the middle period. Poetry became especially popular in this era, and many of the leading writers of the time composed poems as well as essays, short stories, book reviews, and magazine articles. (One of the characteristics of the men and women of letters was their versatility.) In the following poems, reproduced in part below, underline the references to nature and divinity. In the space following each poem, briefly summarize the author's attitude toward nature.

C William Cullen Bryant (1794–1878) of New York was one of the first of these romantic poets and later, as associate editor of the New York *Evening Post*, a patron, correspondent, and reviewer of the later writers. He was also a lawyer and political figure, first as a Jacksonian Democrat and then as a free soiler (one who opposed the extension of slavery into the western territories). His poem "Thanatopsis" was published in 1817.

Thanatopsis

To him who in the love of Nature holds
Communion with her visible forms, she speaks
A various language; for his gayer hours
She has a voice of gladness, and a smile
And eloquence of beauty, and she glides
Into his darker musings, with a mild
And healing sympathy, that steals away
Their sharpness, ere he is aware. When thoughts
Of the last bitter hour come like a blight
Over thy spirit, and sad images
Of the stern agony, and shroud, and pall,
And breathless darkness, and the narrow house,
Make thee to shudder, and grow sick at heart;—
Go forth under the open sky, and list
To Nature's teachings, while from all around—
Earth and her waters, and the depths of air—
Comes a still voice—Yet a few days, and thee
The all-beholding sun shall see no more
In all his course; nor yet in the cold ground,
Where thy pale form was laid, with many tears,
Nor in the embrace of ocean, shall exist
Thy image. Earth, that nourished thee, shall claim
Thy growth, to be resolved to earth again,
And, lost each human trace, surrendering up
Thine individual being, shalt thou go
To mix forever with the elements;
To be a brother to the insensible rock,
And to the sluggish clod, which the rude swain
Turns with his share, and treads upon. The oak
Shall send his roots abroad, and pierce thy mould.
Yet not to thine eternal resting-place
Shalt thou retire alone, nor couldst thou wish
Couch more magnificent. Thou shalt lie down
With patriarchs of the infant world,—with kings,
The powerful of the earth,—the wise, the good,
Fair forms, and hoary seers of ages past,
All in one mighty sepulchre. The hills
Rock-ribbed and ancient as the sun; the vales
Stretching in pensive quietness between;
The venerable woods—rivers that move
In majesty, and the complaining brooks
That make the meadows green; and, poured round all,
Old Ocean's gray and melancholy waste,—
Are but the solemn decorations all
Of the great tomb of man! . . . [8]

Main theme?

_____

_____

_____

D John Greenleaf Whittier, a lifelong Quaker and abolitionist (proponent of the abolition of slavery) from New England was also a newspaper editor, anti-slavery organizer and political candidate, and much read poet. His best known poem was probably "The Barefoot Boy" published in 1855, which was less ethereal and more politically pointed than "Thanatopsis," but drew from the same supply of ideas as Emerson, Thoreau, and Bryant.

The Barefoot Boy

Blessings on thee, little man,
Barefoot boy, with cheek of tan!
With thy turned-up pantaloons,
And thy merry whistled tunes;
With thy red lip, redder still
Kissed by strawberries on the hill;
With the sunshine on thy face,
Through thy torn brim's jaunty grace;
From my heart I give thee joy,—
I was once a barefoot boy!
Prince thou art,—the grown-up man
Only is republican.
Let the million-dollared ride!
Barefoot, trudging at his side,
Thou hast more than he can buy
In the reach of ear and eye,—
Outward sunshine, inward joy:
Blessings on thee, barefoot boy!

Oh for boyhood's painless play,
Sleep that wakes in laughing day,
Health that mocks the doctor's rules,
Knowledge never learned of schools,
Of the wild bee's morning chase,
Of the wild-flower's time and place,
Flight of fowl and habitude
Of the tenants of the wood;
How the tortoise bears his shell,
How the woodchuck digs his cell,
And the ground-mole sinks his well;
How the robin feeds her young,
How the oriole's nest is hung;
Where the whitest lilies blow,
Where the freshest berries grow,
Where the ground-nut trails its vine,
Where the wood-grape's clusters shine;

Of the black wasp's cunning way,
Mason of his walls of clay,
And the architectural plans
Of gray hornet artisans!
For, eschewing books and tasks,
Nature answers all he asks;
Hand in hand with her he walks,
Face to face with her he talks,
Part and parcel of her joy,—
Blessings on the barefoot boy! . . .
Cheerily, then, my little man,
Live and laugh, as boyhood can!
Though the flinty slopes be hard,
Stubble-speared the new-mown sward,
Every mom shall lead thee through
Fresh baptisms of the dew;
Every evening from thy feet
Shall the cool wind kiss the heat:
All too soon these feet must hide
In the prison cells of pride,
Lose the freedom of the sod,
Like a colt's for work be shod,
Made to tread the mills of toil,
Up and down in ceaseless moil:
Happy if their track be found
Never on forbidden ground;
Happy if they sink not in
Quick and treacherous sands of sin.
Ah! that thou couldst know thy joy,
Ere it passes, barefoot boy![9]

Main theme?

_____

_____

_____

E   There is none of the longing for innocence in Edgar Allan Poe's "The Raven" (1845) that we found in Whittier's "Barefoot Boy," in part because Poe's childhood and adult experiences were harsh. Poe (1809–1849) was orphaned at 3 and raised by a relative in Richmond. He briefly attended the University of Virginia and later West Point and lived on his meager earnings as a writer in New York City, Philadelphia, and Baltimore. His short stories and poetry were filled with ironic twists and emotional agony, the dark side of the nature worship and idealism of middle-period literature.

The Raven

Once upon a midnight dreary, while I pondered, weak and weary,
Over many a quaint and curious volume of forgotten lore—
While I nodded, nearly napping, suddenly there came a tapping,
As of some one gently rapping—rapping at my chamber door.

"'Tis some visitor," I muttered, "tapping at my chamber door—
Only this and nothing more."

Ah, distinctly I remember, it was in the bleak December,
And each separate dying ember wrought its ghost upon the floor.
Eagerly I wished the morrow;—vainly I had sought to borrow
From my books surcease of sorrow—sorrow for the lost Lenore—
For the rare and radiant maiden whom the angels name Lenore—
Nameless here for evermore.

And the silken sad uncertain rustling of each purple curtain
Thrilled me—filled me with fantastic terrors never felt before;
So that now, to still the beating of my heart, I stood repeating
"'Tis some visitor entreating entrance at my chamber door—
Some late visitor entreating entrance at my chamber door—
This it is and nothing more."

Presently my soul grew stronger; hesitating then no longer,
"Sir," said I, "or Madam, truly your forgiveness I implore;
But the fact is I was napping, and so gently you came rapping,
And so faintly you came tapping—tapping at my chamber door,
That I scarce was sure I heard you"—here I opened wide the door:—
Darkness there, and nothing more. . . .

Open here I flung the shutter, when, with many a flirt and flutter,
In there stepped a stately Raven of the saintly days of yore.
Not the least obeisance made he; not an instant stopped or stayed he;
But, with mien of lord or lady, perched above my chamber door—
Perched upon a bust of Pallas just above my chamber door—
Perched, and sat, and nothing more . . .

"Prophet!" said I, "thing of evil!—prophet still, if bird or devil!—
Whether Tempter sent, or whether tempest tossed thee here ashore,
Desolate yet all undaunted, on this desert land enchanted—
On this Home by Horror haunted—tell me truly I implore—
Is there—is there balm in Gilead? tell me—tell me, I implore!"
Quoth the Raven, "Nevermore."

"Prophet!" said I, "thing of evil—prophet still, if bird or devil!
By that Heaven that bends above us—by that God we both adore—
Tell this soul with sorrow laden if, within the distant Aidenn,
It shall clasp a sainted maiden whom the angels name Lenore.
Clasp a rare and radiant maiden whom the angels name Lenore."
Quoth the Raven, "Nevermore."

"Be that word our sign of parting, bird or fiend!" I shrieked, upstarting—
"Get thee back into the tempest and the Night's Plutonian shore!
Leave no black plume as a token of that lie thy soul hath spoken!
Leave my loneliness unbroken!—quit the bust above my door!

> Take thy beak from out my heart, and take thy form from off my door!"
> Quoth the Raven, "Nevermore." . . . [10]

Main theme?

_____

_____

_____

Literary Texts as Versions of Secondary Sources

Another of the themes in this era's rich outpouring of literary works was time—in particular the relations between present and past, on the one hand, and present and future on the other. As Walt Whitman wrote, near the end of his life, in a short poem "To The Historian": "You who celebrate bygones/Who have explored the outward, the surfaces of the races . . . / Who have treated of man as the creature of politics, aggregates, rulers and priests/I, habitan of the Alleghenies, treating of him as he is in himself in his own rights/Pressing the pulse of the life that has seldom exhibited itself . . . /I project the history of the future."[11] Whitman warned the historian that he was not the best interpreter of the inner life of people in the past. So, too, Thoreau at Walden saw himself in the stream of history rather than an isolated individual at the edge of the settlements: "I dwelt nearer to those parts of the universe and to those eras on history which had most attracted me."[12]

The connection between the creativity of the author of the historical novel, the imagination of the reader, and the plastic nature of history (after all, we know so little about what really happened), allows modern historical novelists to draw upon history for plot, setting, and dialogue. Buyers of historical novels today find that the evocative detail, the conversations, and the dramatic personal touches in the novel—even those that are invented or based very loosely on ascertainable fact—make far more attractive reading and more persuasive history than the ponderous tomes of the scholars. Some scholars agree with this estimate, and have added dialogue and detail beyond what the surviving primary sources include.[13]

In the middle period, novelists were eager readers of historians, and used history as the background for their short stories and novels. The past fascinated novelists like Cooper and Hawthorne, the former because he was reared in a New York frontier town founded by his father, the latter because he grew up in Salem, Massachusetts, surrounded by history. The way in which these two novelists handled historical themes offers us another window in middle period America, and another chance to practice our skills at reading texts.

Exercise 2: The Historical Novel as Secondary Source

Although we cannot take literally as secondary sources what the historical novelists of the middle period wrote, we can appreciate their insight into human nature and their ability to describe scenes. In the following selections from Cooper and Hawthorne, the author talks about the historical novel and then puts their ideas into practice. Read the selections and then answer the questions that follow.

A Cooper (1789–1851) grew up in the town that his father laid out by Lake Otsego, New York. He was to become the first of the American-born popular novelists. Many of the major characters in *The Pioneers* (1823), the original of Cooper's so-called "leatherstocking tales" about the life of woodsman, Indian fighter, and hunter Natty Bumppo (the hero of *The*

Pathfinder, The Deerslayer, and *The Last of the Mohicans*), came directly from Cooper's youthful experiences. The character Judge Marmaduke Temple was in fact a poorly disguised portrait of Cooper's father, William, and the young heroine, Elizabeth, of his sister. Cooper's powers of description and plot development were almost unrivaled in his time, and made the book a "best seller" that rivaled Sir Walter Scott's novels. In the first passage, Judge Temple has just arrived at the place where he will build his town. In the second, five years later, the landscape has undergone great changes. Read the two passages and answer the questions that follow.

The side of the mountain, on which our travellers were journeying, though not absolutely perpendicular, was so steep as to render great care necessary in descending the rude and narrow path, which, in that early day, wound along the precipices. . . . time was given Elizabeth to dwell on a scene which was so rapidly altering under the hands of man, that it only resembled, in its outlines, the picture she had so often studied, with delight, in childhood. Immediately beneath them lay a seeming plain, glittering, without inequality, and buried in mountains. The latter were precipitous, especially on the side of the plain, and chiefly in forest. Here and there the hills fell away in long, low points, and broke the sameness of the outline; or setting to the long and wide field of snow, which, without house, tree, fence, or any other fixture, resembled so much spotless cloud settled to the earth. A few dark and moving spots were, however, visible on the even surface, which the eye of Elizabeth knew to be so many sleighs going their several ways, to or from the village. On the western border of the plain, the mountains, though equally high, were less precipitous, and as they receded, opened into irregular valleys and glens, or were formed into terraces and hollows that admitted of cultivation. Although the evergreens still held dominion over many of the hills that rose on this side of the valley, yet the undulating outlines of the distant mountains, covered with forests of beech and maple, gave a relief to the eye, and the promise of a kinder soil. Occasionally, spots of white were discoverable amidst the forests of the opposite hills, which announced, by the smoke that curled over the tops of the trees, the habitations of man, and the commencement of agriculture. These spots were, sometimes, by the aid of united labour, enlarged into what were called settlements; but more frequently were small and insulated; though so rapid were the changes, and so persevering the labors of those who had cast their fortunes on the success of the enterprise, that it was not difficult for the imagination of Elizabeth to conceive they were enlarging under her eye, while she was gazing, in mute wonder, at the alterations that a few short years had made in the aspect of the country. The points on the western side of this remarkable plain, on which no plant had taken root, were both larger and more numerous than those on its eastern, and one in particular thrust itself forward in such a manner, as to form beautifully curved bays of snow on either side. On its extreme end an oak stretched forward, as if to overshadow, with its branches, a spot which its roots were forbidden to enter. It had released itself from the thraldom, that a growth of centuries had imposed on the branches of the surrounding forest trees, and threw its gnarled and fantastic arms abroad, in the wildness of liberty. A dark spot of a few acres in extent at the southern extremity of this beautiful flat, and immediately under the feet of our travellers, alone showed, by its rippling surface, and the vapors which exhaled from it, that what at first might seem a plain, was one of the mountain lakes, locked in the frosts of winter. A narrow current rushed impetuously from its bosom at the open place we have mentioned, and was to be traced, for miles, as it wound its way towards the south through the real valley, by its borders of hemlock and pine, and by the vapour which arose from its warmer surface into the chill atmosphere of the hills. The banks of this lovely basin, at its outlet, or southern end, were steep but not high, and in that direction the land continued, far as the eye could reach, a narrow but graceful valley, along which the settlers had scattered their humble habitations, with a profusion that bespoke the quality of the soil, and the comparative facilities of intercourse. Immediately on the bank of the lake and at its foot, stood the village of Templeton. It consisted of some fifty buildings, including those of every description, chiefly built of wood, and which, in their architecture, bore no great marks of taste, but which also, by the unfinished appearance of most of the dwellings, indicated the hasty manner of their construction. To the eye, they presented a variety of colours. A few were white in both front and rear, but more bore that expensive color on their fronts only, while their economical but ambitious owners had covered the remaining sides of the edifices, with a dingy red. One or two were slowly assuming the russet of age; while the uncovered beams that were to be seen through the broken windows of their second stories, showed, that either the taste, or the vanity of their proprietors, had led them to undertake a task, which they were unable to accomplish. The whole were grouped in a manner that aped the streets of a city, and were evidently so arranged, by the directions of one, who looked to the wants of posterity, rather than to the convenience of the present incumbents. . . .

Five years had wrought greater changes, than a century would produce in countries, where time and labour have given permanency to the works of man. To the young hunter and the Judge the scene had less novelty; though none ever emerge from the dark forests of that mountain, and witness the glorious scenery of that beauteous valley, as it bursts unexpectedly upon them, without a feeling of delight. The former cast one admiring glance from north to south, and sunk his face, again, beneath the folds of his coat; while the latter contemplated, with philanthropic pleasure, the prospect of affluence and comfort, that was expanding around him; the result of his own enterprise, and, much of it, the fruits of his own industry.[14]

How does Cooper initially characterize the landscape? What mood did he create?

_____

_____

How had the landscape changed over the course of years? What was the cause of the change?

_____

_____

By the end of the book, the old hunter, Natty Bumppo, has violated the laws that Judge Temple has helped to pass. Natty finds that he must once again go west. The scene has all the sentimentality and moralism we have come to expect from the middle-period writers, but it also has a historical message.

"Don't fear for the Leather-stocking, children; God will see that his days be provided for, and his ind happy. I know you mean all for the best, but our ways doesn't agree. I love the woods, and ye relish the face of man; I eat when hungry and drink when a-dry, and ye keep stated hours and rules; nay, nay, you even over-feed the dogs, lad, from pure kindness; and hounds should be gaunty to run well. The meanest of God's creaters be made for some use, and I'm form'd for the wilderness; if ye love me, let me go where my soul craves to be ag'in!"

The appeal was decisive; and not another word of entreaty, for him to remain, was then uttered; but Elizabeth bent her head to her bosom and wept, while her husband dashed away the tears from his eyes, and, with hands that almost refused to perform their office, he produced his pocket-book, and extended a parcel of bank-notes to the hunter.

"Take these," he said, "at least, take these; secure them about your person, and, in the hour of need, they will do you good service."

The old man took the notes, and examined them with a curious eye.

"This, then, is some of the new-fashioned money that they've been making at Albany, out of paper! It can't be worth much to they that hasn't larning! No, no, lad—take back the stuff; it will do me no sarvice. I took kear to get all the Frenchman's powder, afore he broke up, and they say lead grows where I'm going. It isn't even fit for wads, seeing that I use none but leather!—Madam Effingham, let an old man kiss your hand, and wish God's choicest blessings on you and your'n."

"Once more let me beseech you, stay!" cried Elizabeth. "Do not, Leather-stocking, leave me to grieve for the man who has twice rescued me from death, and who has served those I love so faithfully. For my sake, if not for your own, stay. I shall see you, in those frightful dreams that still haunt my nights, dying in poverty and age, by the side of those terrific beasts you slew. There will be no evil that sickness, want, and solitude can inflict, that my fancy will not conjure as your fate. Stay with us, old man; if not for your own sake, at least for ours."

"Such thoughts and bitter dreams, Madame Effingham," returned the hunter, solemnly, "will never haunt an innocent parson long. They'll pass away with God's pleasure. And if the cat-a-mounts be yet brought to your eyes in sleep, 'tis not for my sake, but to show you the power of him that led me there to save you. Trust in God, Madam, and your honourable husband, and the thoughts for an old man like me can never be long nor bitter. I pray that the Lord will keep you in mind—the Lord that lives in clearings as well as in the wilderness—and bless you, and all that belong to you, from this time, till the great day when the whites shall meet the red-skins in judgment, and justice shall be the law, and not power."

Elizabeth raised her head, and offered her colourless cheek to his salute; when he lifted his cap, and touched it respectfully. His hand was grasped with convulsive fervour by the youth, who continued silent. The hunter prepared himself for his journey, drawing his belt tighter, and wasting his moments in the little reluctant movements of a sorrowful departure. Once or twice he essayed to speak, but a rising in his throat prevented it. At length he shouldered his rifle, and cried, with a clear huntsman's call, that echoed through the woods—

"He-e-e-re, he-e-e-re, pups—away, dogs, away;—ye'll be foot-sore afore ye see the ind of the journey!"

The hounds leaped from the earth at this cry, and, scenting around the graves and the silent pair, as if conscious of their own destination, they followed humbly at the heels of their master. A short pause succeeded, during which even the youth concealed his face on his grandfather's tomb. When the pride of manhood, however, had suppressed the feelings of nature, he turned to renew his entreaties, but saw that the cemetery was occupied only by himself and his wife.

"He is gone!" cried Effingham.

Elizabeth raised her face, and saw the old hunter standing, looking back for a moment, on the verge of the wood. As he caught their glances, he drew his hard hand hastily across his eyes again, waved it on high for an adieu, and, uttering a forced cry to his dogs, who were crouching at his feet, he entered the forest.

This was the last that they ever saw of the Leather-stocking, whose rapid movements preceded the pursuit which Judge Temple both ordered and conducted. He had gone far towards the setting sun,—the foremost in that band of Pioneers, who are opening the way for the march of the nation across the continent.[15]

According to Cooper, what personal values does Natty have that reflect an older way of life?

How does Natty explain why he must leave? What does that suggest about the change from frontier to settlement in American history?

B Hawthorne (1804–1864) was born in Salem and spent much of his life there. His first major work, *The Scarlet Letter* (1850), drew upon the records of the town as well as its ambiance as one of the first Puritan settlements in New England. In the first reading from that novel, Hawthorne discusses the impact of history on him, and by implication, on everyone.

This old town of Salem—my native place, though I have dwelt much away from it, both in boyhood and maturer years—possesses, or did possess, a hold on my affections, the force of which I have never realized during my seasons of actual residence here. Indeed, so far as its physical aspect is concerned, with its flat, unvaried surface, covered chiefly with wooden houses, few or none of which pretend to architectural beauty,—its irregularity, which is neither picturesque nor quaint; but only tame,—its long and lazy street, lounging wearisomely through the whole extent of the peninsula, with Gallows Hill and New Guinea at one end, and a view of the alms-house at the other,—such being the features of my native town, it would be quite as reasonable to form a sentimental attachment to a disarranged checkerboard. And yet, though invariably happiest elsewhere, there is within me a feeling for old Salem, which, in lack of a better phrase, I must be content to call affection. The sentiment is probably assignable to the deep and aged roots which my family has struck into the soil. It is now nearly two centuries and a quarter since the original Briton, the earliest emigrant of my name, made his appearance in the wild and forest-bordered settlement, which has since become a city. And here his descendants have been born and died, and have mingled their earthy substance with the soil; until no small portion of it must necessarily be akin to the mortal frame wherewith, for a little while, I walk the streets. In part, therefore, the attachment which I speak of is the mere sensuous sympathy of dust for dust. Few of my countrymen can know what it is; nor, as frequent transplantation is perhaps better for the stock, need they consider it desirable to know.

But the sentiment has likewise its moral quality. The figure of that first ancestor, invested by family tradition with a dim and dusky grandeur, was present to my boyish imagination, as far back as I can remember. It still haunts me, and induces a sort of home-feeling with the past, which I scarcely claim in reference to the present phase of the town. I seem to have a stronger claim to a residence here on account of this grave, bearded, sable-cloaked, and steeple-crowned progenitor,—who came so early, with his Bible and his sword, and trode the unworn street with such a stately port, and made so large a figure, as a man of war and peace,—a stronger claim than for myself, whose name is seldom heard and my face hardly known. He was a soldier, legislator, judge; he was a ruler in the Church; he had all the Puritanic traits, both good and evil. He was likewise a bitter persecutor; as witness the Quakers, who have remembered him in their histories, and relate an incident of his hard severity towards a woman of their sect, which will last longer, it is to be feared, than any record of his better deeds, although these were many. His son, too, inherited the persecuting spirit, and made himself so conspicuous in the martyrdom of the witches, that their blood may fairly be said to have left a stain upon him. So deep a stain, indeed, that his old dry bones, in the Charter Street burial-ground, must still retain it, if they have not crumbled utterly to dust! I know not whether these ancestors of mine bethought themselves to repent, and ask pardon of Heaven for their cruelties; or whether they are now groaning under the heavy consequences of them, in another state of being. At all events, I, the present writer, as their representative, hereby take shame upon myself for their sakes, and pray that any curse incurred by them—as I have heard, and as the dreary and unprosperous condition of the race, for many a long year back, would argue to exist—may be now and henceforth removed.

Doubtless, however, either of these stern and black-browed Puritans would have thought it quite a sufficient retribution for his sins, that, after so long a lapse of years, the old trunk of the family tree, with so much venerable moss upon it, should have borne, as its topmost bough, an idler like myself. No aim, that I have ever cherished, would they recognize as laudable; no success of mine—if my life, beyond its domestic scope, had ever been brightened by success—would they deem otherwise than worthless, if not positively disgraceful. "What is he?" murmurs one gray shadow of my forefathers to the other. "A writer of story-books! What kind of a business in life,—what mode of glorifying God, or being serviceable to mankind in his day and generation,—may that be? Why, the degenerate fellow might as well have been a fiddler!" Such are the compliments bandied between my great-grandsires and myself, across the gulf of time! And yet, let them scorn me as they will, strong traits of their nature have intertwined themselves with mine.[16]

How did Salem exert its hold on the author? _____
_____
_____

What does he say about his family tradition, in particular its impact on his moral views?
_____
_____

What were his ancestors like? _____
_____
_____

How does he show the difference between their world and his? _____
_____
_____

In the book, Reverend Arthur Dimmesdale has an adulterous affair with young Hester Prynne. Their liaison results in a child. Dimmesdale does not admit his guilt when Hester is shamed and forced to wear a red letter A on her clothing, but seven years later, as he is about to die, he makes a public confession of his sins and seeks her forgiveness. Before he dies he climbs atop the town scaffold and bears his breast literally as well as figuratively. What followed his revelation and death forms the closing passages of the book, and again allows Hawthorne to think about how history works.

After many days, when time sufficed for the people to arrange their thoughts in reference to the foregoing scene, there was more than one account of what had been witnessed on the scaffold.

Most of the spectators testified to having seen, on the breast of the unhappy minister, a SCARLET LETTER—the very semblance of that worn by Hester Prynne—imprinted in the flesh. As regarded its origin, there were various explanations, all of which must necessarily have been conjectural. Some affirmed that the Reverend Mr. Dimmesdale, on the very day when Hester Prynne first wore her ignominious badge, had begun a course of penance,—which he afterwards, in so many futile methods, followed out,—by inflicting a hideous torture on himself. Others contended that the stigma had not been produced until a long time subsequent, when old Roger Chillingworth, being a potent necromancer, had caused it to appear, through the agency of magic and poisonous drugs. Others, again,—and those best able to appreciate the minister's peculiar sensibility, and the wonderful operation of his spirit upon the body,—whispered their belief, that the awful symbol was the effect of the ever active tooth of remorse, gnawing from the inmost heart outwardly, and at last manifesting Heaven's dreadful judgment by the visible presence of the letter. The reader may choose among these theories. We have thrown all the light we could acquire upon the portent, and would gladly, now that it has done its office, erase its deep print out of our own brain; where long meditation has fixed it in very undesirable distinctness.

It is singular, nevertheless, that certain persons, who were spectators of the whole scene, and professed never once to have removed their eyes from the Reverend Mr. Dimmesdale, denied that there was any mark whatever on his breast, more than on a new-born infant's. Neither, by their report, had his dying words acknowledged, nor even remotely implied, any, the slightest connection, on his part, with the guilt for which Hester Prynne had so long worn the scarlet letter. According to these highly respectable witnesses, the minister, conscious that he was dying,—conscious, also, that the reverence of the multitude placed him already among saints and angels,—had desired, by yielding up his breath in the arms of that fallen woman, to express to the world how utterly nugatory is the choicest of man's own righteousness. After exhausting life in his efforts for mankind's spiritual goods, he had made the manner of his death a parable, in order to impress on his admirers the mighty and mournful lesson, that, in the view of Infinite Purity, we are sinners all alike. It was to teach them, that the holiest among us has but attained so far above his fellows as to discern more clearly the Mercy which looks down, and repudiate more utterly the phantom of human merit, which would look aspiringly upward. Without disputing a truth so momentous, we must be allowed to consider this version of Mr. Dimmesdale's story as only an instance of that stubborn fidelity with which a man's friends—and especially a clergyman's—will sometimes uphold his character; when proofs, clear as the mid-day sunshine on the scarlet letter, establish him a false and sin-stained creature of the dust.

The authority which we have chiefly followed—a manuscript of old date, drawn up from the verbal testimony of individuals, some of whom had known Hester Prynne, while others had heard the tale from contemporary witnesses—fully confirms the view taken in the foregoing pages. Among many morals which press upon us from the poor minister's miserable experience, we put only this into a sentence:—"Be true! Be true! Show freely to the world, if not your worst, yet some trait whereby the worst may be inferred!"[17]

How did the people who watched the confession and death of Dimmesdale variously report it?

_____

_____

_____

What does Hawthorne suggest about the way that people make sense of the events of their lives? _____

_____

_____

Looking for the Argument in Literary Texts

Some of the best known authors of the middle period preferred nonfiction writing to fiction. These were the so-called Transcendentalists. They were a group of writers, philosophers, and reformers who saw a close connection between literary work and the perfection of society. Indeed, the movement began in the writings of Unitarian ministers like William Ellery Channing. He and those who followed him believed that people had within them a spark of the divine; as he wrote in 1819, "To me it seems that the soul, in all its higher actions . . . in its aspirations after a pure and unknown joy, and especially in disinterestedness, in the spirit of self-sacrifice, and in enlightened devotion, has a character of infinity."[18] The Transcendentalists would come to include in their number utopian reformers like George Ripley and Amos Bronson Alcott, founders of Brook Farm, literary giants like Emerson, and social reformers like Orestes Brownson and Theodore Parker. But above all, the movement was a literary one.

Exercise 3: Reading Texts as Political Statements

Can we read texts to unravel some of the cultural work of the Transcendentalist writers? As George Ripley, an essayist, philosopher, and promoter of reform in the middle period, wrote of the Transcendentalist authors, they "value literature not as an end, but as an instrument to help the solution of problems, that haunt and agitate the soul."[19] Many Transcendentalist writings openly advocated some kind of reform.

A Because of its often experimental view of the world, its belief in equality, and its love of creativity and learning, Transcendentalism was a more welcoming place to women of intellect than any other movement in American culture at that time. Women were not allowed to enter the professions except school teaching, and then only at the elementary level. They could not vote nor hold public office. They were not admitted to colleges. A few, like Sarah Margaret Fuller (1810–1850), from a middle class Newburyport, Massachusetts, family, were given a classical education at home, but that only whetted their appetite for intellectual stimulation. Fuller went on to be an editor of the Transcendentalist literary magazine *The Dial*, a critic and essayist herself, and one of the most respected minds of her circle. She died in a shipwreck with her husband and child, returning from Europe, in 1850. A selection from an article for *The Dial* entitled "The Great Law Suit" (1843) follows. Read it and then in your own words restate its argument.

> Male and female represent the two sides of the great radical dualism. But, in fact, they are perpetually passing into one another. Fluid hardens to solid, solid rushes to fluid. There is no wholly masculine man, no purely feminine woman.
>
> History jeers at the attempts of physiologists to bind great original laws by the forms which flow from them. They make a rule; they say from observation, what can and cannot be. In vain! Nature provides exceptions to every rule. She sends women to battle, and sets Hercules spinning; she enables women to bear immense burdens, cold, and frost; she

enables the man, who feels material love, to nourish his infant like a mother. Of late she plays still gayer pranks. Not only she deprives organizations, but organs, of a necessary end. She enables people to read with the top of the head, and see with the pit of the stomach. Presently she will make a female Newton, and a male Syren.

Man partakes of the feminine in the Apollo, woman of the masculine as Minerva.

Let us be wise and not impede the soul. Let her work as she will. Let us have one creative energy, one incessant revelation. Let it take what form it will, and let us not bind it by the past to man or woman, black or white. Jove sprang from Rhea, Pallas from Jove. So let it be. . . .

[M]en do *not* look at both sides, and women must leave off asking them and being influenced by them, but retire within themselves, and explore the groundwork of being till they find their peculiar secret. Then when they come forth again, renovated and baptized, they will know how to turn all dross to gold, and will be rich and free though they live in a hut, tranquil, if in a crowd. Then their sweet singing shall not be from passionate impulse, but the lyrical overflow of a divine rapture, and a new music shall be elucidated from this many-chorded world. . . .

It is therefore that I would have woman lay aside all thought, such as she habitually cherishes, of being taught and led by men. I would have her, like the Indian girl, dedicate herself to the Sun, the Sun of Truth, and go no where if his beams did not make clear the path. I would have her free from compromise, from complaisance, from helplessness, because I would have her good enough and strong enough to love one and all beings, from the fulness, not the poverty of being. . . .[20]

Fuller's argument: _____

_____

_____

B Elizabeth Palmer Peabody (1804–1894) of Salem was another remarkable woman whose contributions to the movement were manifold. Related by marriage to Hawthorne and Horace Mann (the Massachusetts public school reformer), Peabody taught school (she introduced the first "kindergarten" classes in America), ran a bookshop, published *The Dial*, and contributed spirited articles to it. One of these concerned Brook Farm, and suggested how it might be turned into a truly communal establishment.

The plan of the Community, as an Economy, is in brief this; for all who have property to take stock, and receive a fixed interest thereon; then to keep house or board in commons, as they shall severally desire, at the cost of provisions purchased at wholesale, or raised on the farm; and for all to labor in community, and be paid at a certain rate an hour, choosing their own number of hours, and their own kind of work. With the results of this labor, and their interest, they are to pay their board, and also purchase whatever else they require at cost, at the warehouses of the Community, which are to be filled by the Community as such. To perfect this economy, in the course of time they must have all trades, and all modes of business carried on among themselves, from the lowest mechanical trade, which contributes to the health and comfort of life, to the finest art which adorns it with food or drapery for the mind.

All labor, whether bodily or intellectual, is to be paid at the same rate of wages; on the principle, that as the labor becomes merely bodily, it is a greater sacrifice to the individual laborer, to give his time to it; because time is desirable for the cultivation of the intellect, in exact proportion to ignorance. Besides, intellectual labor involves in itself higher pleasures, and is more its own reward, than bodily labor . . .

Besides, after becoming members of this community, none will be engaged merely in bodily labor. The hours of labor for the Association will be limited by a general law, and can be curtailed at the will of the individual still more; and means will be given to all for intellectual improvement and for social intercourse, calculated to refine and expand. The hours redeemed from labor by community, will not be reapplied to the acquisition of wealth, but to the production of intellectual goods. This community aims to be rich, not in the metallic representative of wealth, but in the wealth itself, which money should represent; namely, LEISURE TO LIVE IN ALL THE FACULTIES OF THE SOUL. As a community, it will traffic with the world at large, in the products of Agricultural labor; and it will sell education to as many young persons as can be domesticated in the families, and enter into the common life with their own children. In the end, it hopes to be enabled to provide—not only all the necessaries, but all the elegances desirable for bodily and for spiritual health; books, apparatus, collections for science, works of art, means of beautiful amusement. These things are to be common to all; and thus that object, which alone gilds and refines the passion for individual accumulation, will no longer exist for desire, and whenever the Sordid passion appears, it will be seen in its naked selfishness. In its ultimate success, the community will realize all the ends which selfishness seeks, but involved in spiritual blessings, which only greatness of soul can aspire after.[21]

Peabody's argument: _____

_____

_____

C Theodore Parker (1810–1860) was another of the crusading Transcendentalists. A minister who thought that Christianity was a platform for the reform of society, he took on all comers. His series of sermons on the abuses of the working people of Boston, in the 1840s, caused a sensation. Below is an excerpt from one of the sermons, "A Sermon of Merchants," delivered in 1846 and later published in 1852.

. . . In virtue of its strength and position, this class is the controlling one in politics. It mainly enacts the laws of this State and the nation; makes them serve its turn. Acting consciously or without consciousness, it buys up legislators when they are in the market; breeds them when the market is bare. It can manufacture governors, senators, judges, to suit its purposes, as easily as it can make cotton cloth. It pays them money and honors; pays them for doing its work, not another's. It is fairly and faithfully represented by them. Our popular legislators are made in its image; represent its wisdom, foresight, patriotism and conscience. Your Congress is its mirror.

This class is the controlling one in the churches, none the less, for with us fortunately the churches have no existence independent of the wealth and knowledge of the people. In the same way it buys up the clergymen, hunting them out all over the land; the clergymen who will do its work, putting them in comfortable places. It drives off such as interfere with its work, saying, "Go starve, you and your children!" It raises or manufactures others to suit its taste.

The merchants build mainly the churches, endow theological schools; they furnish the material sinews of the church. Hence metropolitan churches are in general as much commercial as the shops . . .

This class owns the machinery of society, in great measure,—the ships, factories, shops, water privileges, houses and the like. This brings into their employment large masses of working men, with no capital but muscles or skill. The law leaves the employed at the employer's mercy. Perhaps this is unavoidable. One wishes to sell his work dear, the other to get it cheap as he can. It seems to me no law can regulate this matter, only conscience, reason, the Christianity of the two parties. One class is strong, the other weak. In all encounters of these two, on the field of battle, or in the marketplace, we know the results: the weaker is driven to the wall. When the earthen and iron vessel strike together, we know beforehand which will go to pieces. The weaker class can seldom tell their tale, so their story gets often suppressed in the world's literature, and told only in outbreaks and revolutions. Still the bold men who wrote the Bible, Old Testament and New, have told truths on this theme which others dared not tell—terrible words which it will take ages of Christianity to expunge from the world's memory.

There is a strong temptation to use one's power of nature or position to the disadvantage of the weak. This may be done consciously or unconsciously. There are examples enough of both. Here the merchant deals in the labor of men. This is a legitimate article of traffic, and dealing in it is quite indispensable in the present condition of affairs. In the Southern States, the merchant, whether producer, manufacturer or trader, owns men and deals in their labor, or their bodies . . . That is slavery. He steals the man and his labor. Here it is possible to do a similar thing: I mean it is possible to employ men and give them just enough of the result of that labor to keep up a miserable life, and yourself take all the rest of the results of that labor. This may be done consciously or otherwise, but legally, without direct violence, and without owning the person. This is not slavery, though only one remove from it. This is the tyranny of the strong over the weak; the feudalism of money; stealing a man's work, and not his person. The merchants as a class are exposed to this very temptation. Sometimes it is yielded to. Some large fortunes have been made in this way. Let me mention some extreme cases; one from abroad, one near at home. In Belgium the average wages of men in manufactories is less than twenty-seven cents a day . . . How much better off are many women in Boston who gain their bread by the needle? yes, a large class of women in all our great cities? The ministers of the poor can answer that; your police can tell of the direful crime to which necessity sometimes drives women whom honest labor cannot feed! . . .

Then, too, there is the temptation to abuse their political power to the injury of the nation, to make laws which seem good for themselves, but are baneful to the people; to control the churches, so that they shall not dare rebuke the actual sins of the nation, or the sins of trade, and so the churches may be made apologizers for lowness, practising infidelity as their sacrament, but in the name of Christ and God. The ruling power in England once published a volume of sermons, as well as a book of prayers, which the clergy were commanded to preach. What sort of a gospel got recommended therein, you may easily guess; and what is recommended by the class of merchants in New England, you may as easily hear . . . [22]

Parker's argument: _____

_____

_____

The writers of the era stressed romantic individualism. One component of that ideology, as you can see from Parker's sermon, was the abhorrence of slavery. Slavery denied to people their individuality. Thoreau, Emerson, Whittier, and Parker, to name but a few, became strong advocates of emancipation of all the slaves. Hawthorne and others became "free soilers" who opposed the extension of slavery to the western territories of the nation. But abolitionists and free soilers in the antebellum years came up hard against a South almost solidly committed to its "peculiar institution" of slavery. In part, the South's commitment to slavery was a matter of measurable quantities rather than literary qualities—the numbers of slaves who lived in the South, the wealth the slaves represented to their masters, the profits of the cotton crop. Historians of the South are well aware of the importance of these numbers and the need to analyze them. To these skills we turn in Chapter Nine.

Notes

[1] Joyce Appleby, Lynn Hunt, Margaret Jacob, *Telling the Truth About History* (New York: W.W. Norton, 1994), 266.

[2] Richard D. Altick, *Lives and Letters: A History of Literary Biography in England and America* (New York: Knopf, 1965), xi, 429.

[3] Lewis Turco, *The Book of Literary Terms* (Hanover, N.H.: University Press of New England, 1999), 149, 156.

[4] Catherine Gallagher, "The History of Literary Criticism" in Thomas Bender and Carl E. Schorske, eds., *The American Academic Culture in Transition* (Princeton, N.J.: Princeton University Press, 1998), 156–157.

[5] Joseph Steven Buckminster, "The Dangers and Duties of Men of Letters," (1809) in Lewis P. Simpson, ed., *The Federalist Literary Mind* (Baton Rouge: Louisiana State University Press, 1962), 97.

[6] Ralph Waldo Emerson, *The American Scholar* (Boston, 1837).

[7] Henry David Thoreau, *Walden* [1854] in Owen Thomas, ed., *Walden and Civil Disobedience* (New York: Norton, 1966), 58–59, 187.

[8] William Cullen Bryant, "Thanatopsis," *North American Review* (September 1817).

[9] John Greenleaf Whittier, "The Barefoot Boy" [1855], *The Complete Poetical Works of John Greenleaf Whittier* (Boston: Houghton Mifflin, 1894), 396–397.

[10] Edgar Allan Poe, "The Raven," *New York Evening Mirror* January 29, 1845.

[11] Walt Whitman, "To The Historian" in *Leaves of Grass* ([1892] New York: New American Library, 1955), 32–33.

[12] Thoreau, *Walden*, 59.

[13] John Demos, "In Search of Reasons for Historians to Read Novels," *American Historical Review* 103 (1998), 1526–1529.

[14] James Fenimore Cooper, *The Pioneers* [1823], James Franklin Beard, ed., *The Writings of James Fenimore Cooper* (Albany: State University of New York Press, 1980), 39–41, 45–46.

[15] Ibid., 454–456.

[16] Nathaniel Hawthorne, *The Scarlet Letter* [1850], ed. Brian Harding (New York: Oxford University Press, 1990), 8–10.

[17] Ibid., 258-260.

[18] William Ellery Channing, "Likeness to God" (1819) in Perry Miller, ed., *The Transcendentalists: An Anthology* (Cambridge, Mass.: Harvard University Press, 1967), 24.

[19] George Ripley, quoted in the introduction to Miller, ed., *The Transcendentalists*, 2.

[20] Margaret Fuller, "The Great Law Suit" [1843] in Miller, ed., *The Transcendentalists*, 460, 461, 462.

[21] Elizabeth Palmer Peabody, "Plan of the West Roxbury Community" [1844] in Miller, ed. *The Transcendentalists*, 466–467.

[22] Theodore Parker, "A Sermon of Merchants" [1846] in Miller, ed., *The Transcendentalists*, 451, 452, 453.

9: Groups, Numbers, and Patterns in History

The Antebellum South

When you write a narrative, you tell a story. You need not decide whether your story is typical or try to compare the subject of your story to other subjects. You are free to ignore questions about larger trends in the past. If all historical writing were narrative in style, however, history would be a very narrow discipline. It would exclude analysis of groups, numbers, and patterns.

In ordinary speech we define *analysis* as the breaking apart of a whole to examine its parts. Analysis is the opposite of *synthesis*, the assembly of the many parts into a whole. Historians must do both analysis and synthesis to understand and explain what happened in the past. Historical analysis does not supplant or preclude narration but rather overlaps it.

History and the Social Sciences

Analytical writing about history is very popular among scholars today. In part this popularity results from the emergence of social history. Social history requires a keen appreciation of the role of groups in society, and social historians often use numerical methods to explain the dynamics of group formation and behavior. Social history also emphasizes long-term shifts in the shape and conduct of groups.

Analytical historical interpretations, including social history, would be impossible without the rise of the social sciences of sociology, economics, and cultural anthropology at the end of the nineteenth and the beginning of the twentieth centuries. Analytical historians are always borrowing concepts and methods from the social sciences. Although narrative historians ordinarily confine themselves to the language and ideas of the people they study—indeed, sometimes these historians' writings begin to resemble the prose style of their subjects—analytical historians reflect vogues in economic research, sociological concepts, and anthropological findings. Returning to the question posed in Chapter 2 of whether history is an art or a science, narrative historical writers would choose the former option, analytical historical writers the latter.

Groups

Narrative focuses on the uniqueness of particular people and events. Analysis requires you to think about similarities and connections among groups of people—for example, families, neighborhoods, communities, and voluntary associations—and groups of things—for example, prices, wages, import and export figures. You cannot find continuities or make comparisons unless you conceptualize history as group activity over time.

To frame analytical questions about how and why groups acted as they did, you must begin to think in terms of the characteristics that define a group. Certain characteristics are obvious to the observer. Other features are not so visible. They have to be found through research.

Exercise 1: What Makes a Group?

This exercise introduces the technique of grouping. Look around the classroom. The people in it can be sorted into different groups in a number of ways. In what four ways might you categorize your classmates?

1. _____
   _____
   _____

2. _____
   _____
   _____

3. _____
   _____
   _____

4. _____
   _____
   _____

Each of these four ways of sorting your class is based on a categorization that you formulated. Each of these categories divides one large group—your class—into smaller groups. Each smaller group is united by one or more salient characteristics. You may have used observable physical variables, like height, age, or gender, to arrange your groups, or selected groups on the basis of observed behavior—habits of dress, attentiveness in class, or personality traits. You may have recalled your classmates' participation in an event (for example, the grades they got on the last exam) to group them. To isolate and examine groups, historians employ categories based on social and economic status, age, and other population criteria, categories derived from time and place, and distinctions growing out of the behavior of their subjects.

Exercise 2: Studying Nearby Groups

You are surrounded by groups and no doubt belong to some. The United States is a nation of joiners. The groups you belong to are not mutually exclusive. They overlap, sometimes in harmony, sometimes in competition for your time and loyalty. One group we all belong to is our neighborhood. A neighborhood is both a group of people living in close proximity to each other and a group of dwellings. David E. Kyvig and Myron A. Marty have prepared a series of questions about neighborhoods for students in their *Nearby History: Exploring the Past Around You* (1982). These questions help you to turn something with which you are already familiar into a subject for historical study. Think about the neighborhood in which you were reared, or, alternatively, the one in which you now reside, and try to answer the following questions about it.

1. What are the boundaries of your home neighborhood? How are they defined? What distinguishes your neighborhood from those around it? _____
   _____
   _____

2. What is the central social focus of your neighborhood? Where do the people in it congregate? _____
   _____
   _____

3. How and why have the size and shape of your neighborhood changed over the years? Has the appearance or disappearance of buildings or open spaces during this time changed your neighborhood? _____
   _____
   _____

4. How do people in the neighborhood travel to work? What kinds of workplaces are there in the neighborhood? How have these changed over the years? _____
   _____
   _____

5. Who lives in the neighborhood? What family ties, religious ties, or ethnic ties predominate among these people? Have these characteristics changed? If so, how? _____
   _____
   _____

6. How does the neighborhood fit into the larger community (city, county, or other larger place)? What historical events brought people in the neighborhood together? What events caused them to divide among themselves? _____
   _____
   _____

By considering these questions, you have begun the analytical history of your neighborhood. Although you are telling its story, you cannot tell the story without focusing on groups and measuring changes in them.

Exercise 3: Identifying Groups in Historical Writing

Often, a historical account that appears to be purely narrative actually deals with groups, and analytical historians often use the writing of narrative historians to select appropriate groups for study. For this exercise, read the two following passages and underline the groups that the author discusses. Remember, a group can be a collection of persons or of things. We have underlined the first group in each passage to help you get started.

> **A** Demographic mobility was so much a part of life in the slaveholding South <u>that those who yearned for stability</u> were often frustrated. Complaints were most

common among the wives of slaveholders who missed the society they left. "I feel almost friendless," a Tennessee mistress wrote to her Virginia friend. "The intimacy of dear and loved relatives have been broken by the bitter pill of separation leaving a faint hope of meeting on earth. I feel exceedingly desolate and lonely." . . . It was women who most consistently protested the wandering ways of their slaveholding husbands. They wrote of their loneliness on the frontier, complained of being left alone for long stretches while their spouses searched for lands out west, and objected when the decision to move was announced.[1]

B [Visitors to free African-American communities on the coastal islands of Georgia and South Carolina during the Civil War] described ties between kin in different immediate families. "The country people" [one visitor observed] "regard their relations more than the city people; they often walk fifteen miles on a Saturday night to see a cousin." [Another visitor] agreed: "Their affection extends to the whole family. If a cousin is in want, they admit the claim [on them]." Other observers of the wartime Sea Islanders noticed binding ties between members of different immediate families.[2]

Numbers

Thinking about historical events in terms of groups of people or groups of things is the first step in writing analytically. The next step is to select precise measures of differences and similarities within and between groups and changes in group characteristics over time. The most precise measures of differences and changes are numerical—the analytical historian must use numbers.

Exercise 4: Hidden Counting

A vociferous critic of analytical writing once complained that only those things that cannot be counted are ever really important. This statement overlooks the fact that every historian—whether engaged in narration or analysis—resorts to hidden counting. The following two passages are filled with hidden *quantifiers*, words that indicate rates or quantity. Find them and underline them. We have underlined the first two quantifiers in each passage to get you started.

A Dueling was a vitally important institution in the antebellum South. The practice first appeared in <u>common</u> use in America among revolutionary war officers during the 1770s and <u>quickly</u> spread to the rest of the nation, but it retreated into the South by the early nineteenth century. It flourished in the slave states even though it was both against the law and widely condemned in public. Even in states without anti-dueling statutes common law prosecution was possible. But Southern prosecutors, unlike their Northern counterparts, rarely enforced laws against dueling. When a possibility of enforcement existed, duelists crossed borders [of states] or even dueled on borders in order to create just enough ambiguity in legal jurisdiction to discourage indictment. Even when duelists did come to trial, Southern juries almost never found them guilty. If dueling laws provided that public officers swear they had never fought duels, Southern legislatures routinely passed special exception laws.[3]

B Owners [of slaves in the antebellum South] had <u>various</u> methods of providing religious training. <u>Most</u> of them believed it "pernicious and evil" for slaves to preach at their own services or prayer meetings. Nevertheless, some permitted it. The master or overseer usually attended such meetings, as required by law—and the preacher, naturally, was a trusted slave. In a number of southern towns the bondsmen attended their own churches . . . controlled by a governing board of whites and served by a white pastor. . . . In the regions of small slaveholding, whites and blacks commonly belonged to the same churches; on the large plantations only the domestics accompanied their masters to worship. When there were mixed congregations the slaves sat in the galleries, or were grouped together at the rear. Sometimes they attended special services on Sunday afternoons.[4]

Quantification

No historian can avoid using words like *rise, fall, many,* and *few.* Analytical writers are especially open about and sophisticated in **quantification**, the measurement of trends or characteristics of data through mathematical methods. The particular method of calculation or measurement is called **statistics**. Statistical methods need not be difficult to understand.

Properties or characteristics of subjects like age, height, and sex are **variables**. They vary from person to person or from thing to thing. If we are looking at groups, we want to know the range and most common features of such variables within each group. Some types of historical evidence about groups lend themselves readily to counting.

Interval data such as wages, prices, population figures, and the number of homicides committed in a given period of time are inherently numerical. Your age and income are interval data. Interval data can be expressed in integers (whole numbers) and decimals. The most common statistical summary measure of interval data is the **mean**, or **average**. For example, to calculate the average number of slaves that each Georgia slaveholder possessed in 1850, the historian adds up the number of slaves recorded in the state by the U.S. census of 1850 and then divides that total by the number of slaveholders in the state, also recorded in the same census. An average can be misleading if "outliers"—cases on the extreme high or low end of the distribution of data—are too numerous or too scanty.

Nominal data (sometimes called **categorical data**), such as racial and ethnic categories, gender, and region, are less amenable than interval data to statistical manipulation. There is no inherent or measurable quantitative difference between red hair and black hair, for example. Even so, nominal data can still be counted. To measure the most important characteristics in a set of nominal data, the historian calculates the **mode**, the most common qualitative characteristic of the cases of that particular variable. To answer the question "Was the typical slave male or female," one would count the number of male slaves and compare that total to the number of female slaves. The gender with the larger count would be the mode. Modes can be calculated for any collection of nominal data.

Exercise 5: Recognizing Types of Data

The distinction between interval data and nominal data is basic to all quantification. With practice, you will easily recognize the difference. For this exercise, select any page of your textbook, and identify on it an example of interval data and an example of nominal data.

1. interval _____

_____

_____

2. nominal _____

_____

_____

Displaying Quantification: Tables

Analytical historians often integrate the results of their quantification into the body of their writing, instead of calling attention to percentages, averages, or other measures in any way. By incorporating numbers into their prose, these historians minimize the disruptive effect that their statistical calculations might have on the flow of their account. On other occasions, analytical historians interrupt their prose accounts with tables, figures, or other obtrusive forms of quantitative display. These quantitative displays can be compared in impact and function to long block quotations in a narrative. Both break the flow of the page in order to force the reader to pay attention to the evidence rather than to the argument. Behind each such quantitative exhibit is a twofold task: first, to give a full, clear, and informative presentation of the data; second, to spotlight the most important relationships within the data.

Tables summarize and tabulate the characteristics of variables—that which you are counting. Tables are appropriate for both interval and nominal data. They are always comparative—that is, they compare one variable against another or show how a single variable changes over time or place. One variable is displayed across the top or bottom of the table in a row or rows. The second variable is displayed down the table in columns. At the intersection of each column (reading up and down) and each row (reading from side to side) is a cell with an entry:

	Column 1	Column 2
Row 1	cell (entry)	cell (entry)
Row 2	cell (entry)	cell (entry)

If you were to analyze the entries in a two-by-two table (having two columns and two rows), you would compare the entries in the four cells. Your comparison would tell you how the row variables and the column variables relate to each other.

Some variables in our comparison are *dependent* variables and some are *independent* variables. The **dependent variables** are the phenomena that are our subject. In our analysis, we are trying to explain changes in dependent variables—that is, we are trying to find out what they depend on. The **independent variables** are what we look at to explain changes in the dependent variables. For example, the size of the antebellum cotton crop (the dependent variable) varied over time. To determine what might have caused that variation one might look at changes over the same span of time in *independent* variables such as the size of the labor force, the acreage devoted to cotton production, and the introduction of new techniques. The first two of those independent variables are interval data; the last is nominal data, for it is hard to quantify technological change (although one can quantify some of the results of new technologies).

Exercise 6: Reading Tables

Examine Tables A and B. Answer the questions after each of them.

Table A Cotton Production in the South, 1790–1860

Year	1790	1820	1840	1860
Cotton bales	4,000	73,222	1,347,098	3,841,416
Number of slaves	697,897	1,538,098	2,487,213	3,957,760

Source: Paul Boyer et al., *The Enduring Vision: A History of the American People* (Lexington, Mass.: D.C. Heath, 1990), 1:353.

1. What does Table A reveal about changes in the extent of cotton farming in the United States between 1790 and 1860? _____

   _____

   _____

2. What does it reveal about the number of slaves? _____

   _____

   _____

3. Are the two sets of data interval or nominal? _____

   _____

   _____

4. Do the two sets of data co-vary (that is, go up and down together)? _____

   _____

   _____

5. What does your answer to the previous question suggest about the use of slaves in cotton production? _____

   _____

Table B Life Expectancy of African-American Women

Period	Expectation of Life
1850–1860	27.8 years
1880–1900	25.0
1920–1930	34.4
1940–1950	55.6
1950–1960	66.6

Source: Reynolds Farley, *Growth of the Black Population* (Chicago: Markham, 1970), 58–75.

1. What was the change in life expectancy for African-American women between 1850–1860 and 1880–1900? _____

   _____

   _____

2. Between 1900 and 1960? _____

   _____

   _____

3. Are the data in the table interval or nominal? _____

   _____

   _____

4. What does the variation in the life-expectancy data before and immediately after the Civil War tell you about the problems faced by the newly freed slaves? _____

   _____

   _____

Displaying Quantification: Graphs

The data in graphs can always be given in table form, but graphs are much more visually dramatic. There are three common types of graphs: pie graph, bar graph, and line graph.

The **pie graph** is a circle with wedges representing the percentage that each group or category contributes to the whole. A pie graph divides up the total evidence into its parts. Pie graphs are excellent for cross-sectional displays that show the distribution of a single variable at any one time. They are often used to exhibit the proportion of the total vote that different political parties received in a given election year. Pie graphs may be used with nom-

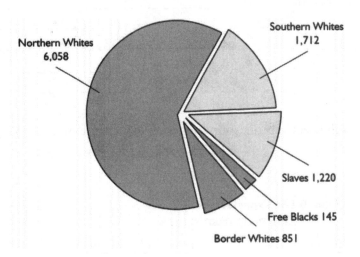

FIGURE 9.1 *Population of Males 10 to 49 Years of Age in 1860 (in thousands)*
Reproduced from Roger Ransom, *Conflict and Compromise: The Political Economy of Slavery, Emancipation, and the American Civil War,* (New York: Cambridge University Press, 1989).

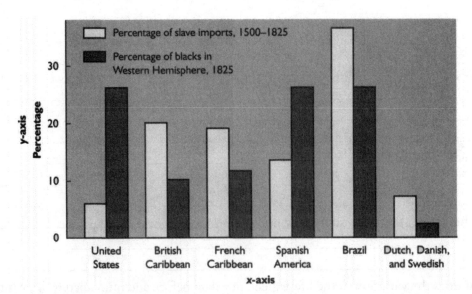

FIGURE 9.2 *Distribution of the Black Population (Slave and Free) in 1825 Compared to the Distribution of Slave Imports, 1500–1825*
Reproduced from Robert William Fogel and Stanley L. Engerman, *Time on the Cross: The Economics of American Negro Slavery* (New York: W.W. Norton & Company, 1974).

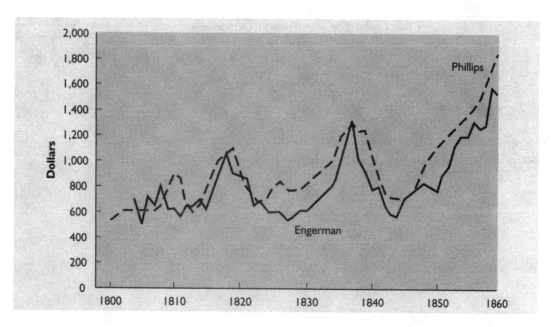

FIGURE 9.3 *Price of a Prime Male Slave, New Orleans, 1800–1860, according to estimates of economists Stanley Engerman and Stuart Phillips*
Reproduced from *Agricultural History* 62, no. 3 (Summer 1988), the Agricultural History Society.

inal or interval data but are most effective with nominal data. If you wanted to show the percentage of people of different ethnic origins in the United States in 1860, you would use a pie graph. Figure 9.1 shows a pie graph.

Bar graphs show quantities. The extent, amount, or number of each category or group is represented by a rectangle whose base is the *x*-axis of a graph. The *y*-axis of the graph depicts the quantity. For example, a bar graph would be an excellent display of the differences in slave populations of various regions. Bar graphs can be used with interval or nominal data but usually are chosen for interval data. Figure 9.2 shows a bar graph.

A **line graph** shows changes in data over time or compares changes in quantities against each other. A line graph begins with a scattergram, a plot of data points having an *x* and a *y* coordinate. If the *x* coordinate is "time"—that is, a year or some other period of time—and the *y* coordinate is the measure of some variable—such as the sale value of slaves in each time period—the line graph will show the change in the cost of buying a slave over time. Line graphs are commonly used to show the increase and decrease of profits of a business, rates of interest, and other economic data. When such data are plotted against time, the time periods must be uniform. Any two variables that have some relationship to each other can be made into a line graph. Line graphs work best with interval data, but they can also be used to plot changes in nominal data over time. Figure 9.3 shows a line graph.

Exercise 7: Graphing Data

Each of the following three data sets best lends itself to one kind of graph. Try your hand at turning each set into the appropriate sort of graph. You may need to do some experimenting with rough sketches to decide which type of graph best suits which data set. All data was taken from the Bureau of the Census, *Historical Statistics of the United States* (1975), Part 1.

**Data Set 1 The Population of the South,
1800–1860** (in thousands of people)

1800	2,622	1840	6,951
1810	3,461	1850	8,983
1820	4,419	1860	11,133
1830	5,708		

Your graph for Data Set 1 should show how dramatically population in the South was rising throughout this period. Use the space below to draw your graph.

**Data Set 2 Southern Population, by Age Group, in
1860** (in thousands of people)

Under 5	3,066
5–14	3,206
25–44	2,605
45–64	377
Over 64	44

Your graph for Data Set 2 should highlight the fact that the population of the South was predominantly under the age of 45 on the eve of the Civil War. Draw it below.

**Data Set 3 Rural/Urban Population
Distribution in the South,
1860** (in thousands of people)

Rural (percent)	Urban (percent)
10,791 (88%)	1,497 (12%)

Data Set 3 uses percentages. Does that suggest to you the type of graph that will best display the data? Draw it below.

Numbers over Time

On a graph, linear data may have a positive slope (Figure 9.4a) or a negative slope (Figure 9.4b). Inflation of prices for consumer goods is linear and positive, as is the rise in gross national product and population growth. Infant mortality rates and the size of families in modern societies are both linear and have a negative slope (meaning they decreased more or

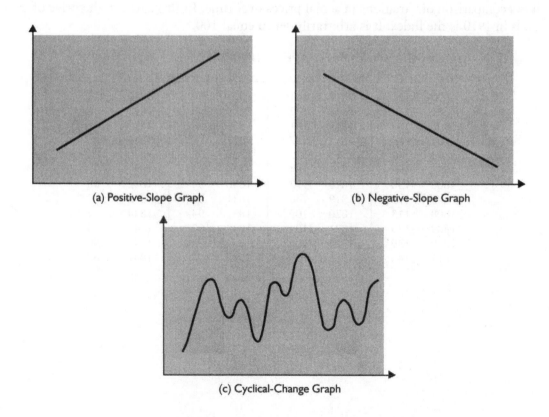

(a) Positive-Slope Graph

(b) Negative-Slope Graph

(c) Cyclical-Change Graph

FIGURE 9.4 *Line Graphs Indicating Three Kinds of Change over Time*

less steadily over time). Of course, the line is just an approximation of the actual distribution of the data. The line, like the words we use to describe what the line demonstrates—*increasing*, *growing*, *decreasing*, or *shrinking*—is just a device to depict a trend or direction of change over time.

The change in cotton production from 1790 to 1860 was linear. On a line graph, the plotted data would resemble a straight line with an upward slope. Production grew very quickly and steadily, despite several periods when demand fell sharply and cotton prices declined.

Many historical changes are not linear at all but come and go in cycles or even more complex patterns. If we were to graph such cyclical change—for example, the cycles of boom and bust that characterized the antebellum U.S. economy—our graph would look like the tracks on a roller coaster (Figure 9.4c). The antebellum economy, fueled by speculation over land and staple crops, was inherently unstable. Analytical historians have linked this instability with Americans' attitudes toward business and profits and have connected political differences of opinion, such as the difference of opinion over slavery between northerners and southerners on the eve of the Civil War, with the two regions' different responses to business cycles.

Exercise 8: Linear or Cyclical Change over Time?

Following is another data set from the *Historical Statistics of the United States*. Plot the data points on the *x*- and *y*-axes in Figure 9.5, using the *x*-axis for years and the *y*-axis for prices. Connect the data points with lines, making a line graph. The *index* is a baseline figure that allows comparison of variations in actual prices over time. In this data set, the price of these goods in 1910 is the index. It is arbitrarily set to equal 100.

Data Set 4 Wholesale Food Price, 1800–1847 (index is price in 1910, set to = 100.)

1800	157	1812	141	1824	99	1836	128
1801	177	1813	172	1825	100	1837	132
1802	132	1814	181	1826	98	1838	128
1803	135	1815	187	1827	100	1839	126
1804	142	1816	172	1828	99	1840	102
1805	162	1817	184	1829	100	1841	90
1806	150	1818	172	1830	94	1842	80
1807	142	1819	140	1831	98	1843	77
1808	113	1820	109	1832	94	1844	72
1809	129	1821	102	1833	100	1845	84
1810	139	1822	109	1834	93	1846	96
1811	140	1823	108	1835	107	1847	87

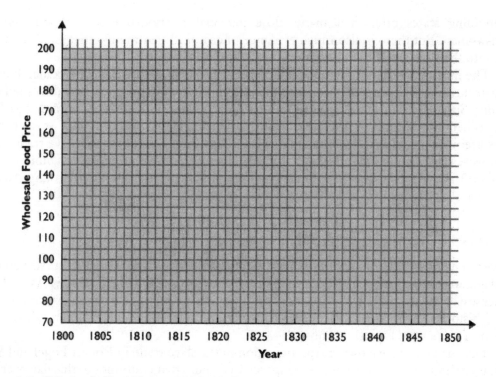

FIGURE 9.5 *Wholesale Food Prices, 1800–1847*

Is the variable (wholesale food price) linear or cyclical? _____

_____

_____

Patterns in the Past

Analytical historians seek patterns, regularities, and continuities in the past. An analytical study of southern planters' wives before the Civil War, for example, would begin by asking when these women married, how many children they had, what their place in the plantation economy was, and how they managed their household affairs. The analytical historian collects data to answer these and other questions about as many plantation wives as possible. The aggregation, or piling up, of individual cases is vital, for the analytical historian measures typicality and frequency. A single piece of evidence (for example, one of the letters mentioned in the first passage in Exercise 3), might be quite moving but misleading. The analytical historian will not be content with anecdotal evidence, no matter how colorful or detailed it is.

Just as the authors of narratives arrange their facts in different ways, so analytical historians differ about the meaning of their evidence. Controversies among analytical historians often revolve about claims of typicality. When the analytical historian examines any single piece of evidence—one point on a graph, one entry on a ledger, one piece of correspondence or diary entry—he or she asks whether that piece of evidence fits the larger pattern of evidence or is an exception to that pattern.

Over the past few decades, no subject in early American history has raised more controversy among analytical historians than the treatment of slaves in the South before the Civil War. Deliberate brutality may have been rare: the typical master or mistress in the slaveholding states often had many close personal relationships with bondsmen and bondswomen. But there is also much evidence of casual ill treatment—that is, ill treatment built into the system itself.

The most troubling of these systemic brutalities was the internal slave trade. The sale of husbands and wives away from each other and children away from parents disrupted slave families. Slave traders were busy entrepreneurs, and although some were regarded as "low-lifes," others were leaders in their community. The analytical questions that present themselves are: How central to the economy of the antebellum South was the slave trade? How often were slave families disrupted by the sale, gift, or bequeathal of one or more of their members? Did slave owners breed slaves for sale—giving inducements to young African-American slaves to bear children in order that they might later be sold?

Exercise 9: Evaluating Analytical Arguments

There are many oral accounts of the breakup of slave families from slaves who escaped from bondage, were freed by their masters, or became free during and after the Civil War. These stories are deeply moving, but were the events they describe the rule or the exception? Analytical historical writing directly tackles the question of whether the events recalled in the slave narratives were typical or unusual.

The analysis of slave owners' participation in the slave trade in Robert Fogel and Stanley Engerman's *Time on the Cross* (1974) sparked a dispute that continues to this day over how analytical historians are to assess data on slave trading. Economists Fogel and Engerman sought to prove, using statistical analysis of plantation records and auctioneers' records, that few slave families were disrupted by the sale of their members. Following is an excerpt from Fogel and Engerman's proof, and a rebuttal by historians Herbert Gutman and Richard Sutch. There are questions after each selection for you to ponder.

A Abolitionists claimed that southern planters deliberately tried to "breed" slaves, as though African-American babies were a crop to be harvested and sold. Such breeding was never admitted by planters, but slaves were in fact sold. There was a slightly higher fertility rate among slave mothers in parts of the South where land was no longer suitable for intensive agriculture. Abolitionists argued that instead of using their slaves to grow crops, planters in such parts of the South arranged for slave mothers to become pregnant more frequently. Fogel and Engerman deny this.

> The evidence put forward to support the contention of breeding for the market is meager indeed. . . . the evidence consists largely of unverified charges made by abolitionists and of certain demographic [population] data. However, subsequent corrections . . . have shown that rates of return on [money invested in male and female slaves] were approximately the same. And the many thousands of hours of research by professional historians into plantation records have failed to produce a single authenticated case of the "stud" plantations alleged in abolitionist literature . . . The demographic argument for the existence of slave breeding is based on two principal observations. First, the slave-exporting states [of Virginia and Maryland] had fewer slaves in the age group fifteen to twenty-nine, and more at very young and old ages, than the slave-importing states [in the deep South]. Second, the fertility rate, measured as the ratio of children under one year to women aged fifteen to forty-nine [the childbearing years] was slightly higher in the exporting than in the importing states. Neither of these demographic observations is sufficient to establish the existence of breeding for the market. The deviations of the age distribution in import-

ing and exporting states existed not only for slaves but for free men. As such they are proof that both free men and slaves migrated from east to west. But this point has never been in contention. What is in contention is the claim that the slave migration took place through market trading [that is, slave selling] instead of through the migration of whole plantations . . . [even if slaves were bred for market, few were sold "down the river"]. Only 16 percent of the interregional movement of slaves took place through market trading. This small movement, an average of about twenty-five hundred persons per year [produced very little profit]. Indeed, one could more easily make a case for the indispensability of the sweet potato crop [to the economy of the South than the slave trade], since this item brought in more income to slaveowners than the interregional sale of their bondsmen.[5]

1. According to Fogel and Engerman, what motive drove all planters' behavior? _____

_____

_____

2. What two kinds of evidence do Fogel and Engerman consider? _____

_____

_____

3. How do they dismiss the first kind of evidence? _____

_____

_____

4. How do they handle the second kind? _____

_____

_____

5. What do they conclude? _____

_____

_____

6. Fogel and Engerman compared two different sets of figures on age distributions—slave *women* and free*men*. Might this inconsistency in any way weaken their argument? _____

_____

_____

B Fogel and Engerman found strong critics in Herbert Gutman and Richard Sutch. Gutman and Sutch agreed that the profit motive was central to slavery but read the data on slave births in the upper South quite differently from Fogel and Engerman.

The issue of slave breeding has been somewhat confused because participants in the debate have failed to define the term adequately. One of the present writers has defined it rather broadly as any practice of the slave master intended to cause the fertility of the slave population to be higher than it would have been in the absence of such interference. So defined, "breeding" includes the use of "rewards" for childbearing, the encouragement of early marriage and short [breast-feeding] periods, and the provision of both pre- and postnatal medical care [for the mother and the infant], as well as practices more reprehensible to modern as well as to many nineteenth century sensibilities. . . .

Whatever the definitions of "breeding," demographic evidence contained in the 1850 and 1860 censuses provides strong circumstantial evidence of the prevalence of inducements to childbearing, particularly in the so-called "breeding" states of the Atlantic seaboard and along the northern border of legal slavery. Slave women in these states exhibited higher fertility than did those of the importing regions, and their fertility rates approached the upper bounds of human capacity.[6]

1. How do Gutman and Sutch define slave breeding? _____
   _____
   _____

2. Have they in any way changed the Fogel and Engerman definition? _____
   _____
   _____

3. If slave breeding is defined as any measure—including nutritious diets and medical care—that results in a higher birthrate, could some slave masters have provided these benefits to pregnant slaves out of compassion, rather than out of a desire to breed and sell slave children for profit? _____
   _____
   _____

4. What do Gutman and Sutch conclude about the meaning of elevated fertility rates in the upper South? _____
   _____
   _____

5. Do you find the argument of Gutman and Sutch or of Fogel and Engerman more convincing? Why? _____
   _____
   _____

6. Think about the definitions of slave breeding and the question of what motivated slave masters to act as they did. Is 16 percent a small number of "interregional movements" of slaves, as Fogel and Engerman claim, or a large number of disruptions of family life?
   _____
   _____

Fogel and Engerman and Gutman and Sutch transformed thousands of historical records listing individual slave sales into an exciting argument. Their grouping of data, use of numbers, and determination of patterns in the numbers would be quite convincing were it not for the fact that they thoroughly disagree with each other. They have employed highly sophisticated statistical tools to test the validity of their conclusions, yet they remain as far apart in their conclusions as one can imagine.

Critics of quantification in historical scholarship would be quick to cite the controversy over slave breeding as proof that the entire enterprise of quantitative history is doomed to failure. Before you consent to this dismal conclusion, though, remember that narrative historians challenge one another's findings all the time. A more enlightened inference about analytical history from the controversy over slave breeding is that, in their efforts to discover the truth, the analytical historians have probed far more deeply into the subject than they could have without the tools of quantification. In the end, historical writing, with or without numbers, remains the creative act of human imagination—and such ventures will always lead to controversy.

At the opposite end of the spectrum from analysis among the varieties of history is biography. As you will see in the next chapter, biographers are even more prone to controversy than analytical historians.

Notes

[1] James Oakes, *The Ruling Race: A History of American Slaveholders* (New York: Vintage, 1982), 87.

[2] Herbert G. Gutman, *The Black Family in Slavery and Freedom, 1750–1925* (New York: Pantheon, 1976), 92.

[3] Kenneth S. Greenberg, *Masters and Statesmen: The Political Culture of American Slavery* (Baltimore: Johns Hopkins University Press, 1985), 24.

[4] Kenneth M. Stampp, *The Peculiar Institution: Slavery in the Ante-Bellum South* (New York: Knopf, 1956), 160–161.

[5] Robert William Fogel and Stanley L. Engerman, *Time on the Cross: The Economics of American Negro Slavery* (Boston: Little, Brown, 1974), 1:78–86.

[6] Herbert Gutman and Richard Sutch, "Sexual Mores and Conduct," in Paul A. David et al., *Reckoning with Slavery* (New York: Oxford University Press, 1976), 154–161.

10: Biography: Life and Times

Abraham Lincoln, Frederick Douglass, and Their Generation

————•———•———•————

Throughout his majestic *Decline and Fall of the Roman Empire* (1765), eighteenth-century English historian Edward Gibbon lamented that history was often little more than an organ of hatred or flattery. In his day and our own no branch of historical study is more prone to this vice than biography, the account of the thoughts and deeds of individuals. At the same time, there is no question that biography remains the most popular branch of historical writing.

The Virtues and Vices of Biography

The sterling virtues of biography are obvious. Allan Nevins, one of the twentieth century's leading biographers, argued that the best biography should persuade the reader that the subject of the biography "lived, moved, spoke, and enjoyed a certain set of human attributes. We must not merely be shown what he did, but what he was, and why he was that kind of man."[1] Although Nevins wrote before most historians (women included) began to take the interest in women's history that has led to a virtual revolution in the practice of the historian's craft, his statement applies just as well to women as to men. Biography "humanizes the past,"[2] making it possible for us to relive a world otherwise strange to us.

Biography is one way of writing about history. The study of a person in a crucial moment in time can help anyone interested in the events and movements of that day understand why that person developed as he or she did. As Garrett Mattingly, the biographer of Catherine of Aragon, informed his readers, "Two things in her story have chiefly fascinated me: the way the decisions of a person by no means gifted with genius but strategically placed may influence the course of history, and the way that the divided loyalties common in thoughtful persons during a time of rapid change may affect their conduct in unexpected ways, and consequently give a twist, sometimes, to remote events."[3]

The vice lurking among the virtues of biography is that biographers may assign too great a role to their subjects, suggesting that all history depends on the whims or wiles of strategically placed people. This theory once dominated biographers' thinking. Thomas

Carlyle, one of England's greatest biographers, insisted that great men were the makers of great events. Ralph Waldo Emerson, after reading Carlyle, concluded that all history is nothing more than biography. In a reaction to this oversimplified view of historical causation, later American and English historians retorted that the great man or woman was merely the spokesperson or the representative of great masses of people, speaking in a language that they understood and thereby moving them to action.

Biographers and Biographies

Although one may debate the virtues and vices of biography, there is no question that good biography makes fascinating reading and opens up the past to us through the eyes of the biographer's subject. In an essay written shortly before she died, Barbara Tuchman explained that she wrote her Pulitzer Prize–winning biography of General Joseph Stilwell, U.S. military adviser in China during the Second World War, to help her readers understand American-Asian contacts. She used Stilwell as "a human vehicle" to carry her readers back to a critical period in the relations between the United States and its Asian friends and enemies. As she recounted Stilwell's trials and tribulations, Tuchman made America's experience in China "comprehensible to the reader."[4] In the end, the best biographers must strike a balance between seeing the past through the eyes of their subjects without letting the biases and aims of the subject distort the reader's view of the past.

Most biographers come to respect and like their subjects, appreciating the difficulties that their subjects faced and sharing the joys and sorrows their subjects experienced. For example, Nevins became the great defender of millionaire oil magnate John D. Rockefeller, a man much criticized by other scholars. Some biographers learn to dislike their subjects. Robert Caro, a biographer of the late President Lyndon Baines Johnson, admitted that "knowing Lyndon Baines Johnson—understanding the character of the thirty-sixth president of the United States—is essential to understanding the history of the United States in the twentieth century." Johnson was a great man whose decisions changed the course of history, and the broader outlines of his life illustrated "a panorama vast in scope: the panorama of the westward movement in America." Nevertheless, Caro concluded, "The more one follows his life, the more apparent it becomes that alongside the thread of achievement running through it runs another thread, as dark as the other is bright, and as fraught with consequences for history: a hunger for power in its most naked form, for power to . . . bend others to his will."[5] Of course, everyone, whether great or ordinary, has vices as well as virtues. The successful biographer enables the reader to see the virtues and vices of the subject from the inside, as though the reader knew the subject intimately.

Exercise 1: How Biographers See Their Subjects

Different biographers often view the same person very differently; hence biography is the most subjective of all the forms of history. Biographers disagree about what sort of personality their common subject had and about how that person altered the course of history. Biographers even disagree about how their subject looked and sounded, as this exercise, based on biographies of Abraham Lincoln, illustrates. Read the excerpts from three biographies of Abraham Lincoln, and answer the study questions about them.

"A. Lincoln," as he signed his name, remains one of the United States' most beloved presidents. His assassination at the end of the Civil War made him a martyr to the cause of the Union, but in life he revealed little of himself, even to his political allies. Asked to compose an autobiographical statement in December 1859 for the upcoming presidential campaign, he scribbled a few humorous lines about his "undistinguished family" and his meager schooling. He went on, "If any personal description of me is thought desireable, it may be said, I am, in height, six feet, four inches, nearly; lean in flesh, weighing, on an average, one hundred and eighty pounds; dark complexion, with coarse black hair, and grey eyes—no other marks or brands recollected."[6] Laconic, self-deprecating, protecting himself with humor—that was A. Lincoln. Here is how the biographers saw the man:

A He looked like a farmer, it was often said; he seemed to have come from prairies and barns rather than city streets and barber shops; and in his own way he admitted and acknowledged it; he told voters from the stump that it was only a few years since he had worn buckskin breeches and they shrank in the rain and crept to his knees leaving the skin blue and bare. The very words that came off his lips in tangled important discussions among lawyers had a wilderness air and a log-cabin smack. The way he pronounced the word "idea" was more like "idee," the word "really" more like a drawled Kentucky "ra-a-ly." As he strode or shambled into a gathering of men, he stood out as a special figure for men to look at; it was a little as though he had come farther on harder roads . . . as though he had been where life is stripped to its naked facts and it would be useless for him to try to put on certain pretenses of civilization.[7]

1. Do you think this biographer liked Lincoln? _____

_____

_____

2. Judging from the passage you just read, do you think you would have liked Lincoln at first sight? _____

_____

_____

3. What about this biographer's technique caught your attention? _____

_____

_____

4. In particular, does the biographer use common or colorful terms? _____

_____

_____

5. Do these terms capture Lincoln's own way of speaking? _____

_____

_____

B As [Lincoln] cultivated the deceptively simple homespun stance of a stump speaker . . . so he also cultivated the artlessness of the circuit-riding storyteller. He would memorize those stories, walking around with clippings from newspapers or magazines or even with a comical book until he had them by heart and could slip them into conversations, interviews, or speeches on any occasion. . . . These stories had a practical, everyday value. As president, Lincoln used them to save time and temper. Under prodding from reporters, his secretary John Hay often tried to pry stories [out of Lincoln] for the sake of stories, but in the White House Lincoln listened. When he had to talk, stories helped keep that talk short, sweet, and to the point.[8]

1. How does this biographer's approach to Lincoln differ from the approach in the first reading? _____

_____

_____

2. In particular, is it more or less sympathetic? _____

_____

_____

3. What does this biographer tell us about Lincoln's personality? _____

_____

_____

> **C** Lincoln's renowned sense of humor was related to his passion for secrecy. Again and again self-important delegations would descend upon the White House, deliver themselves of ponderous utterances upon pressing issues of the war, and demand point-blank what the President proposed to do about their problems. Lincoln could say much in a few words when he chose, but he could also say nothing at great length when it was expedient. The petitioners' request, he would say, reminded him of "a little story," which he would proceed to tell in great detail, accompanied by mimicry and gestures, by hearty slapping of the thigh, by uproarious laughter at the end—at which time he would usher out his callers, baffled and confused by the smoke-screen of good humor, with their questions still unanswered.[9]

1. What is the difference between the Lincoln in selection **C** and the Lincoln in selection **B**?

_____

_____

2. Does the biographer in selection **C** approach Lincoln from a new direction? Care less for the man? See Lincoln as two men—one public and the other private?

_____

_____

_____

The Biographer's Imagination

How can biographers see the same person so differently? In Lincoln's case, perhaps the discrepancies can be attributed to his passion for secrecy and his self-lacerating sense of humor. Lincoln knew how to fabricate public masks and hide behind them, to bury inner feelings and project an image. The biographers' job is to go where their subjects' contemporaries could not go—into the subject's inner life. Biographers' views vary so widely because they express the biographers' own imaginative capacity to probe into the recesses of their subjects' lives. Visualize a model posing for a portrait by different artists—say Rembrandt, Goya, and Picasso. Would you not expect each portrait to look different? Biography is first and foremost an art form, and biographical portraits are works of art.

Biographers take primary sources and transform them, reshaping original words and pictures into new, more revealing words and pictures. For example, much of what we know about Abraham Lincoln's married life is based upon the recollections of the young man Lincoln took into his office in 1844, William Herndon.

Herndon was a complex man about whose habits and abilities scholars disagree. In *A. Lincoln, Prairie Lawyer* (1960) John Duff opines that "the garrulous, windy, opinionated, prodigiously indiscreet Herndon, oracularly sure of himself and forever spouting dicta, was certainly not the happiest choice Lincoln could have made" as a partner in the law firm.[10] Historian David Donald believes that "there was something almost pathetic" in the way Herndon, a bright but unfocused man, sought knowledge.[11] A lawyer by trade, he was more of an intellectual than a working attorney and only his partnership with the more down-to-earth Lincoln ensured Herndon any regular income. Herndon did bring to the partnership political connections in the Whig party and growing commitment to radical reformism, including abolition of slavery. These commitments did not always sway the older Lincoln, but they influenced his thinking.

Herndon's *Life of Lincoln*, written (with the help of a young clerk, Jesse Weik) and published near the end of Herndon's life in 1889, is filled with opinion, unsubstantiated tales, and attacks on Lincoln's and Herndon's personal and political enemies. The modern editor of the work, Paul M. Angle, has decided that "confidence in his power of intuitive perception was, in fact, a dominant characteristic of William H. Herndon. Time after time he relied implicitly upon this faculty."[12] According to Angle, Herndon did not consciously lie about Lincoln, but he did treat his own hunches as though they were facts.

Exercise 2: How Biographers Use Sources

In 1842, Lincoln married Mary Todd (see Figure 10.1). Lincoln's parents were poor farmers; Todd's were well-to-do Kentucky slaveholders. A planter's daughter, Todd seemed an unlikely match for Lincoln.

William Herndon and Mary Todd took an instant dislike to one another. Privately, Herndon spread rumors about Mary Todd's bad temper and Lincoln's prior and purer love

FIGURE 10.1 *Abraham and Mary Todd Lincoln*
Abraham Lincoln courtesy of the Library of Congress. Mary Todd Lincoln courtesy of Corbis Images

for Ann Rutledge. After Lincoln's assassination, Herndon began to publicize his animosity for Mary Todd Lincoln, and she privately fumed, " '[It] will not be *well with* [*Herndon*]— if he makes the least disagreeable or false allusion in the future. He will be closely watched. W. H. [Herndon] may consider himself a ruined man, in attempting to disgrace others, the vials of wrath, will be poured upon his own head' "[13] Mary's biographer, Jean Baker, surmised, "No doubt Mary Lincoln remembered how the men of Lexington [Kentucky, where she was reared] had defended their lady loves with their swords and pistols."[14] As you read Herndon's account, bear in mind the animosity between Herndon and Todd.

> That a lady as proud and as ambitious to exercise the rights of supremacy in society as Mary Todd should repent of her marriage to [Lincoln] surely need occasion no surprise in the mind of anyone. Both she and the man whose hand she accepted . . . reaped the bitter harvest of conjugal infelicity. . . . Mrs. Lincoln, on account of her peculiar nature, could not long retain a servant in her employ. The sea was never so placid but that a breeze would ruffle its waters. She loved show and attention, and if, when she gloried her family descent or indulged in one of her strange outbreaks, the servant could simulate absolute obsequiousness or had tact enough to encourage her social pretensions, Mrs. Lincoln was for the time her firmest friend. One servant . . . told me that . . . the secret of her ability to endure the eccentricities of her mistress . . . [was] that Mr. Lincoln gave her an extra dollar each week on condition that she would brave whatever storms might arise, and suffer whatever might befall her, without complaint. It was a rather severe condition, but she lived rigidly up to her part of the contract. The money was paid secretly and without the knowledge of Mrs. Lincoln.[15]

Biographers have regarded Herndon's views on Mary Todd Lincoln as a major, indispensable primary source on the life of Lincoln. Following are selections from three biographers based on Herndon's recollections. Each biographer gives Herndon's accusations a different twist. Answer the questions after each passage.

> **A** Lincoln was indulgent as a father and left the upbringing of the children largely to "Mother," who was forebearing and overstrict by turns. Her whole nature took on a sort of instability as time went on. Devoted, even possessive toward her husband, she was eager to make him happy. But small matters upset her and brought on fits of temper. Servants found her difficult to please . . . Lincoln bore it all as best he could, taking her tongue lashings, yielding to her whims whenever possible, offering excuses to the neighbors, trying to make allowances for the affectionate wife and mother he knew she was at heart. When her upbraidings became unbearable he would not talk back or censure her, but simply slip off quietly to his office.[16]

How does this biographer balance criticism of Mary Todd, drawn from Herndon, with a more sympathetic view of Lincoln's wife?

_____

_____

_____

> **B** Mary's temper did not mellow with age. Neighbors, in time, adjusted to her loud, shrill voice, hysterical outbursts, and imagined fears. At the fierce explosions of anger everyone scurried for shelter. One after another, servants who resented her hectoring and felt exploited left; only those whom Lincoln secretly paid extra stayed. Mary indiscrimi-

nately scolded everyone around her, the children excepted, and on the slightest provocation flew into a fury, though once quieting down she tried to make amends.[17]

1. To what extent does this biographer rely on Herndon's view of Mary Todd?

_____

_____

_____

2. Is this account closer to Herndon's than the account in selection **A**? _____

_____

_____

_____

    C Mary Lincoln's critics have held that her bad temper drove off her domestic workers, but such judgments remove her from her time and place. Everyone had difficulty keeping hired girls. In fact, the entire problem of finding and retaining good domestic help was a chronic concern for middle-class women. . . . Unlike the well-trained slaves of her childhood recollections, the independent daughters of Sangamon County's [Illinois] farmers required constant supervision in specific tasks such as the seasonal exigencies of housecleaning. Hired girls did not consider themselves servants, and they did not expect to be in service long. . . . Mary Lincoln on occasion did not have help because she refused to pay the market price, and it is her parsimony more than her bad temper that her employment [of servants] record reveals.[18]

1. Does this biographer credit or discredit Herndon's account? _____

_____

2. How does this author shift the reader's perspective by offering new information?

_____

_____

    The biographer has a coworker in the transformation of a real life into a biography. The coworker is the subject herself or himself. All of us, during the course of our lives, think about where we have been, what we have done, and how others have seen us. In our letters, diaries, and recollections we not only rethink but remake our own lives, and such materials make possible a continuous interaction between the biographer and the subject, even if the subject is no longer alive.

Exercise 3: The Interaction Between Biographer and Subject

You can explore the interaction between the subject's perception of himself or herself and the imagination of the biographer in the following excerpts from two versions of Frederick Douglass's autobiography, recalling his earliest youth. Douglass, seen in Figure 10.2, fled slavery in Maryland and became a leading abolitionist. During the Civil War he was Lincoln's adviser and emissary, though the two men did not always agree. Later, he served the United States as an ambassador. Douglass, passionate and dignified, wrote a series of autobiographies. The earliest was published in 1845. Selection **A** is taken from this volume.

Selection **B** comes from the final version of his autobiography, published in 1892, shortly before he died. Specific questions follow the two selections.

> **A** [1845] My mother and I were separated when I was but an infant—before I knew her as my mother. It is a common custom, in the part of Maryland from which I ran away, to part children from their mothers at a very early age. Frequently, before the child has reached its twelfth month, its mother is taken from it, and hired out on some farm a considerable distance off, and the child is placed under the care of an old woman, too old for field labor. For what this separation is done, I do not know, unless it be to hinder the development of the child's affection toward its mother, and to blunt and destroy the natural affection of the mother for the child. This is the inevitable result.[19]
>
> **B** [1892] Living thus with my grandmother, whose kindness and love stood in place of my mother's, it was some time before I knew myself to be a slave. I knew many other things before I knew that. Her little cabin had to me the attractions of a palace. Its fence-railed floor—which was equally floor and bedstead—upstairs, and its clay floor downstairs, its dirt and straw chimney, and windowless sides, and that most curious piece of workmanship, the ladder stairway, and the hole so strangely dug in front of the fireplace, beneath which grandma placed the sweet potatoes, to keep them from frost in winter, were full of interest to my childish observation. . . . It was not long, however, before I began to learn the sad fact that this house of my childhood belonged not to my dear old grandmother, but to some one I had never seen, and who lived a great distance off . . . called by grandmother, with every mark of reverence, "Old Master." Thus early did clouds and shadows begin to fall upon my path.[20]

Consider the differences in the two accounts. The first is didactic, as though part of a lecture on the evils of slavery. The second is more personal, sentimental, and self-revealing. Why did the first, written in 1845, when Douglass's memory of his childhood ought to have been fresh and detailed, give a much shorter description of his childhood in his grandmother's cabin than did the autobiography he wrote in 1892?

FIGURE 10.2 *Frederick Douglass in 1855 and ca. 1885*
(left) Courtesy of the National Portrait Gallery, Smithsonian Institution/Art Resource, New York.
(right) Courtesy of the Library of Congress.

_____

_____

_____

Might Douglass have had different purposes—different faces that he wanted the public to see—in 1845 and 1892? Bear in mind that in 1845, Douglass was a leading abolitionist speaker and organizer throughout the Northeast.

_____

_____

_____

Exercise 4: Biographers' Use of Autobiography

Douglass's life has fascinated biographers. Not only did Douglass escape from slavery to lead a rich and eventful life in the North, but he was a brilliant writer and public speaker as well. Douglass's autobiography has been the most important primary source for his biographers, but they have come away from the various versions of the autobiography with different impressions of its author. The following selections from three of his biographers concern the portions of the autobiographies you have already read. As you examine the passages, consider how the biographers have transformed Douglass's revelations about his early childhood. Questions follow each passage.

A Frederick, as a small child, led a rather carefree life in his grandmother's cabin, but when he was about seven he felt for the first time the bitter reality of slavery.[21]

1. Which of Douglass's versions has this biographer adopted? _____

_____

_____

2. How much space (and importance) does this biographer assign to Douglass's early childhood life? _____

_____

_____

B It was a happy time, one he would remember always as the most golden period of his life. He was as free as a bird; he could do anything he liked . . . As for Frederick, he was, in his own words, a "spirited, joyous, uproarious, and happy boy," without a care in the world. But gradually, as he grew older, the shape of things to come hove into hazy view. He learned that he was something called a *slave*, and that his grandmother and most of the others in his family were slaves also. There was a mysterious being, called "Old Master," who controlled their lives and who could make them all, even his grandmother, do anything he wanted them to do.[22]

1. What does this biographer emphasize in his account of Douglass's childhood? _____

_____

_____

2. Which version does he follow? _____

_____

_____

C Douglass wrote later of his boyhood in [his grandmother's] cabin as "spirited, joyous, uproarious, and happy," but drew a picture of the surrounding area that does not just reflect what he saw as a child. His description of the "worn-out sandy desert-like appearance of the soil," the "general dilapidation of its farms," and the "ague and fever" that rose from the Tuckahoe [plantation] is more a metaphor for the barrenness of slavery than the recollection of a six-year-old. It does, however, return attention from the idyllic to the realities of carving out a living in this remote country. . . . If the small house was indeed in the woods, as Douglass remembered it, the problem of providing food was immediate; you cannot grow vegetables under trees . . . In this realm [his grandmother] Betsy became legendary. Intelligent and physically powerful, she had made herself an expert in fishing and farming. . . . Douglass's stress on the impressive competence of his grandmother in what might have been thought of as masculine functions . . . is significant. . . . For the rest of his life Douglass looked to women as confidants, companions, and sources of strength. They rather than men could be . . . counted on. . . . They could also be the source of immense anguish.[23]

1. What new elements and perspectives does the third biographer introduce into the account? _____
_____
_____

2. How close does he stay to Douglass's own words? _____
_____
_____

3. How does he transform or penetrate what Douglass says to gain insights into the hidden, personal feelings of the man? _____
_____
_____

Biographers, as you have seen, identify with their subjects. One of the first important facts they must ponder about their subject is his or her sex. In middle-period America (1800–1860) sex defined private and public roles to a far greater extent than it does today. Women were disfavored in the public arena. Not only were they denied the right to vote and hold office, but genteel women were not even supposed to be out in the evening without an escort. Nineteenth-century men certainly claimed that women had to be protected from the rough-and-tumble of public life as "mothers of the race." In reality, women worked as hard as men, often outside the home. In much of the plantation South, slave women constituted the majority of the field gangs. Responding to simple facts like these, many historians have begun to argue that in the study of women what is important is not biological differences—sex—but socially constructed roles. When we study gender—relations between women and men—we capture a fuller historical reality than when we study women in isolation.

The debate over women's history versus histories of gender leads naturally to the question of whether it is easier for a woman than for a man to write about a woman. Did you notice that one of the selections in Exercise 2 was much more sympathetic than the others to Mary Todd Lincoln. The sympathetic account was written by Jean Baker. The others were the work of men. Perhaps women understand the travails and triumphs of women better than a man might and see things that a man might miss. Women were the primary givers of child care then, as they are now. Can male historians understand bearing, birthing, and caring for children as well as female historians? The implications of the question go to the very heart of the historical discipline. One can raise similar questions, for example, about the ability of non–African-American scholars to write about the African-American experience. Would a negative conclusion about that imply that African-American historians can only write about African-American subjects?

Exercise 5: Does Gender Matter in Biography?

In this exercise you will read two selections from biographies of Sojourner Truth (see Figure 10.3). Sojourner Truth was born in 1797 on a Hudson River valley farm, a slave to a Dutch farmer. Slavery was legal in New York until 1827, and Truth, with her five children, was sold and purchased like any southern slave among the Dutch and English families of the region. After she was freed, she moved to New York City, then to a utopian community in Northampton, Massachusetts, and then to Michigan. In the course of her travels, she realized that her style of public speaking and prayer, along with her devout belief in God and the injustice of slavery, made her an effective abolition advocate. Her emotional public speaking was similar to that of the great evangelists of the age. Her *Narrative* (1850), however, was told to others, for she never learned to read and write. That fact notwithstanding, she bravely joined male colleagues on the podiums of public meetinghouses to inveigh against the evils of the "peculiar institution" of slavery. During the Civil War, she helped black people flee slavery, and after the war she helped relocate them in the North. She died in 1883 in her Battle Creek, Michigan, home, a legend in her own time.

A Carleton Mabee, in a biography of Truth, discusses her illiteracy.

Because Truth found that she could not learn to read or write the letters of the alphabet, and that they seemed to become jumbled before her eyes, it seems probable—a probability that is not known to have been directly proposed in previous studies about Truth—that Truth had a learning disability which at the time might not have been understood. Perhaps she had irregular visual perception that jumbled the letters of the alphabet for her, more of a problem than her glasses could correct. (During much of her life, Truth recalled in her old age, she had worn glasses for ironing.) Such a perceptual disability could have seriously frustrated her in her attempts to learn to read or write. Today experts believe that perhaps 10 to 15 percent of Americans have reading disabilities, but they also believe that with determination and appropriate guidance, these disabled can usually learn to read. In her time, the appropriate guidance was not likely to be available. Perhaps the cause of her not learning to read, then, can best be understood as the interaction of her experience of slavery, the development of her character, and her probable learning disability.

When she was young, Truth seemed to allow her lack of learning to lead her to undervalue education. After she became a public speaker for reform, she displayed signs of negative attitudes toward intellectual education, perhaps disdaining it because it was beyond her reach. Speaking in a church, she ridiculed "Greek-crammed" preachers. Speaking at a college, she ridiculed the students for writing down notes on what she said, advising them instead to keep notes as she did in her head. . . .

For her personally, instead of allowing her illiteracy to weigh her down as much as it might have, she learned to use it to her advantage. To avoid clashing with someone over religious doctrine, she would say that if she could read the Bible she might see the matter differently. As a speaker, she would play provocatively with her illiteracy, as in this one-liner that won her applause: "I tell you I can't read a book, but I can read de people."

FIGURE 10.3 *Sojourner Truth in 1864*
Courtesy of the Library of Congress

Remarkably, she seemed to be able to use her illiteracy to lift herself up into a high pulpit from which she then could more effectively scold an audience, as she did once thus: "With all your opportunities for readin' and writin', you don't take hold and do anything." For many of Truth's listeners, her lack of literacy and culture contributed to her fascination, and of course, shrewd as she was, she knew it, and played it up.[24]

1. In your own words, restate the author's view of Truth's response to her own illiteracy.

_____

_____

2. Does the author regard Truth's illiteracy as a flaw or defect? _____

_____

_____

B Erlene Stetson and Linda David look at the same facts.

Although Sojourner Truth lived in a print culture in which books were being dissociated from oral production, she herself remained an oral producer, and it is misguided to see Truth's orality as a pathology, a condition of negation. "She has rare natural gifts; a clear intellect; a fine moral intuition and spirited insight, with much common sense," wrote Lucy Stone in the official organ of the American Woman's Suffrage Association; "She never could read, and often said, that all the great trouble of the world came from those who could read, and not from those who could not, and that she was glad she never knew how to read." This view lay at the heart of Truth's political vision. Perhaps in agreement with Audre Lorde that *"the master's tools will never dismantle the master's house,"* Truth seems never to have believed that what was taught by the white patriarchal culture could be unlearned; it was best not to learn it at all. Truth saw "through a millstone" that Western culture hung around the neck of her people; looking around her, seeing who had literacy and who did not, she rightly saw it not as a condition of human adequacy but as an effect of dominance. Acquiring literacy did not mean moving from defective humanity to plenitude; it meant acquiring a political tool that could be useful in negating racist theories that enslaved Africans could be defined by their inability to decipher Western print. Truth had chosen a different tool for the hoeing of this field. She used her speaking voice as the unalienated inheritor of a great oral tradition. . . .

Her need to speak aloud to God was in conflict with the constraints imposed on the speech of enslaved people, but Truth became certain that if she "were to present her petitions under the open canopy of heaven, speaking very loud," that God would hear her. So that "she could speak louder to God, without being overheard," she built herself a shelter on an island in a stream "by pulling away the branches of the shrubs from the centre, and weaving them together for a wall on the outside, forming a circular arched alcove, made entirely of the graceful willow." On such a training ground one of the great orators of the nineteenth century perfected her skills.

Talking aloud was Truth's calling, and her audience was broad. "She held almost hourly converse with, as she supposed, the God of the universe," wrote Lucy Colman. From the refugee camp at Mason's Island in the Potomac during the Civil War, Truth wrote, "I do not know but what I shall stay here on the Island all winter and go around among the Freedmen's camps. They are all *delighted* to hear me talk." With the characteristic reserve of literate black men toward Truth, William Still wondered at her audacity: "She would dauntlessly face the most intelligent and cultivated audiences, or would individually approach the President of the United States as readily as she would one of the humblest citizens." Wendell Phillips praised her power "to move and bear down a whole audience by a few simple words." Her improvisatory style used the material of the moment to incorporate the shifting needs of her audiences into her performances.[25]

1. In your own words, describe how Stetson and David characterize Truth's illiteracy.

_____

_____

2. Do they regard her "talking to God" as a strength or a weakness? _____

_____

_____

3. In what ways do Mabee's and Stetson and David's accounts differ? _____

_____

_____

4. How might this difference be explained by the considerations that we laid out in the introduction to this exercise? _____

_____

_____

Writing Biography

We conclude this chapter with a short biographical assignment. Step one is to prepare a chronology. A biographical chronology is a time line on which you place important dates in your subject's life. These include events in which the person participated and events that were important to the person. The chronology should include **objective material** (dates of birth, marriage, children's births, and information about occupation, education, public service, and military service) and **subjective material** (dates that the subject himself or herself regarded as important). The latter category might include meetings with other people, political events, travel, the reading of a particularly influential book or article, or similar moments in the subject's life. A chronology can be very detailed, but as with any historical writing, you must know what to omit as well as what to include. A chronology that is too detailed might have an entry for every day of the subject's life—surely too many entries for most biographies, although some biographers approach this level of detail.

Exercise 6: Preparing a Chronology

Choose a person—such as a parent or other close relative—with whose life you are quite familiar. On a separate sheet of paper prepare a chronology of important objective and subjective dates in his or her life. You may interview your subject and ask for additional information from other family members. Seek information about education, employment, travel, and family matters. When you have finished a preliminary chronology, return to your sources and decide whether you have omitted any important episodes in your subject's life; if you have, include these. Your chronology should be about two pages long and resemble the following model:

> date #1   event
> date #2   event
> and so on . . .

Exercise 7: Life and Times, or Context

Your chronology is only the skeleton of a life. The names and dates in it are bare bones until you put flesh on them by putting them into historical context. What was happening when your subject lived? Some of these events directly changed your subject's life or influenced your subject's thinking. Others were too remote to affect your subject. You must decide which contemporary events merit inclusion in your biography. Historical context is essential in a biography. Included in the immediate context is your subject's family, regional and ethnic background, his or her neighborhood, and the cultural (religious, ethnic, educational) and social circle in which he or she moved. Included in more general context are the political events and economic changes that shaped your subject's life.

Decide which national events and movements are important enough to merit treatment in your biography. What you include or omit is up to you. Examine the dates on your chronology. Using newspapers, the library, your textbook, and interviews with your subject, your subject's friends, relations, and coworkers (if possible), link those events or movements to the corresponding dates in your chronology. On a separate sheet of paper, write a paragraph associating each entry in your chronology with relevant outside events. For example, if your subject went to college between 1965 and 1969, you may decide to tie his or her experiences to the protests over the Vietnam War, the switch to open enrollment in many colleges, or increasing emphasis on science in the college curriculum in those years.

Exercise 8: The Inner Dimension of Biography

The inner dimension of biography is your subject's feelings, ideas, and perceptions of the world. Biographers must assess their subject's thoughts and emotions empathetically. Seeing the world as the subject saw it is the most difficult yet the most important task that a biographer can attempt.

Talk to your subject about his or her beliefs, ideas, and opinions. Determine how these relate to the important events in his or her life. If your subject is not available, attempt to gather information from those who knew your subject. To complete your biography exercise, select one issue or event that was important to your subject. Write a page on what your subject thought about that issue. Give evidence to support your interpretation of your subject's views. You may quote your subject, but you need not believe everything he or she says. Your subject's own words are primary sources and must be treated with the cautions described in Chapter 3.

_____
_____
_____
_____
_____
_____
_____
_____
_____
_____
_____
_____
_____
_____
_____
_____
_____
_____
_____
_____
_____
_____

The lives of Lincoln and Douglass came together in the Civil War. Lincoln asked Douglass to recruit African-American soldiers for the Union cause, and Douglass served with energy. At the same time, Douglass pleaded for equality for African-Americans, giving voice to a moral stance that was not popular among many political leaders of his day. For a time, Lincoln resisted the urging of Douglass and others to turn the Civil War into a struggle over equality, but reformers like Douglass continued to elevate the war effort into a struggle for the freedom of all peoples, and gave its terrible costs a moral dimension. They believed that history taught moral lessons and clung to that belief even when, after Reconstruction was abandoned, most other Americans turned their backs on the suffering of the freed men and women. In Chapter 11, we turn to these "big questions."

Notes

[1] Allan Nevins, *The Gateway to History* (New York: Doubleday, 1962), 355.

[2] Ibid., 348.

[3] Garrett Mattingly, *Catherine of Aragon* (New York: Vintage, 1941), vii.

[4] Barbara W. Tuchman, *Practicing History* (New York: Knopf, 1981), 65.

[5] Robert A. Caro, *The Years of Lyndon Johnson: The Path to Power* (New York: Knopf, 1982), xvi, xvii, xix.

[6] Abraham Lincoln, December 20, 1859, in Mario M. Cuomo and Harold Holzer, eds., *Lincoln on Democracy* (New York: HarperCollins, 1990), xlv, xlvi–xlvii.

[7] Carl Sandburg, *Abraham Lincoln: The Prairie Years* (New York: Harcourt, 1926), 1:303–304.

[8] P. M. Zall, "Abe Lincoln Laughing," in Gabor S. Boritt and Norman O. Forness, eds., *The Historian's Lincoln* (Urbana: University of Illinois Press, 1988), 11–12.

[9] David Donald, *Lincoln Reconsidered: Essays on the Civil War Era*, 2nd ed. (New York: Vintage, 1956), 67–68.

[10] John J. Duff, *A. Lincoln: Prairie Lawyer* (New York: Holt, Rinehart & Winston, 1960), 97.

[11] Donald, *Lincoln Reconsidered*, 39.

[12] Paul M. Angle, ed., *Herndon's Life of Lincoln* (Greenwich, Conn.: Fawcett, 1961), 35.

[13] Mary Todd Lincoln, November 1866, quoted in Jean Baker, *Mary Todd Lincoln: A Biography* (New York: Norton, 1987), 268.

[14] Ibid., 269.

[15] Angle, *Herndon's Life of Lincoln*, 338–341.

[16] Benjamin P. Thomas, *Abraham Lincoln* (New York: Knopf, 1952), 90–91.

[17] Oscar Handlin and Lillian Handlin, *Abraham Lincoln and the Union* (Boston: Little, Brown, 1980), 86–87.

[18] Baker, *Mary Todd Lincoln*, 106, 107.

[19] Frederick Douglass, *Narrative of the Life of Frederick Douglass, An American Slave* (Boston: Anti-Slavery Office, 1845), 2.

[20] Frederick Douglass, *Life and Times of Frederick Douglass*, ed. Rayford W. Logan (1892; reprinted, New York: Collier, 1962), 30–33.

[21] Nathan Irvin Huggins, *Slave and Citizen: The Life of Frederick Douglass* (Boston: Little, Brown, 1980), 4.

[22] Dickson J. Preston, *Young Frederick Douglass: The Maryland Years* (Baltimore: Johns Hopkins University Press, 1980), 37–39.

[23] William S. McFeely, *Frederick Douglass* (New York: Norton, 1991), 8, 9.

[24] Carleton Mabee, *Sojourner Truth: Slave, Prophet, Legend.* (New York: New York University Press, 1993).

[25] Erlene Stetson and Linda David, *Glorying in Tribulation: The Lifework of Sojourner Truth* (East Lansing: Michigan State University Press, 1994), 11–12.

11: Big Questions: Inevitability, Morality, and the Lessons of History

Civil War and Reconstruction

Historians cannot avoid asking "big questions"—questions that go beyond what they have found in their sources. A big question may be compared to the shell of a nut. The meat of the nut is the historian's account, but the shell of the nut confines and shapes that account. Big questions may not be answerable, at least not through conventional means of narration, analysis, and biography, but they remind us of the complexity and significance of the historian's discipline. This chapter explores three of the big questions that shape every historical account: Are certain events inevitable? Is the historian permitted moral judgment? Can we learn from the past?

Inevitability

First, the question of inevitability: was an event, a movement, or a development inevitable, or could it have been avoided? For historians the question of inevitability begins with a simple query. We ask, If a certain person had acted differently, would the outcome of the story have been altered? This question is contrary to fact (after all, the person acted as he or she did), but the hypothetical "what if" focuses our attention on *contingencies*, accidents or unplanned actions that can change the course of history. The classic example is the tale of the "want of a nail." For the want of a nail, a messenger's horse lost a shoe. Without the shoe, the horse went lame. Without the horse, the messenger was not able to deliver the message on time. Without the message, the general did not know where his enemy was, and his army was defeated.

The missing nail was a contingency, and history is filled with them. Harriet Beecher Stowe was not a general, but her dramatic tales of "Uncle Tom's Cabin," serialized in newspapers and then published in book form in 1852, galvanized antislavery opinion in the North. Would the Civil War have been fought had she not aroused the consciences of her readers? When Stowe visited Lincoln, early in 1863, he greeted her with "so you're the little woman who wrote the book that made this great war." If, for some reason, Stowe had never set pen to paper, would the Civil War have come when it did—or at all? Her decision

207

to write *Uncle Tom's Cabin* was not a contingency, but its momentous impact on the debate over abolition of slavery could not have been foreseen—or could it? If the Civil War was inevitable, then the publication of *Uncle Tom's Cabin* was only one cause among many.

We can broaden our perspective on questions of contingency and inevitability by turning from individual actions to major events. We all ask ourselves whether wars could have been averted, plagues evaded, and people saved from the effects of their own folly. The ancient Greek Stoics, a group of philosophers who profoundly influenced Western thought, believed that all history was cyclical. In these cycles, nations rose, shone, decayed, and fell, to be replaced by other nations that would in their turn suffer the same fate. No people and no nation could escape from this unchangeable law of history.

Eighteenth-century European and American Enlightenment leaders looked to the idea of progress for deliverance from these cycles of rise and decay. Through progress in science and technology and the spread of education, these thinkers argued, people could save themselves and their nations from ruin. Throughout the nineteenth century and into the first decade of the twentieth century, educated Americans and Europeans embraced this idea of progress. Having conquered much of the world and made great strides in science and the arts, Western peoples saw history in terms of one straight, upward motion. This line marked the decline of barbarism and the rise of Western civilization. Most Europeans ignored the baneful effects of their imperialism.

In the twentieth century, however, world wars, totalitarianism, and mass destruction of civilian populations gave pause to advocates of the theory of progress. Some historians, like Arnold Toynbee, went back to the Stoic ideal and warned about the rise and fall of Western civilization. Other scholars selected some period of the past as a golden age and extolled it over the present. Few historians still believe that progress is automatic. The simple faith of nineteenth-century historians in the inevitability of progress has vanished like a dream at morning.

Exercise 1: Was the Civil War Inevitable?

Are great cataclysms inevitable? Could the Civil War have been delayed or averted? Did the division between the free North and the slave South make conflict irrepressible, as William Henry Seward told a meeting of voters in 1858, or could some compromise have been found, similar to the Missouri Compromise of 1820 or the Compromise of 1850? Read the following passages reflecting historians' opinions about the causes of the Civil War. After each, indicate whether the author thinks the Civil War was inevitable or avoidable. Explain your answer.

> **A** People fight under the stress of hyperemotionalism. When some compelling drive, whether it be ambition, fear, anger, or hunger, becomes supercharged, violence and blood-letting, thus far in human history, seem "inevitable." Now why was emotion in the United States in 1861 supercharged? . . . [there was] a deep seated enjoyment of political activity by Americans which proved dangerous. They gave themselves so many opportunities to gratify their desire for this sport. There were so many elections and such constant agitation . . . A great disruptive fact was the baneful influence of . . . [political] campaigns never over, and of political uproar endlessly arousing emotions. . . . This constant agitation certainly furnishes one of the primary clues to why the war came. It raised to ever higher pitch the passion-rousing oratory of rivals. They egged one another on to make more and more exaggerated statements to a people pervasively . . . isolated and confused.[1]

B The Abolitionists now felt themselves carried along by the tide of events and urged and pushed Lincoln [not to compromise]. But the moderates and the doubters were a powerful party for all that. The accusation of the South, describing Lincoln as the despot trying by brute force of arms to do violence to free American states, found echoes in the Northern [Democratic] press and in the Congress . . . But why go on piling up instances and particulars? I am quite ready to concede the point. The American people had suddenly found themselves in the Civil War and the majority in none of the sections [of the country] had deliberately willed it. . . . Does it prove that the war might therefore have been avoided? Is it not rather one more proof of the general truth that the course of history is not governed by the conscious will of the majority?[2]

C Had the economic systems of the North and the South remained static or changed slowly . . . the balance of power [in the federal government] might have been maintained indefinitely by repeating the [compromise] . . . tactics of 1787, 1820, 1833, and 1850 . . . But nothing was stable in the economy of the United States or in the moral sentiments associated with its diversities. Within each section of the country, the necessities of the productive system were generating portentous results. . . . shifting with mechanical precision the weights which statesmen had to adjust in their efforts to maintain the . . . peace [between North and South].[3]

D War causation tends to be "explained" in terms of great forces. Something elemental is supposed to be at work, be it nationalism, race conflict, or quest for economic advantage. With these forces predicated, the move toward war is alleged to be understandable, to be "explained" and therefore to be in some sense reasonable. [But] Warmaking is too much dignified if it is told in terms of broad national urges . . . or of compelling . . . ambitions. When nations stumble into war, or when peoples rub their eyes and find they have been dragged into war, there is at some point a psychopathic case. Omit the element of abnormality, of bogus leadership . . . and diagnosis [of the causes of war] fails.[4]

Exercise 2: Identifying Turning Points in History

It is easy from a distance, writing in generalities, to take sides on the question of the inevitability of the Civil War. It is not nearly so easy to rewrite the history of the days and weeks before the first shot was fired on the Union garrison at Fort Sumter in the harbor of Charleston, South Carolina. Were there moments when a different decision by a key individual might have changed the course of history?

The following passages trace the crisis at Fort Sumter in the winter and spring of 1861. If Governor Francis W. Pickens of South Carolina, President-elect Lincoln, and their many advisers had not acted as they did, what would have resulted? After each paragraph, write in the space provided what the key decision was and how the decision might have been different. These mental exercises are called "hypotheticals" or "contrary-to-fact" speculations. Obviously, events turned out as they did. But by trying to conceive alternative scenarios in our own minds, we can better understand the motives of individuals and the larger issues of the times. Be historically minded in your approach to the exercise: White southerners feared that their slaves would be taken from them and, perhaps worse, freed in their midst. The president and his newly victorious Republican party were not about to give up the spoils of their victory or give in on their campaign promise to stem the advance of slavery.

> **A** However much the border South wished to avoid a confrontation between [the North and South], by April of 1861 both Jefferson Davis [President of the Confederate States of America] and Abraham Lincoln had good reason to seek one. Neither president wanted war, but both had to have an end to the ambiguity surrounding the secession crisis. During his first month [of March] in office Lincoln could afford to stall. He needed to form his administration, he hoped that the great mass of Southern whites would "come to their senses," and he sought support for the Union among the border states. Davis, too, required time to construct his government and to proselytize [for support] among the slave states still in the Union. By April, though, both governments had done what they could about the border South; people and governments on both sides had begun to clamor for decisive action.

1. What key decisions lay before Lincoln? _____

   _____

2. What crucial decisions did Davis have to make? _____

   _____

> **B** At [Fort] Sumter [in the harbor of Charleston, S.C.] the situation had become critical. Major Anderson [commander of the Union garrison at the fort] and his garrison were running out of food. Women and children, dependents of the troops, left the fort in early February; but even without the extra mouths to feed, Anderson calculated that he would be starved out before mid-April. To retain Sumter the United States would have to send in supplies. To be rid of the Union presence in Charleston Harbor the Confederacy would then be compelled to open fire on the resupply ship or the fort or both. Both sides accepted the confrontation then and there.

1. What problems did Major Anderson face? _____

   _____

2. How might he have resolved them? _____
_____

3. What were Lincoln's choices now? _____
_____

C On April 7 a federal fleet sailed for Charleston to resupply Anderson's garrison. A day later the Confederate commissioners in Washington received a letter, dated March 15 but held back by [new secretary of state William Henry] Seward, stating that the United States had no intention of abandoning Sumter. The same day, April 8, Robert Chew of the United States State Department arrived in Charleston and personally read a message from his President to Governor Pickens [of South Carolina] which explained that Lincoln planned to send provisions to Fort Sumter but would not send more troops or arms. After Pickens had heard his tidings, Chew left in some haste.

1. What decision did Lincoln make? _____
_____

2. How did he present the decision to Governor Pickens? _____
_____

3. How might Lincoln have acted differently? _____
_____

D Pickens promptly relayed Lincoln's message to the Confederate military commander at Charleston, General P. G. T. Beauregard, who passed the news on to his commander in chief in Montgomery [Alabama, still the capital of the Confederacy]. Then it was Davis's turn to act. All along he had believed that war was inevitable, and although he did not wish to fire the first shot, he perceived no alternative. Accordingly, on the tenth [of April, his] secretary of War Walker sent orders by telegraph to Beauregard to demand evacuation [of Sumter] and to reduce [by force] the fort should the demand be refused.

1. What options did Davis have when Beauregard informed him of Lincoln's plan?
_____
_____

2. How did Davis respond? _____
_____

E At two o'clock on the afternoon of April 11, Beauregard sent a written demand to Anderson. Two of the General's aides, Colonel James Chesnut and Captain Stephen D. Lee, presented the note to Anderson with appropriate formality. No one involved in the Sumter confrontation missed the drama and import of what was happening. Beneath the courtesy and fastidious propriety of the proceedings, however, were the hard facts that Anderson refused to move and Beauregard meant to move him.[5]

1. Did Beauregard have any choice but to behave as he did? _____
_____

2. Did Anderson have any choice? _____

_____

3. How might they have averted actual conflict, if they so chose? _____

_____

Exercise 3: Contingency and the Incidents of War

The opposite of inevitability is contingency. No branch of history is more concerned with contingency, unpredictability, and accident than military history. Students of battle are always asking counterfactual questions: what if the attack had been pressed home, or the reinforcements had come sooner, or the commander had only known. . . . ? No battle in American history has raised more of these questions than Gettysburg. Fought over the course of three hot days, from July 1 through 3, 1863, and involving almost 200,000 soldiers of the Army of the Potomac and the Army of Northern Virginia, Gettysburg was regarded by many then and is still seen as a turning point in the war. William Faulkner once wrote that for every thirteen-year-old white southern boy, it was always one o'clock on July 3, just before George Pickett's Virginia Division began its fateful charge up the slope toward the Union line on Cemetery Ridge. Yet it may be argued that the Confederates' failure to press their success against the Union forces on the first day of combat foreordained the final result of the battle. On that day, General Robert E. Lee's troops had flanked and partially broken the ranks of the 1st and 11th Corps of General George Meade's defenders. Had Lieutenant General Richard Ewell's Confederate infantry pushed on to the knob at the northern edge of Cemetery Hill and swarmed across Culp's Hill, in the rear of the Union position, the course of the war might have changed. Gary W. Gallagher, one of our foremost experts on the Civil War, summarizes the conventional story of a lost opportunity:

> Lost opportunities on July 1 loomed large because the troops of [A.P.] Hill and Ewell had gained a decided advantage over their opponents north and west of Gettysburg by midafternoon. To many Southern observers it seemed that one more round of assaults would have carried Cemetery Hill and Culp's Hill and sealed a major victory. Loath to engage the enemy in the first place, Lee had reached the field in time to recognize the opening presented by Hill's earlier decision to commit two divisions and had sought to press the Confederate advantage. But first Hill and then Ewell declined to renew the offensive, observed their critics, affording the desperate Federals time to patch together a strong line on high ground below the town. Their failure set the stage for two more days of bloody battle during which the commanders of the Second and Third corps became little more than bystanders in a drama dominated on the Confederate side by Lee and Longstreet.[6]

It is true that in memoirs written after the war was over, both General Lee and General Winfield Scott Hancock, who commanded the Union's Second Corps, judged that had Ewell pressed forward he could have driven the disorganized U.S. infantry from both hills. In fact, Lee had given an order orally to Ewell through an aide to take the hill in front of Ewell "if practicable."

Lee commonly gave orders to subordinates in such polite language, expecting the orders to be obeyed. Ewell, however, was new at his job. His corps had just been created out of remnants of the recently deceased General Thomas ("Stonewall") Jackson's corps, General James P. Longstreet's corps, and a newly formed division. And Ewell was a punctilious man; he took orders literally.

One of Ewell's brigade commanders had brought word that Union troops had been spotted on his own flank. The Confederate cavalry, which should have been screening the Confederates' march into Pennsylvania, was instead on the far side of the Army of the Potomac. Ewell thus had no clear intelligence reports about Union strength. Just like Lee earlier in the day when the battle had begun inadvertently, Ewell was hesitant to launch an attack into a position that might hold uncounted Union troops. His officers could see Union troops strongly fortifying the heights above Gettysburg—the target of Ewell's attack. In addition to everything else, Ewell's troops were tired. They had marched for many days over unfamiliar territory (they had no accurate maps of southeastern Pennsylvania) and had fought long and hard on July 1. And Ewell's third division had not yet reached the front. As Ewell nevertheless readied his two divisions to move forward again, he was told that General Lee and General Ambrose P. Hill, whose troops had routed the Union divisions in front of them, had decided not to advance any farther that day. Thus, no help would be coming

FIGURE 11.1 *Lieutenant General Richard Stoddert Ewell*
Courtesy of the Medford Historical Society Collection/Corbis Images

from Hill's men. Finally, the day was coming to a close. No one on Ewell's staff was eager to bring on a major battle in the darkness. Given what Ewell knew and what he did not know, what decision was he to make? You decide. _____

_____

_____

Does anything in Ewell's expression, pose or demeanor (see Figure 11.1) suggest to you why he acted as he did? _____

_____

_____

If Ewell had acted differently, then the Confederate Army of Northern Virginia might have driven the Union Army of the Potomac from the ridges surrounding Gettysburg. But with hindsight, we know that such a victory would not have opened the way to Washington, D.C., to the Confederates. Nor would the North have lost its will to fight, any more than the South did after Vicksburg fell to General Ulysses Grant or after General Lee retreated from Pennsylvania in the aftermath of Gettysburg. It may be that victory in battles does not determine the outcome of wars. Union armies in the East had already suffered grievous defeats at Fredericksburg and Chancellorsville, but the war did not end with these defeats. Antietam and Gettysburg were great losses for the Confederacy, but the war continued. Was it then inevitable that the North would win—given its greater industrial output, its ability to feed itself even when many of its young men were in the armed services, and its larger free population base? These advantages did tell in time, but many historians insist that northern victory in the war resulted directly from northern victory on the battlefields of the West. Does the answer to the big question of inevitability then lie in the details—millions of historical contingencies? Or, to paraphrase Napoleon, does history favor the big battalions? Will the strong always defeat the weak?

Moral Responsibility

In Exercise 2 you discovered that even for men and women who believe in free will, some choices do not come easily. The choice between honor and autonomy, on the one hand, and the prospect of war, on the other, was not one that southern leaders or northern politicians welcomed. The extreme case of this dilemma is not uncommon in history: a person coming to believe that what appears to be a choice is no choice at all, that every road leads to the same ending place. Is the resulting series of events then inevitable? In this sense, the coming of the Civil War was a tragedy that many foresaw but none seemed able to prevent. Does this apparent paradox mean that no one bore any moral responsibility for the 1 million casualties—dead, wounded, and missing—and the billions of dollars of damage to homes and workplaces? Is such responsibility justified by the emancipation of 4 million people held in perpetual bondage?

In the twentieth century, the question of moral responsibility—and moral judgment—has become a second big question for historians. After so many human cataclysms—Adolf Hitler's attempt to destroy European Jewry, Stalin's atrocities in the Soviet Union, Japanese militarists' experiments with chemical and germ warfare, American aerial assaults on Japanese population centers, and countless other cases of barbarous conduct by "civilized" governments—questions of guilt have become inescapable historical issues. May the historian assign blame?

All writing, historical and otherwise, is filled with implicit moral judgment. The words we choose can never be wholly neutral, nor do we want them to be. To persuade and inform readers, history must touch moral sensibilities. Without some judgment of their subjects' actions, historians' writing would simply disintegrate like a mummified parchment unwrapped in the sunlight. At the same time, historians do not want to patronize or override the moral belief systems of their subjects. Doing so would violate the basic tenets of historical-mindedness—to see the past through the eyes of the people who lived then.

Can one escape from the dilemma by asserting that there is one moral code that all Americans, past and present, share, and then using this code to judge Americans' conduct in the past? Historians have written volumes about Americans' belief in liberty, opportunity, and equal protection of law. These words capture moral ideals celebrated in our politics and written into our laws, but the words have not always been translated into real liberty, opportunity, and equal protection. Must we then conclude that moral pronouncements so prominent in our legal and political speech are either self-delusions or deliberate lies? If so, can historians presume to substitute their own modern moral sensitivities for the moral values of the people they are studying?

Exercise 4: Identifying Moral Judgment in Historical Accounts

The era of Reconstruction has raised as many moral questions as any period in our history. In this exercise, excerpts from historians' accounts of Reconstruction demonstrate a variety of moral judgments, both implicit and explicit. Underline historians' words implying a moral stance in each passage, and answer the questions at the end of each.

A President Lincoln's successor, President Andrew Johnson, began reconstruction of the Confederate states immediately after the close of hostilities, allowing former Confederate leaders and soldiers to swear loyalty to the Union and alter their states' constitutions to forbid slavery. The governments of these "presidentially reconstructed" southern states then wrote "Black Codes" that denied to former slaves full equality under law.

> In effect, the Black Codes made all Negroes free but not equal to whites in civil rights, made the ex-slaves roughly equivalent to the free Negroes of slave times . . . the Black Codes created a class of Americans excluded by law because of race and color from the capacity to protect itself in courts equally with whites through testimony, to be fully responsible for marketplace decisions, or to live without fear of prejudiced application of criminal justice. . . . the notorious vagrancy and apprentice clauses commonly placed unemployed and minor [underage] blacks whose parents lacked funds under white employers' control, and permitted employers to exercise penal [criminal law] authority.[7]

1. What did the authors find to be the purpose of the Black Codes? _____

_____

_____

2. What is the authors' opinion of the Black Codes? _____

_____

_____

B Recoiling at reports of the ill treatment of former slaves under the Black Codes and equally worried that the Republican party would gain few votes in the South if former slaves and unionists were not supported by the federal government, the Republicans in Congress took charge of Reconstruction. Here are two historians' opposing views of the new turn of events. Underline the moral terms.

Even when the former Confederates were rather firmly in control of Southern state and local governments in the early postwar years, violence was an important part of the pattern of life. In 1866 the head of the [federal] Freedman's Bureau [to help former slaves] in Georgia complained that numerous bands of [white] ruffians were committing "the most fiendish and diabolical outrages" on the freedmen. The former slaves themselves made many representations to Congress and the President that they were in constant danger of physical harm at the hands of the former Confederates. Northern teachers of freedmen frequently saw their efforts literally turn to ashes as local white opponents set fire to the Negro schools . . . If violence was an integral part of the old order and even of the new order controlled by former Confederates, it was only natural that it would be a prime factor in any move to oppose the still newer order administered by those whom the former Confederates regarded as natural enemies [from the North].[8]

1. What did the author think of the former Confederates? _____

_____

Of the agents of the Freedman's Bureau? _____

_____

Of the purposes of Reconstruction? _____

_____

In the autumn of 1866 and through the winter and summer of 1867 strange men from the North were flocking into the black belt of the South, and mingling familiarly with the negroes, day and night. These were the emissaries of the Union League Clubs . . . Organized in the dark days of the war to revive the failing spirit of the [northern] people, they had become bitterly partisan clubs with the conclusion of the struggle, and, the Union saved, they had turned with zest to the congenial task of working out the salvation of their [Republican] party. This, they thought, depended on the domination of the South through the negro vote. Sagacious politicians, and men of material means, obsessed with ideas as extreme as those of [the radical Republicans] they dispatched agents to turn the negroes against the Southern whites and organize them in secret clubs. Left to themselves, the negroes would have turned for leadership to the native southern whites [their former masters] who understood them best. This was the danger. [It was] imperative, then, that [the negroes] should be taught to hate—[the white southerners] . . . Over the plantations these [Union League] agents wandered, seeking the negroes in their cabins, and halting them at their labors in the fields, and the simple-minded freedmen were easy victims of their guile.[9]

1. What are this author's views of southern whites? _____

_____

Of freed men and women? _____

_____

Of Union League agents? _____

_____

_____

2. What is his opinion of Republican political recruiting in the South? _____

_____

_____

C The "Reconstruction Amendments" to the United States Constitution (the Thirteenth, Fourteenth, and Fifteenth Amendments) ended slavery, told state governments they must afford equal protection under the law to all persons, and barred discrimination in voting on the basis of race. A series of Civil Rights Acts from 1866 through 1875 gave teeth to these amendments. Former slaves and free African-Americans were soon taking on important posts in the congressionally reconstructed governments. Underline the moral terms.

> The Negroes were seldom vindictive in their use of political power or in their attitude toward native whites. To be sure, there were plenty of cases of friction between Negroes and whites, and Negro militiamen were sometimes inordinately aggressive. But in no southern state did any responsible Negro leader, or any substantial Negro group, attempt to get complete political control into the hands of the freedmen. All they asked for was equal political rights and equality before the law. . . . Negroes did not desire to have political parties divided along racial lines; rather, unlike most white Democrats, they were eager to drop the race issue and work with the whites within the existing party framework.[10]

1. What are this author's views of freedmen's conduct in the Reconstruction era? _____

_____

_____

2. What is his stance on Reconstruction? _____

_____

_____

D The best hopes of the Republican Reconstruction governments were dashed and the worst fears of their Democratic opponents were confirmed when many of the economic projects designed to put the South on its feet again crashed down in bankruptcy. Corruption, widespread throughout the United States, had an especially disheartening effect in the South, according to the author of the next passage. Underline the moral language.

> Corruption through bribery and extortion had brought great damage to the railroads [planned and built in the South by the new governments]; yet this form of corruption was the least important kind. If the term is broadened to include other, more subtle betrayals of the public interest, "corruption" involved almost every man and measure of the Reconstruction period. Many corporations did not deserve [government] aid. A systematic railroad policy could not endow all lines equally. Yet the legislature gave support to undeserving roads, not because the projects seemed good, but because the representatives, blinded by local prejudices and impractical visions, allowed themselves to place local gain above sectional and state good. State pride corrupted legislators. . . . selfishness, in all its

forms, made the railroad aid programs a jumble of different subsidies and encrusted the financial burdens on taxpayers. Here was the real corruption . . . not only a corruption of ethics, but a corruption of judgment. The latter was by far the more serious of the two.[11]

1. What is this author's view of the problem of Reconstruction economics? _____

_____

_____

2. What is his final judgment on Reconstruction? _____

_____

_____

The Lessons of History

Beneath the historians' disparate views of Reconstruction, embedded in explicit and implicit judgments, were the authors' moral visions. For some of these historians, Reconstruction was a tragedy because it burdened the former Confederates with military occupation and political subjugation or because it never fulfilled the ideals of equality under law or racial fair play. Historians writing about Reconstruction cannot help expressing their moral judgment; their language, like all language, is inherently moralistic, and no author can escape its constraints.

If even the most conscientious and fair-minded historian cannot help but engage in implicit moral judgment, few historians have been so explicit or so bold as Howard Zinn, who wrote: "I start, therefore, from the idea of writing history in such a way as to extend human sensibilities, not out of this book into other books, but into the going conflict over how people shall live, and whether they shall live."[12]

A third big question that preoccupies not only historians but everyone who takes the study of history seriously is, Does history teach lessons we can use today and tomorrow? The philosopher Santayana wrote that those who forgot history were fated to relive it. In his day, this applied to the makers of World War I, who, after nearly a century of peace, disregarded what great wars did to nations. Yet a mere generation after the Great War, Europeans were again locked in mortal combat. It is easy to see the differences between the First and Second World Wars, but we can still wonder whether the makers of World War II misread the lessons of history. Adolf Hitler had seen firsthand the horrors of the First World War—he served in the German army on the western front and was wounded in the last year of the war—yet he drew from history the lesson that Germany should avenge a bitter defeat rather than pursue peace. To the leaders of England and France, the Great War had taught other lessons; and, blinded by these, they failed to realize the threat that Hitler posed to peace. It is tempting to agree with historian Martin Duberman that the only lesson history teaches is that there are no lessons, only "bitter disappointment" for those interested in "changing the present" through knowledge of the past.[13]

However real our fears may be that political leaders never learn lessons from history, modern policymakers and social scientists still desire to use the past to help governments avoid repeating disastrous mistakes. *Thinking in Time*, the title of Richard Neustadt and Ernest May's attempt to raise the "historical consciousness" of our political leaders, suggests that such an endeavor is urgently needed. Neustadt and May conclude that a study of the past, even the brief study allowed to busy policymakers (not unlike the brief time you can give to history in your crowded class schedule and your hectic days at school), can be valuable if leaders ask the question, What would a little more study, a little broader study, gain?

It is remarkable, they maintain, how much more accurate predictions about the present and the future would be if decisionmakers were to take just one more step into the past.[14]

You may well ask, If the task of predicting the future from the past is possible, why have wise and well-informed leaders so often—almost regularly—led their peoples into disaster? The answer may be that history—like weather storms or the disruptions of motion in fluids—is dependent on small differences, variations of individual action so minute, so easily lost in the welter of mass movements, that they are not easily perceived at the time, much less recovered by later scholars. These minute variations in the initial conditions of two otherwise apparently similar events may produce, at the end of a long chain of human actions and responses, very different outcomes. Physicists call this the "butterfly effect"—the theory that the wind currents that a butterfly in Georgia creates will affect the weather in London, England. Were the butterfly resting the next day and all else remained the same, the weather would be different in London, for minute variations will have wider and wider effects until they change the world in which we live. Thus we return to the first theme of this chapter, "for want of a nail."

Exercise 5: Learning from the Past

The last exercise in this book, like the first exercise in Chapter 1, requires you to think rather than write. Reviewing in your mind the materials on American history you have studied this term, ask yourself what lessons in our past may point the way to a better future. For example, can you apply what you have learned about race relations to today's debate over minority rights and Affirmative Action plans at your college or school? How does your knowledge of that part of our past help you to predict what will happen in the future of race relations? Is future conflict inevitable? Can compromises be found that make everyone a winner? Or must there always be victors and vanquished? What is your view?

_____

_____

_____

Much of what you have learned this term would serve well those who decide our nations' fate. Perhaps, if you find yourself in that role, you will use the skills that you have mastered to prove Neustadt and May right. Bear in mind, however, that the human past is not recaptured in straight lines or in easy-to-solve formulas of economic or political interaction. Like nature itself, human history is the "rough, not rounded, scabrous, not smooth . . . pitted, pocked, and broken up, the twisted, tangled, and intertwined" expression of the human condition.[15]

Notes

[1] Roy Franklin Nichols, *The Disruption of American Democracy* (New York: Macmillan, 1961), 502–504.

[2] Pietr Geyl, *Debates with Historians* (New York: Meridian, 1958), 249–250.

[3] Charles Beard and Mary Beard, *The Rise of American Civilization* (New York: Macmillan, 1927), 2:3–4.

[4] James G. Randall, "A Blundering Generation," in *Lincoln the Liberal Statesman* (New York: Dodd, Mead, 1947), 36–64.

[5] Emory M. Thomas, *The Confederate Nation, 1861–1865* (New York: HarperCollins, 1979).

[6] Gary W. Gallagher, "Confederate Corps Leadership on the First Day at Gettysburg," in Gallagher, ed., *The First Day at Gettysburg* (Kent, Ohio: Kent State University Press, 1992), 30–31.

[7] Harold M. Hyman and William M. Wiecek, *Equal Justice Under Law: Constitutional Development, 1835–1875* (New York: Harper & Row, 1982), 320.

[8] John Hope Franklin, *Reconstruction After the Civil War* (Chicago: University of Chicago Press, 1961), 152–153.

[9] Claude G. Bowers, *The Tragic Era: America After Lincoln, The Dark That Followed the Dawn of Peace* (1929; reprint, Boston: Houghton Mifflin, 1962), 198.

[10] Kenneth M. Stampp, *The Era of Reconstruction, 1865–1877* (New York: Random House, 1967), 168–169.

[11] Mark W. Summers, *Railroads, Reconstruction, and the Gospel of Prosperity: Aid Under the Radical Republicans, 1865–1877* (Princeton: Princeton University Press, 1984), 116–117.

[12] Howard Zinn, *The Politics of History* (Boston: Beacon Press, 1970), 35–36.

[13] Martin Duberman, *The Uncompleted Past* (New York: Dutton, 1971), 356.

[14] Richard E. Neustadt and Ernest R. May, *Thinking in Time: The Uses of History for Decision Makers* (New York: Free Press, 1986), 232–246.

[15] James Gleick, *Chaos: Making a New Science* (New York: Viking, 1987), 94.